Career Barriers:
How People Experience, Overcome, and Avoid Failure

Career Barriers:
How People Experience, Overcome, and Avoid Failure

Manuel London
State University of New York at Stony Brook

LEA LAWRENCE ERLBAUM ASSOCIATES, PUBLISHERS
1998   Mahwah, New Jersey   London

Lawrence Erlbaum Associates, Inc., Publishers
10 Industrial Avenue
Mahwah, New Jersey 07430

Library of Congress Cataloging-in-Publication-Data

London, Manuel.
Career Barriers : how people experience, overcome, and avoid
failure / Manuel London.
     p. cm
  Includes bibliographical references and index.
   ISBN 0-8058-2579-7 (cloth : alk. paper). —ISBN 0-
8058-2580-0 (pbk. : alk. paper)
   1. Career development. 2. Employment motivation. 3.
Alienation (Psychology) 4. Motivation (psychology) 5. Suc-
cess in business.
  I. Title
  HF5381.L6558   1997   97-22282
  650.14—dc21   CIP

Books published by Lawrence Erlbaum Associates are printed
on acid-free paper, and their bindings are chosen for strength
and durability.

Printed in the United States of America
10 9 8 7 6 5 4 3 2 1

For Marilyn

Contents

Preface

This book is for people who are experiencing, or have experienced, career barriers and want to learn constructive responses. It is also for students at the start of their careers and seasoned employees who want to avoid career barriers or be prepared to deal with them. In addition, the book is for managers, human resource professionals, and researchers who want to understand how people confront career barriers.

We tend to think of careers in a positive way. When we are young, we have high expectations; we look ahead to wonderful accomplishments and we are certain that our hard work, career devotion, and arduous preparation will pay off. Whether our career goal is to make a fortune, gain recognition and status, or do interesting and challenging work, there's nothing we cannot do! We are energized and raring to go. Many of us sacrifice time with our family or friends for the sake of our career. Some of us delay starting a family or decide not to marry in order to devote ourselves fully to our profession.

We do not anticipate what might happen if our career goals are not met. We do not worry much about hitting the glass ceiling, we do not anticipate that the company to which we devote our lives will downsize and put us out on the street at age 50, we do not believe that by age 30 we will have achieved the most responsible position we will ever have, and we do not foresee having an abusive boss who places unreasonable demands on our time and energy. We also cannot imagine that our creative ideas will go unrewarded, we do not believe we are capable of making an error that cannot be fixed, and we do not view ourselves having a physical illness or handicap. We know such things happen, but we do not plan or prepare for them any more than we anticipate other unpredictable, unfortunate events in our lives.

However, career barriers are not unusual and never have been. They are ordinary experiences. They can happen to anyone in any walk of life—executive or secretary, artist or mechanic, physician or janitor. Some career barriers pop up out of nowhere, like a major accident. Others emerge slowly from the daily pressures of life. People feel them deeply and painfully regardless of how and why they happen. Consider the young faculty member who fails to get tenure, the politician who loses an election, the employees who lose their jobs because of a company merger, the worker whose function is outsourced (i.e., the firm decides to hire an outside company to do the work), and the business person whose trusted partners break away to start their own firm down the street. Consider how we react when the economy turns sour; business does not turn out as rosy as we had hoped; our boss has no compassion, only demands; or a younger, seemingly brighter person is hired.

The mid-1980s through the early and mid-1990s were a time of considerable organizational churn. Announcements of corporate mergers, joint ventures, and new technologies were often accompanied by forecasts of layoffs. This seems to be continuing with no end in sight. These events have changed the way people conceive of a career. College graduates today recognize that they may work for eight or nine different companies during the course of their lives. Some foresee having two or three different careers. People try to avoid being dependent on others for their employment security; they want to be in control of their own development, and they create their own opportunities. Those who accomplish this are the lucky ones. Insightful people begin planning for a new career before they reach midlife. However, even the best-laid career plans go awry.

Career barriers make us feel hopeless and out of control. We may feel like a grain of sand in a storm—all we can do is go with the flow, and we may be washed out to sea in the process. We may feel like a chess piece—the focus of attention but at another's mercy. In this case, we may have a minor role (pawn) or a major role (queen), but someone else is making the decisions, and even the decision maker is reacting to someone's else's moves and we become the sacrificial lamb. We may feel like a bumper-car driver. We can enjoy the fun, get bashed and be bashed, or stay away from the fray and miss the excitement and rewards, but at least we have some control. Alternatively, we may feel like a camp fire. We know we are important, but before we know it, dinner is over and we are burned out (or stomped out). Some people encounter career barriers because of physical problems brought on by an accident or illness. Still others create their own career barriers. They make a career choice that did not pan out, or they were unable to make the grade.

There is no easy way to prevent or overcome a career barrier. Just as many forces may cause the barrier—often forces beyond our control—many factors make overcoming the barrier difficult. New jobs are not readily available, especially for older workers. Financial obligations cannot be ignored so we can go back to school and start afresh. Time, waning motivation, and possibly bitterness all work against us. However, it helps to have "insurance"—for instance, starting out with a good profession or job, working hard, having fun, maintaining an optimistic attitude, continuing one's education, having a balanced life with good friends and a life partner, and financial planning.

My goal in this book is to help the reader understand how people react to career barriers and how people develop constructive ways of coping with them. Throughout the book, I draw on original cases and data from interviews with people who faced different types of career barriers. I describe how people react to, and make sense of, unfortunate events in their lives, and I apply this to how people make sense of career barriers when they occur. I consider how and why some people cope constructively, while others do not. I explore how our resilience and support from others help get us though tough times and emerge with a sense of renewal and career growth. I also suggest how we can manage career barriers and prepare for, or even prevent, career barriers through foresight, planning, and education. These methods suggest what managers and organizations should do to help their employees who are, or may soon be, facing career barriers. Although the book focuses on the perspective of the person who has been, or may be, affected by a career barrier, the material should be of interest to a broad range of readers—in particular, academics who study careers, practitioners in the fields of training and development, and government officials who set public policies that affect displaced workers.

My interest in career barriers is an extension of my work on career motivation. My initial work on career motivation was done at AT&T in the early 1980s. There I focused on determining what makes some young people want to get ahead—to advance, earn more money, and achieve positions of power and responsibility—whereas others are content with fewer outward signs of success as long as they have a well-balanced, satisfying life. The research I conducted with Douglas Bray suggested that one important factor was the support and encouragement young managers received early in their careers. Some work environments foster motivation and goal achievement through attention to individual development. In such environments, young people are viewed by the company as resources for the future, and their development is inextricably linked to the firm's future success. The importance of development and moving ahead infects the motivation of newcomers. Employees are devastated when this type of environment turns sour—for instance, opportunities diminish or employees do not make the grade. Other work environments emphasize meeting immediate business objectives. Young people are expected to do their job assignments to meet current business objectives. These firms discourage attention to development and focus young people's attention on other aspects of their lives where they can seek fulfillment. Even when the environment does not raise expectations, however, some employees feel stymied and grow discontent. They may not realize it at first, but over time their career interest wanes or they seek other avenues for career satisfaction.

Doug Bray and I conceptualized career motivation in terms of three major components: *career insight* (understanding ourselves and the work environment); *career identity* (the direction of our career goals); and *career resilience* (the ability to overcome career barriers baseu on our self-efficacy, need for achievement, and willingness to take reasonable risks). Resilience stems from positive reinforcement for doing well, and it is largely formed before people start their careers. However, it can be strengthened (or diminished) depending of support in the work environment. Career insight and identity stem from information about possible career opportunities, organizational expectations, and performance feedback.

Recognizing the importance of such information to career motivation, I subsequently conducted research on how people learn about themselves and others through feedback. I was particularly interested in feedback processes that collect information about a manager's performance from the manager's subordinates, peers, supervisors, and customers and provide this information as input for development—a process called *360-degree feedback*. Key questions here are whether people are open to such information—whether they are willing to use the information to alter their behavior or make decisions about their future. Research on life stages, career development, and learning suggests that people are most open to learning during times of trauma.

People can learn while facing the stress and self-questioning that accompanies a career barrier. However, this is not an easy process. Learning requires considerable self-understanding and environmental support. The organization can play a vital role in limiting a person's pain and creating opportunities. However, despite generous severance packages and outplacement services, many organizations have been little help to people who lose their jobs, suffer job stress, face unreasonably demanding bosses, or suffer physical handicap or chronic illness. Most of the burden falls on the individual and the individual's family. Assistance can come from employers, government agencies, educational institutions, and religious organizations. Training and human resource professionals, counselors, and managers have much to learn about how to help people avoid career barriers or develop constructive responses when they occur. I hope this book contributes to helping people face this challenge.

I am grateful to the advanced graduate students in SUNY-Stony Brook's Center for Human Resource Management program who identified people who had faced career barriers, conducted interviews, and collected data. As they interviewed people, they supported and contributed to the psychological theory and practical ideas I discuss here. I also benefited from numerous colleagues whose creative energy and ideas stimulated my thinking. In particular I am grateful to Edward Mone, with whom I have written several articles and books on the role of human resource development in changing organizations. I also appreciate James Smither's contributions to my thinking and writing about feedback and careers research. I would like to thank my fellow faculty members at Stony Brook, in particular, Gerrit Wolf, Jeff Casey, and Subimal Chatterjee, who are always available as a sounding board for new ideas. Last but not least, I am grateful to my wife Marilyn, to whom this book is dedicated. She has continuously refined her skills as performing artist and administrator and successfully balanced work and family roles, all the while putting up with my compulsive work habits. Her love and devotion has kept me going. Also, I thank my sons David and Jared whose anticipated careers are a neverending topic of discussion and planning.

—*Manuel London*
Stony Brook, New York

Introduction

Some people have modest career goals. They want to have a secure job, earn a middle-class salary, have some responsibility and challenge, and have time for their family and friends. Other people want to advance rapidly, be in a position of leadership, earn a sizable salary, own a lavish home, and have prestige and status in their profession and the community. Whether their career goals are modest or ambitious, however, they may face barriers to achieving these goals. Age and accompanying physical changes may reduce their energy and abilities. A supportive boss or an encouraging family member may be lost, diminishing their feelings of support and encouragement. They may lose their jobs, have fewer chances for promotion, or be pressured to do more with less.

This book defines career barriers, considers how people react to them, and offers ways to overcome and prevent them. Some barriers creep up slowly. Although there is plenty of time to adjust, there is also plenty of time to avoid or deny the encroaching problem. These are *incremental* barriers because they become evident a bit at a time, and they do not impose tremendous hurdles that are impossible to overcome. Their effects may be temporary. Other barriers happen suddenly and impose traumatic changes on a person's life. These barriers are *framebreaking*. They may be permanent, and they cause tremendous uncertainty about how or whether they can be overcome. Some barriers that arise incrementally seem framebreaking because they are not recognized until it is too late.

Examples of career barriers are *loss* (e.g., loss of one's job or of one's support system); *handicap* (absence or loss of physical or mental ability through injury or debilitating chronic illness); *change* (new job, employer, work location); *conflicts* (between people or roles expected of one person); *unrealistic expectations or work demands*; *discrimination* (unfair treatment/harassment); *unfavorable performance feedback*; and *negative aspects of positive events* (e.g., promotion leading to increased responsibility, demands, and corresponding stress). These may occur as a result of the individual, the situation, or both.

Understanding how people respond to roadblocks to goal accomplishment requires considering the intersection of emotional and thought processes. These processes affect how people think about, cope with, and hopefully overcome career barriers. How we think about a career barrier and the extent to which we are able to identify and carry out constructive coping strategies depends on our resilience in the face of adversity and the support and training available in our environment.

In this book, I review sources of support for overcoming career barriers. I suggest how people learn new, more effective ways for evaluating and coping with tough career situations. I consider how people learn from experience as they manage adverse situations and find new directions for self-fulfillment. The organizing framework for the book is a model for understanding reactions to career barriers. The components of the model are emotional and thought processes in reacting to career barriers, the processes of making sense of the barrier over time, and trying various ways of coping. I consider how the person's resilience affects these components. I also consider the kind of support from the environment that can help overcome career barriers. In doing so, I draw on interviews with people who have experienced career barriers to show how people can cope more effectively with career barriers.

The ideas in this book should help people who are faced with career barriers, or who might be in the future, learn how to:

- Analyze and cope with their emotions.
- Evaluate the barrier realistically (make accurate judgments as to why the barrier occurred and its likely consequences).
- Identify viable coping strategies that deal with their emotions and change the situation.
- Assess what they have learned about themselves and the career environment (their employer, job opportunities).
- Devise tracking mechanisms and a readiness to revise or change strategies to deal with the career barrier more effectively.
- Strengthen their career resilience, insight, and identity.

TOWARD A MODEL OF REACTIONS
TO CAREER BARRIERS

The approach I take in this book builds on models of responses to job loss—probably the most devastating career barrier. The results from research on job loss have much to offer in understanding the effects of other traumatic career barriers. Career barriers have multiplier effects in that they result in a number of stressful conditions. This is especially true of job loss, which can lead to problems with money, family, social standing, and self-image. In their 1992 landmark study of displaced employees in the steel and aerospace industries, Leana and Feldman developed a job loss model that incorporated characteristics of the context (e.g., whether job loss is permanent or temporary), thought processes (for instance, about how difficult finding a new job will be), and emotional and physical reactions (psychosomatic illnesses). These lead to problem-focused coping strategies—that is, strategies that change the situation, such as finding another job. They may also lead to symptom-focused coping strategies, such as seeking medication to relax and reduce anxiety and depression.

My approach in this book is to consider basic psychological processes that explain how people react to career barriers. These include (a) thought, emotions, and their interaction; (b) the effects of our resilience and hardiness on how we react to stress; (c) thought processes—how we compare information about ourselves and the environment to standards, whether we process the information carefully or carelessly, and whether we attribute the reason for the career barrier to ourselves or factors beyond our control; (d) strategies for coping with stress, including direct confrontation and psychological defense mechanisms; (e) how we develop insights about ourselves, others, and the situation; and (f) our career motivation—patterns of personality characteristics, needs, and interests that comprise career resilience, career insight, and career identity.

In Fig. I.1, I outline the variables and relationships that explain how people react to career barriers. The central processes are sizing up the situation and establishing and implementing a coping strategy. Compared to incremental barriers, framebreaking barriers result in stronger emotions and more careful (mindful) thinking about why the barrier arose, how much control we have, and possible coping strategies. People who are resilient and have external support develop constructive coping strategies. Those who are vulnerable, lack support, or both, develop defensive explanations for the barrier and ineffective or possibly destructive coping responses. This is a cyclical process in that people reassess a career barrier over time as they try various coping strategies and as the situation evolves. Constructive coping strategies reduce the cycles needed to overcome the barrier successfully.

Here is what the model means:

- Different career barriers have different effects on us. Incremental barriers may be devastating, but they arise slowly, maybe imperceptibly, and may not have strong emotional effects. However, they may lead to chronic negative emotions, such as depression. Framebreaking barriers—those viewed as more

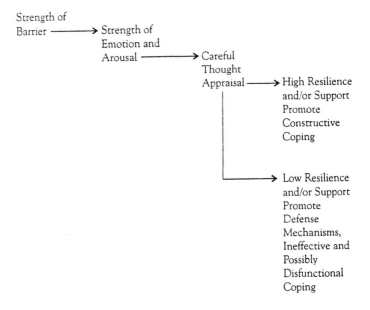

Fig. I.1. A model of responses to career barriers.

severe and traumatic—tend to be sudden events. Other characteristics that make them traumatic are that they offer us little or no choice or opportunity for control, are not subject to negotiation (or, if they are, require tough bargaining), are visible to others, have uncertain outcomes, are self-induced, isolate us from others, and have long-term or permanent effects. The more traumatic the event, the more we are likely to pay attention to the event, evaluate its meaning, and have strong emotions about it.

- Different types of events, including career barriers, give rise to different emotions. For instance, loss leads to sadness; frustration leads to anger. Tough, unpleasant situations generally evoke strong negative emotions.
- Emotions are tied to thoughts. Emotions influence the extent to which we think about unpleasant information carefully or carelessly (in a quick, automatic way) and the extent to which carefully thinking through our predicament results in accurately determining the reasons for the career barrier. The more traumatic the barrier, the more it gives rise to negative emotions, and these in turn prompt careful information processing.
- We may come to believe that the reason for a framebreaking career failure was beyond our control such that we cannot change or influence the situation. Alternatively, we may come to believe that we can do something about

the situation. If, after careful thought, we decide that we were to blame in some way for the failure, we are likely to understand what we can do differently to reverse the situation or set out on a new, more constructive course.

- Incremental career barriers generate less emotion and are less arousing than framebreaking changes. Consequently, we are likely to process information about them carelessly. We discard, ignore, or, in other ways, rationalize information we get that suggests we are failing. For example, we might believe that negative feedback about our performance says more about the person who is giving it than it does about us—a conclusion we might reach when we believe that we are being blamed by someone who is jealous of us.

- Thoughts and emotions affect how we evaluate and cope with the situation. Sometimes this evaluation occurs before the event actually happens as when we are able to anticipate that we are walking into a problem. We continue our assessment as the situation evolves and as we try various coping strategies.

- Our thoughts and emotions give rise to our judgments about why the failure occurred, and this in turn leads us to one or more coping strategies. After careful thought, we might conclude that the failure was not our fault. This might make us feel better. Alternatively, we might conclude that we lack control and are unable to change. This might cause us to feel resigned, frustrated, angry, or any combination thereof. As a result, we withdraw from the situation and do not take any actions that could help.

- There are several ways of coping with a career barrier. One is to change our behavior. Another is to change our interpretation of the barrier and the reasons why it occurred. This latter approach is a psychological defense that makes us feel better in the short run but could be dysfunctional (and maybe even destructive) in the long run. Coping strategies that change our behavior in a positive way and thereby affect the situation directly are likely to have long-term constructive outcomes.

- Constructive ways of coping include establishing new alliances, searching for new goals and alternative behaviors, searching for an explanation, generating and testing different ways of reacting, seeking evidence to support or reject our conclusions, and seeking counseling.

- Destructive or dysfunctional coping strategies include punishing ourselves, pitying ourselves, or giving up.

- Strategies that we do not think through carefully but that may have positive outcomes include copying others who are successful; hitting by chance on the right reason for events, a reasonable response, or both; or simply letting things happen without taking deliberate action (e.g., job loss leads to unemployment insurance, retraining, and a new job).

- Strategies that we do not think through carefully but that may have negative outcomes include lowering our energy level, jumping to a false conclusion, floundering, denying the barrier, continuing negative behavior, continuing commitment to a lost cause or dead end, quitting, increasing our dependence on others, or feeling apprehensive about being evaluated.

- Our psychological makeup or personality may help us face a career barrier in a constructive way. This is called *resilience* or *hardiness*. People who are high in resilience need to achieve, believe in their ability to make positive things happen, feel they are able to control events, are willing to take reasonable risks, need to establish why things happen to them, and are willing to search for negative feedback about themselves and the their interpretations of events.

- Our resilience coupled with the support we receive from the environment affect the extent to which a career barrier influences us negatively. Resilience and support help us to withstand the barrier and limit its negative impact.

- Resilience promotes optimism and hope. This encourages us to think carefully and develop insights about ourselves that may help us react to, and overcome, a career barrier. When this analysis leads us to more accurate judgments about ourselves and the situation, we are likely to take action that has positive outcomes. Lack of resilience promotes feelings of dependence and depression, and we are likely to have trouble devising constructive coping strategies.

- Our supervisor can be the cause of a career barrier in several ways—for instance, unfair, negative performance assessments and personnel decisions, not to mention the possibilities of abuse, harassment, and discrimination. However, our supervisor can help us overcome a career barrier. Supportive supervision includes goal setting, feedback, role modeling, listening and two-way communication, reinforcement, negotiation, persuasion, help in diagnosing reasons for career barriers, suggestions for behaviors, and facilitating or changing environmental conditions. As such, the supervisor can become a change agent, facilitator, coach, monitor, and educator.

- Interventions such as counseling and training can help us interpret a career barrier accurately; deal with strong, negative emotions; and formulate coping strategies that remove the barrier or change career directions.

SUMMARY

Career barriers can be devastating in many respects. They arouse strong emotions. Moreover, people are not always clear about what is happening to them. Understanding how we react to career barriers entails recognizing our emotional and thought processes as the barrier occurs and has an impact on us.

Some people facing a career barrier process information carefully and objectively. They are able to get beyond their disappointment, anger, frustration, and a host of other emotions. Other people are overwhelmed by their emotions, flounder for want of direction, and take a long time to rebound. The conclusions people reach about the barriers affecting them determine how they will manage the situation. Recognizing the reasons behind the barrier—the extent to which it can be controlled, reversed, ignored, or overcome—will help us devise coping strategies.

BOOK OUTLINE

This book is divided into four parts: What Is a Career Barrier? (chapter 1), How People React to Barriers (chapters 2–5), Ways to Help People Overcome Career Barriers (chapters 6–7), and Ways to Avoid Career Barriers in the Future (chapter 8). Interviews for this book were conducted with people who had recently experienced career barriers, and case examples in many of the chapters were drawn from these interviews. They offer the reader a deeper understanding of how people react to career barriers, develop constructive and sometimes destructive or dysfunctional coping strategies, and benefit from a variety of sources of support.

Chapter 1 describes characteristics of career barriers (e.g., how suddenly they arise, the extent to which they are permanent, the clarity of their effects) and different types of barriers (e.g., discrimination, job loss, job stress, an abusive supervisor, a bad business decision). Career barriers are somewhat in the eye of the beholder, because the event that seems traumatic to one person may be a growth experience to another.

Chapter 2 focuses on emotions, thoughts, and their relationships as they affect how people respond to negative life events. Emotions stem from individual characteristics, such as a person's tendency to be angry, and from the situation, for example, the dynamics of the situations causing a natural emotional response, such as grief or frustration. Emotions influence the way people process information about events. Thought processes begin when we categorize information. Positive or neutral (everyday) events that we expect to happen can be interpreted mindlessly. Negative events, however, force our attention to a variety of information; further, strong emotions interfere with our processing the information accurately. Positive outlooks such as a sense of optimism, reduce negative emotional reactions. Chapter 2 suggests how to assess people's thought and how emotional responses to a career barrier can be understood and made more productive—for instance, by asking them to think about the importance of the situation, the extent to which they blame themselves or others, their belief that the situation can be changed, and their feelings of guilt and sadness.

Chapter 3 describes ways people cope with career barriers. It shows that how an individual evaluates the career barrier influences whether he or she will cope in a constructive or destructive way. People cope constructively when they appraise information thoroughly and realistically. They cope dysfunctionally when they deny or ignore information or set unrealistically high goals and behave in a way that guarantees failure in order to say that no one could have done better under the circumstances. Although strong emotions last a long time and guide how people respond to the career barrier, a negative emotional urge is usually accompanied by a secondary urge to modify behavior in recognition of possible consequences. Also, people interpret events in ways that avoid unpleasant feelings. This tempers the negative effects of emotions, but possibly at the expense of constructive coping. For instance, defense mechanisms—such as denial—may protect an individual's self-image and prevent taking positive action to counter a career barrier. Chapter 3 describes problem-focused coping (behavioral actions to handle or overcome the barrier) and symptom-focused coping (dealing with the emotions) for negative performance feedback and job loss, two common career barriers.

Career motivation consists of three parts: career resilience, insight, and identity. In chapter 4, I describe how resilience contributes to insight and identity. Insight allows people to assess career barriers accurately. People may need to revise their career insight (views of their strengths and weaknesses and work demands). They may also need to establish a career identity as they revise their career goals and perhaps embark on a new career direction. Resilience provides the foundation for doing this successfully. However, people who have weak career resilience may develop a misguided sense of themselves and a dysfunctional or fruitless career identity. Reinforcement, performance feedback, and information about career opportunities are necessary to get them back on track.

Chapter 5 looks more closely at career resilience and an associated concept called *hardiness*. These characteristics predispose individuals to respond constructively to career barriers. People who are high in career resilience have self-confidence, need to achieve, are willing to take reasonable risks, and need to evaluate events and circumstances. Hardiness affects people's resistance to stress. People who are hardy are high in *commitment* (the tendency to involve oneself in tough situations), *control* (the tendency to feel and act as if one is influential in the face of tough situations rather than helpless), and *challenge* (the belief that change rather than stability is normal in life). They evaluate career barriers in an optimistic, positive way, and they cope with them constructively. Fortunately, resilience and hardiness can be learned. Some people learn the hard way by having to overcome career barriers. Others learn by watching their peers. Still others have the insight to use their resilience to avoid negative situations altogether.

Chapter 6 makes the transition from individual characteristics that affect reactions to career barriers to situational conditions that promote constructive coping strategies as well as increase positive individual characteristics, such as resilience. I cover environmental conditions that support career resilience (e.g., positive reinforcement for a job well done), insight (e.g., goal setting and career information and performance feedback), and identity (e.g., opportunities for leadership and advancement). I describe an environment that supports continuous learning as one in which knowledge and skill acquisition are essential responsibilities of every employee's job and this is supported by the organization's training, evaluation, and reward systems. I also consider how older workers' career motivation can be enhanced, for instance, by rewarding workers for mentoring younger employees, rehiring retirees for temporary full- or part-time work, and allowing phased retirement positions.

Chapter 7 continues this discussion of situational support by describing programmatic interventions for organizations to help employees cope constructively with career barriers. The chapter suggests that identifying, clarifying, and prioritizing values is a way to understand and manage career transitions. A questionnaire for measuring reactions to career barriers and other stressful work situations is presented as a tool in self-assessment and counseling. The chapter covers methods for counseling, teaching self-management, supporting self-control, and learning useful coping skills. Additional examples of support mechanisms are computer-based counseling, outplacement counseling, hotlines, and teaching self-management techniques. A number of examples of training programs for displaced workers are described. These are often cooperative efforts between government agencies, local universities, and corporations. They give people training in job search skills and methods for dealing with the emotional aspects of job loss and rejection.

Chapter 8 provides recommendations to help people prevent career barriers. I describe how many people will have more than one career in their lifetimes. I also examine how the changing nature of work is determining new skills and areas of knowledge that people need to acquire. I suggest that continuous learning is the best way to avoid a career barrier, or at least to minimize the effects of a barrier if one should arise. Employers may provide resources to help us be continuous learners, but each of us must take responsibility for our own development.

Ninety interviews were conducted to understand how people appraise and cope with different types of career barriers. Selected cases derived from these interviews are reported in several of the chapters and in Appendix A. The cases are listed and summarized in Appendix B. The methods used and quantitative analyses are provided in Appendices C and D. The data show differences between job loss and other types of career barriers; how different people (e.g., older workers, women, professionals) react to career barriers; relationships between emotions, stress, appraisals; and coping strategies. Also, the results show the importance of career motivation and support for career motivation to coping with career barriers constructively.

I

What Is a Career Barrier?

1

Examples and Types of Barriers

Some career barriers hit you in the face, they come unexpectedly, and are nothing short of traumatic. They have severe negative effects on employees and their families. Other barriers emerge slowly—perhaps imperceptibly. Changes in the situation occur incrementally and eventually amount to a career barrier. Corresponding emotions, such as frustration and anger, build up slowly as well. In this chapter I describe characteristics and types of career barriers. Then I present an overview of the exploratory interview study I used to gain a deeper understanding of how people react to a host of career barriers. First, consider two cases.

JOB LOSS: THE ULTIMATE CAREER BARRIER
(CASE 1.1)

Abe is a 58-year-old married man with two children over the age of 20. An electrical engineer, he had worked for a defense contractor in the aerospace industry for 26 years before being laid off. For most of his career with the defense contractor, he felt his job was secure. The work environment was friendly and mostly stress-free. Also, he felt the work was important, not only to the company but to the country.

Job security become a concern for Abe in 1989 as defense spending was cut. Abe was assigned to a new project, but felt this might be short-lived. He thought that receiving jobs in the company seemed to be due to who you knew rather than what you could do. The firm merged with another contractor, and Abe watched as numerous colleagues lost their jobs. Morale in the firm reached a low point. Abe was used to sharing his work with his family, and he continued to keep them informed as times got rough. He hoped this would prepare them if he was laid off. Nevertheless, he occasionally took out his anger on them. He became doleful and somber, and had trouble sleeping.

During his last year with the firm Abe began looking for a job elsewhere, but had no luck. After the inevitable layoff, he discovered that jobs were available in software engineering, and he took classes to move into this field. Although he went on several interviews, it seemed that his age was a barrier. Younger people with less experience were cheaper to hire. After 2 years of looking for a job and the employment situation in the region getting worse, Abe found a position as a consulting engineer for a small firm. He had less autonomy and disliked the constant monitoring. Also, once the project was completed, the consulting assignment was over. He continues to look for other consulting assignments and is thinking about starting his own firm.

This case shows what it means to be a grain of sand in the storm of organizational change. It is a typical case of a displaced engineer—someone who had a secure job for many years but fell victim to an organizational downsizing. Although Abe foresaw the change, he did nothing about it until after he was laid off. After some retraining, he struggled to find a niche as a consultant. Now consider someone who was also forced out of his job late in his career.

ANOTHER VICTIM OF DOWNSIZING
(CASE 1.2)

Bernie is a 58-year-old married man with five children and had been with his current employer in the same position for 22 years. He worked as an executive assistant to the administrative county judge. A management change brought a new administrative judge who forced Bernie to retire after working with him for 7 months. The new judge wanted "his own man" as his assistant. The judge made Bernie's life miserable, treating him in disrespectful, unprofessional ways. In Bernie's opinion, this lowered morale in the unit and increased the pressure on all the staff.
Ironically, after Bernie was forced to retire, the new judge lost his position and was placed in another assignment. Although this was of some consolation to Bernie, he did not mire in self-pity and a negative attitude. He reasoned that his retirement was beyond his control. Now a real estate salesman, he feels he is in a people-oriented business. He believes he is gaining a good reputation and doing more business because of it.

This case shows what it means to be a pawn at the mercy of a tough boss. Bernie is an example of the "typical" older worker who was forced out. Fortunately, he was able to find a new avenue for employment.

CHARACTERISTICS OF CAREER BARRIERS

Career barriers vary along at least three dimensions: (a) *clarity*, the individual's understanding of the barrier's causes and consequences; (b) *costs* in terms of the financial losses and emotional suffering; and (c) the *certainty* or irreversibility of the barrier. For both Abe and Bernie, job loss had high costs. There was not much either of them could do to avoid the layoff, and perhaps they denied the situation or hoped it would go away. They were able to find other places for themselves—other ways to bolster their self-esteem and continue to make a living, although Bernie seemed to be more successful at this than Abe.

Clarity, cost, and certainty of the career barrier combine to make the barrier more traumatic, for instance, when the individual realizes that a negative event is definitely going to happen but does not understand why or what to do about it. In general, the stronger these characteristics, the greater the impact of the barrier on the employee's emotions, thoughts, and actions. Here are some of the components of these characteristics of career barriers.

Clarity

A person's understanding or grasp of the situation is lower when the barrier is:

> *Sudden*—A career barrier that arises without warning results in surprise and shock.
>
> *Involuntary*—The individual had no choice about the barrier happening. For instance, it might have resulted from an organizational change such as a merger. Contrast this with a barrier that occurred by choice, that is, the employee made a decision or behaved in a way that precluded him or her from career opportunities (e.g., decided not to apply for a job; decided not to work harder; lacked important knowledge or work skills; or did not know how to search for, demand, or request a career opportunity).
>
> *Unclear*—The causes and consequences of the barrier and its long-term impact on one's life are unclear. The event may be puzzling to the employee. The employee realizes that a desired career goal has been denied or will not be available, but the employee is unsure who is to blame and how to deal with the situation. for instance, whether it is worth trying to change it or whether it is better to give up on the goal.

Costs

The costs of a career barrier are higher when the barrier is:

Visible to others—The career barrier is public knowledge. For instance, others know that the employee was denied a promotion, did not receive a raise, or was fired. This is likely to make the career barrier all the more salient and require a public reaction, even if this reaction does not match how the employee really feels. For example, saying "It doesn't really matter" or "I didn't want the promotion anyway" may save face but still requires internal coping to deal with feelings of rejection and lower motivation.

Has an effect on other people—A career barrier is likely to seem worse to the employee if he or she is the only one affected than if others were affected similarly. When a career barrier is a shared experience, people available for commiseration and possibly taking joint actions to fight or in other ways deal with the situation. Employees may devote energy to organizing protests or helping each other seek other career opportunities through personal, one-on-one relationships or community efforts (for instance, ways to encourage new businesses in the region that in turn will generate new career opportunities).

Affects other aspects of life—The career barrier has effects on other aspects of life beyond career, such as family, health, leisure pursuits. This can be thought of as the multiplier effect. Price (1992) reviewed the literature on the mental health effects of job loss. He found that the impact of job loss included the effects of financial strain, marital difficulty and conflict, reduced affiliation in personal and social networks, and financial loss (e.g., loss of house or other personal property). For married workers, the spouse and family provided a strong support system that had protective effects on mental health. Being married provided a strong support system.

Certainty

A barrier is more certain, definite, or unequivocal when it is:

Permanent—The career barrier is not going to change. Waiting it out will not alter the situation. The employee does not see a way to alter or reverse the situation after it has occurred. The obverse is that the individual is able to change, influence, or overcome the barrier directly (by one's own decisions, negotiations, or action) or indirectly (by influencing others' decisions or actions). Of course, the same career barrier may seem insurmountable to one person, whereas another looks for loopholes or other alternatives.

Trauma

Traumatic changes are those that occur suddenly without explanation, have high costs, and are immutable. Overall, the more the aforementioned characteristics are prevalent, the more uncertain the individual is likely to be about how to react to, and cope with, the situation. On the other hand, the slower and more imperceptibly the barrier arises, the lower its impact on other aspects of life; the more easily the situation can be changed or reversed, the less traumatic the barrier and the easier it is to determine what to do or feel comfortable doing nothing, at least in the shortrun.

TYPES OF CAREER BARRIERS

Abe and Bernie provide examples of job loss. However, this is just one type of career barrier. Table 1.1 lists types and examples of career barriers many people actually face and even more worry about. Abe and Bernie may have experienced several of these as their careers progressed, even without realizing it. Barriers can stem from factors that are external to the individual and beyond the individual's control (Swanson & Tokar, 1991; Melamed, 1996). These may be general environmental factors such as economic trends (cost cutting, mergers), global markets and competition, demographics/the labor market, and new technology. There are also specific organizational, environmental, or situational changes or conditions. They may be stimulated by general environmental trends or by events that are organization-specific, such as restructuring, the decision to close a plant, adoption of a new technology, job redesign, quality of supervision, and increased work load demands, all of which may lead to career barriers. Other barriers stem from organizational actions that affect specific individuals, such as being fired or being passed over for promotion.

Barriers can also stem from the individual. General individual characteristics that may influence career progress are intelligence and certain aspects of personality, such as aggressiveness (or lack thereof). Individual characteristics that may influence career progress include the ability to learn and do particular work. Non-job-related individual characteristics, especially age, race, gender, and physical appearance, may hamper a person's

TABLE 1.1

Types and Examples of Career Barriers

General organizational/environmental barriers
    Limited career opportunities
    Technological change
    Changing business climate
    Early career ceiling

Specific organizational, environmental, and situational barriers
    Job demands
    Poor supervision
    Organizational change
    Business failure
    Multirole conflict
    Uncertainty about the future
    Disapproval by others
    Lack of Information
    Company Relocation
    Underutilization
    Electronic monitoring

Organizational actions that affect specific individuals
    Job loss
    Whistle-blowing
    Job stress
    Denial of tenure
    Demotion
    Passed over for promotion
    Job transfer

General individual barriers
    Physical or mental disability
    Low motivation
    Desire for a nontraditional lifestyle
    Lack of self-confidence
    Indecision
    Overqualified for the job market
    Career transition late in life

Job-specific individual barriers
    Poor job performance
    Disaffection with one's career
    Inadequate experience/training
    Physical disability

Non-job-related individual barriers
    Discrimination or Unfair Treatment
    Immigrant status
    Nonwork Losses

career; this occurs through the unfair discrimination or bias of those responsible for evaluating and making decisions about these individuals. As such, these career barriers have, in part, a social and societal explanation. Other sources of career barriers may not be work related at all, such as a personal loss or a physical disability that makes it hard to go on.

Following are some examples of the way these career barriers occur. Note that some of the examples could fit under more than one type of career barrier. For instance, physical disability could lead to discrimination or it could be a bona fide reason that precludes a person from a particular career or that halts an ongoing career.

General Organizational/Environmental Barriers

Changing business climate: The dynamic and changing business environment is catalyst for changes in how people view their careers. There is a need for the organization and the individual to recognize and manage changing perceptions of career.

Early career ceiling: Athletes face early career barriers and the need for career transition. Even the most successful athletes face early retirement as their physical abilities decline and younger, more able teammates and competitors come on the scene. This can be a difficult and disruptive process for many athletes given the early and enduring identification, familiarity, and preference athletes have for their sport (Baillie & Danish, 1992).

Specific Organizational, Environmental, and Situational Barriers

Business failure: Entrepreneurs are no strangers to business failures. Starting a business often requires total dedication, and losing the business can be an emotionally devastating, not to mention financially draining, experience. Nevertheless, it can be a critical learning experience that promotes future business success.

Multirole conflict: Problems or demands from one's family (spouse, children) or friends may distract the individual's attention from working toward a career goal or may even demand that the individual give up the goal or settle for something less. For instance, responsibility for children may mean that the employee cannot travel or relocate. Commitments to a recreational sports team or a community organization may take time and energy away from pursuing a career goal. Sex-role conflicts may occur when, for instance, a husband expects his wife to contribute to the family income and take care of the children and home.

Uncertainty about the future: Trying to look ahead and make career choices about likely opportunities is difficult. Some career options promise (but do not guarantee) opportunities (e.g., the recruiter telling the college senior, "Work for us and you will be in our fast track management development program" or the boss telling the experienced manager, "Transfer to a job overseas and you will be rewarded later"). Increasingly, even promises are hard to come by. Nevertheless, feelings of career uncertainty can be frustrating, can stymie the individual's motivation, and can actually prevent the person from following a particular career path.

Disapproval by others: Significant others may disapprove of a career direction or goal perhaps because of lack of status or opportunities for employment and advancement. Parents may not want their child to major in a discipline that does not seem to have a future. They worry whether the student will be able to find a job after graduation and may not see the broader opportunities that could become available.

Lack of information: One of the reasons for uncertainty may be lack of information. This might seem easily resolved, at least when information is available. However, people may not know how to acquire necessary information—for instance, what one has to learn to get a particular job, start one's own business, or get help.

Company relocation: An organization may decide to move its operations, giving employees the "choice" to go along or lose their jobs. Other regions of the country may present better job opportunities, but the employee may not want to disrupt their family members' lives and community ties.

Underutilization: Employees often become frustrated when their jobs cease to use their skills to the fullest or give them a chance to learn.

Electronic monitoring: Electronic monitoring may produce stress through work overload, exhaustion, loss of control, little decision-making latitude, and negative computer feedback (Saxton, Phillips, & Blakeney, 1991; Schleifer & Shell, 1992). This stress is greater for those who have trouble meeting work standards enforced through electronic monitoring.

Organizational Actions That Affect Specific Individuals

Job loss: Job loss may be viewed as challenging experience rather than an insurmountable barrier. For instance, in a study of 59 professional women who involuntarily lost their jobs, family flexibility was most predictive of viewing the job loss as a growth experience. Having financial resources and low pre-job-loss satisfaction also predicted viewing the job loss in terms of career growth (Eby & Buch, 1995). For 456 male displaced professionals, avoiding financial hardship, emotional acceptance of the job loss, and the opportunity to leave a dissatisfying job were predictive of viewing the job loss as a growth experience.

Job stress: Job stress may stem from many sources. It could come from a new boss who has higher standards and work demands, an insensitive and abuse supervisor, coworkers who are uncooperative, and increased work load. Among university teachers, heavy work load was a frequently cited reason for considering job change. Female teachers were more likely than men to consider job change as a result of job stress (Blix, Cruise, Mitchell, & Blix, 1994).

Denial of tenure: Many positions have probationary periods. This may be a matter of months or a year (in the case of government civil service employees or unionized positions in the private sector). In other cases, the tenure decision may be made 5 or 6 years after starting the job (as in the case of college or university faculty members). Denial of tenure can often be appealed. Some people in this situation give up, their motivation declines, and they leave the field altogether. Others recover and strengthen their motivation, seek an extension, double their efforts to demonstrate their worth, seek better opportunities elsewhere, or any combination thereof.

Demotion: Having to move to a lower level job can be highly embarrassing and certainly makes further advancement unlikely. It may also mean using fewer skills and having less responsibility. However, a demotion can have benefits—for instance, the chance to work less hard and develop nonwork interests. If the demotion is to a job in a new area (e.g., a manager of a technical function moving to sales or marketing), the job change may be a chance to learn new skills and advance in the new area.

Passed over for promotion: Watching others receive promotions can also be tough experience. It may mean losing face in front of others and being denied more money, benefits, status, and privileges, not to mention new challenges, responsibilities, and the chance for further advancement. Having been denied a promotion once may be viewed as reaching a career plateau.

Job transfer: Transferring to a different job in the organization at the same level in the same organization (a lateral transfer within an organization) can impose threats and increase job demands. Transferred employees sometimes feel they are starting from scratch in that they need to show their worth in a new situation. However, the payoff may be worthwhile. In a sample of 225 employees, rotation was predicted by career antecedents such as tenure and performance and was related to career to outcomes such as promotion and salary, positive feelings, and perceptions of skill acquisition (Campion, Cheraskin, & Stevens, 1994). In general, job change can be exciting, enhancing opportunities for personal and professional growth as well as new career options and experiences. However, it can also be tumultuous and distressful and have an adverse effect on quality of life (Black & Loughead, 1990).

General Individual Barriers

Lack of self-confidence: The individual does not believe in his or her ability to attain a desired career goal. The individual might say "I am not smart enough" or "I cannot stack up against the competition."

Indecision: Uncertainty and lack of information can make one indecisive. Some people have trouble making decisions to begin with; they shy away from commitments, or are afraid of being wrong. They might not know how to identify the possibilities or trying them out.

Overqualified for the job market: A person may want employment and be willing to accept a job that does not fully utilize his or her skills. Certainly, this would be desirable in a tight job market. Also, the individual may see this as a way to enter an industry and hopefully move up from there. However, employers may shy away from people who are overqualified for fear they will leave at the first opportunity for more pay and responsibility.

Career transition late in life: Consider older workers who try to change their careers. Transition issues include dealing realistically with negative perceptions of older workers and recognizing the advantages of the mature career changer (Newman, 1995).

Job-Specific Individual Barriers

Poor job performance: Negative feedback can be devastating. In general, feedback is a touchy issue. Employees rarely want it, and supervisors often shy away from giving feedback, whether positive or negative. Performance appraisals are often completed halfheartedly, and sometimes are not even given to the employee. A negative appraisal can be viewed as a career barrier. It can result in carefully considered internal causal attributions and constructive coping strategies ("What can I do to improve?"). Alternatively, it can result in a defensive, hastily arrived at conclusion that others are to blame ("I need to get away from this boss!"; I deal with these issues in London, 1995a, 1995b.)

Dissatisfaction with one's career: A series of small failures may add up to dissatisfaction with the field. Changes in work conditions (the environment, funding and other resources, work load) may also make a career less appealing.

Inadequate experience/training: Increasing skill and knowledge requirements may preclude the individual from career opportunities and may even decrease the individual's performance. Advancing technology, competition from younger workers, and changing organizational goals may require continuous learning. People who do not keep up with their fields or do not learn other disciplines may miss out on career opportunities.

Physical disability: People who experienced physical trauma through an accident, the sudden onset of a debilitating illness (e.g., a stroke, cancer), or an increasingly debilitating chronic illness are likely to find their careers disrupted. As with other career barriers, the severity of the disability, their resilience, and sources of support will determine the extent to which the disability becomes a barrier. Newspapers frequently highlight the remarkable "comeback" achievements of individuals who have been severely injured. (Recall the actor Christopher Reeves, who is pursuing writing, directing, and speaking opportunities despite almost total paralysis and the inability to breathe without a respirator.)

Non-Job-Related Individual Barriers

Discrimination: People are denied access to a career goal or negative decisions are made about them on the basis of their race,

religion, age, handicap, gender, sexual orientation, physical appearance, or other personal characteristics that are not related
to the job. Reaching the "glass ceiling"—not being promoted
beyond a certain point—is a common barrier faced by women.
Being an immigrant: People often immigrate to other countries
do so for political reasons, religious reasons, economic reasons,
or a combination of these. Often they lose professional credentials (e.g., the Russian physician who cannot practice in the
United States), suffer discrimination, need to learn a new language—not to mention find new customers, struggle to make
ends meet, and strive for better opportunities for their offspring.
Being a refugee makes difficult occupational situations seem
more difficult. In a 2-year interview study of 1,169 adult Southeast Asian refugees resettling in Vancouver, British Columbia,
and a comparison sample of 319 permanent residents of the city,
it was shown that underemployment did not jeopardize the
mental health of permanent residents as much as refugees
(Beiser, Johnson, & Turner, 1993).

Nonwork Losses As Career Barriers

What happens outside of work can become a career barrier. This may
include family demands or nonwork interests, which may spill over to
affect career motivation. Examples are the loss of a significant other
through death or divorce, being elected to a demanding office of a
community group, taking up an engaging hobby, and no longer being able
to pursue a valued hobby. Such events may create career barriers by
decreasing job performance or limiting the accessibility of certain career
opportunities. For instance, someone who was injured and requires
special treatments cannot easily relocate when their company moves
unless similar resources are available in the new location.

Multiple Simultaneous Career Barriers

Different career barriers may occur together. Consider the plight of older
workers: They may face age discrimination, physical decline, changing work
demands, changing business environments, and perhaps job loss. Immigrants face lack of skills, language difficulties, and discrimination. Individuals who lost their jobs due to corporate downsizing may face age

discrimination, competition from others looking for jobs at the same time, and family pressure not to relocate.

Subjective Nature of Barriers

A career barrier is not just an objective event. It must be perceived as a barrier by the individual who is affected. Barriers are very much in the eye of the beholder. The same event may be perceived as a barrier to one person and an opportunity to another. That is why some people say that losing their job was the best thing that ever happened to them. Others never recover. People who rarely change jobs may perceive themselves to be further behind in their career than those who change jobs frequently (Herriot, Gibson, Pemberton, & Pinder, 1993). On the other hand, lower pay for women, job loss, and being passed over for promotion are objective events. Career-related events have objective qualities that cannot be denied, such as *loss* (e.g., the removal of a desired source of reward) and *punishment* (an aversive situation; Perrez & Reicherts, 1992). How one perceives or interprets these qualities determines how a person reacts to them.

Anticipating Career Barriers

Career barriers can have effects before they actually occur. For instance, the anticipation of career barriers may influence career choice. Internal barriers, such as a low self-concept or low motivation to achieve, may prevent a person from undertaking a challenging career (Perrez & Reicherts, 1992). Perceptions of external barriers, such as anticipated discrimination, may also prevent an individual from entering a particular profession.

The numbers and types of anticipated barriers tend to vary by gender, according to a 1991 study of 558 students (313 female and 245 male; Perrez & Reicherts, 1992). Women perceived a significantly higher likelihood of confronting sex discrimination and interference of children in their career progress whereas men perceived a higher likelihood of sex-role conflict, difficulties from marriage and children, and physical disability.

Learning From Tough Experiences

Career barriers can become learning experiences that prevent future barriers or lead to more constructive actions when new barriers arise. McCall, Lombardo, and Morrison published a study in 1988 of "lessons" executives said they learned from various work-related hardships (see also

McCall, 1994). These lessons included: (a) *set and implement agendas* (e.g., regarding technical and professional skills, details about one's business, and long-term strategy), (b) *handle relationships* (e.g., those involving political situations, ways to get others to implement solutions, understanding other people's perspectives, and how to work with executives, negotiate, and deal with conflict); (c) *maintain basic values* (e.g., recognize that you cannot manage everything alone and that you need to be sensitive to the human side of management); (d) *watch your temperament* (e.g., be tough when necessary, show and feel self-confidence, cope with situations beyond your control, persevere through adversity, cope with ambiguous situations, use—do not abuse—power), and (e) *develop personal awareness* (e.g., the balance between work and personal life and a recognition of personal limits and blind spots).

This suggests that we can learn about how people react to, and cope with, career barriers by studying people whose careers have derailed. These may be people who overcame barriers to goals, people who derailed and failed to recover, people who established careers despite handicaps, or successful people who have been through personal or organizational transitions without missing a beat.

CAREER ASSESSMENT INTERVIEW

Recording a person's life story can be a way to understand continuity and change within lives over time (Cohler, 1991). It can be used to make sense of lived experiences, especially adversity. The record can be evaluated by those reading it. Explanations can be sought for the origins, impact, and resolution of adversity. This necessitates teasing out the teller's causal attributions that serve as defense mechanisms (e.g., blaming others for negative events or blaming the past for the present; Kaplan, 1991).

In order to explore reactions to career barriers in this book, advanced human resource graduate students conducted interviews with a total of 90 people who, within the last 2 or 3 years, had been through a major career transition (not just a job change), faced a major career barrier (e.g., was repeatedly denied a promotion, was displaced by a downsizing, was fired, experienced a period of high stress), or overcame a handicap to find a job. The individual could still be confronting the situation. The goal was to identify a diverse group of people at different career and life stages who encountered different types of career barriers.

While this was an opportunity sample of individuals known by the interviewer to have experienced a career barrier, the stories helped us gain a deeper understanding of how people react to a host of career barriers. The interviews were minimally structured. The students were encouraged to have a free-flowing discussion during which they could ask probing questions. The interviewers were directed to cover the following areas:

- Biographical characteristics—occupation, employer, age, gender, education, marital status, children, time with current employer, time in current job, brief career history.
- Career barrier or change—how the career barrier started, the environment (job, organization, supervisor, coworkers, family support, available information), how long the transition lasted, and any identifiable stages of the transition.
- Reactions and actions—what the interviewee did to cope, resolve the situation, make the change, etc.; how the interviewee felt (emotions); what helped (personal characteristics or situational conditions that made things better); what hurt (e.g., personal characteristics or situational conditions that made things worse).
- The current situation.
- Outcomes—positive and negative; what the interviewee learned from the experience.

The interviewers summarized each interview in a four- to six-page narrative report addressing each of the areas in the interview discussion. Selected cases, summarized from these reports, are presented in several chapters and in Appendix A. A catalogue of the cases organized by type of career barrier is presented in Appendix B.

SUMMARY

This chapter described characteristics and types of career barriers. Barriers can be described along three dimensions: their clarity, cost, and certainty. The more unclear, costly, and certain the barrier, the more traumatic it feels and the less the individual knows what to do about it. Carrier barriers are more traumatic when they occur with little or no warning, have pervasive effects on other parts of one's life, and cannot be changed or reversed.

Career barriers may arise from downturns in the economy, organizational changes, decisions that affect certain individuals, general individual characteristics, job-related individual characteristics, non-job-related individual characteristics, and unfavorable life events that spill over to work. Several tough situations can occur together, compounding the career barrier.

Career barriers are subjective in that the same event may be traumatic to one person and a liberating experience to another. Although career barriers can help a person learn how to handle and avoid negative situations in the future, this is learning the hard way.

The next chapter examines how people react to career barriers and try to make sense of them. First, however, we look at some additional case examples.

FROM THE CASE FILE

The two cases described earlier in the chapter deal with the effects of layoff: an engineer affected by the decline in the defense industry, and a man in late career forced to retire by a new boss. Here, now, are three cases that deal with other major career barriers: discrimination, downsizing, and other organizational changes. In the first case, a young attorney was the victim of sex discrimination. In the second, a long-term clerk's job was disrupted when the senior partners in her firm left. Finally, a midcareer executive faced sudden unemployment.

SEX DISCRIMINATION (CASE 1.3)

This is another example of a pawn—this time a young professional woman who faced gender discrimination:

The case focuses on Alicia, a 30-year-old junior attorney married with no children. She complained about being assigned all the "grunt" work in her firm. She was not allowed to perform to her potential, and was stuck doing clerical-type work. Promised raises never materialized. The partners kept placating her with promises of pay raises and advancement while continuing to demand rush jobs below her capabilities. At the time Alicia was interviewed for the study, she was just coming to grips with understanding that she was being unfairly treated. She was starting to search for another job rather than try to change the firm.

A CHANGE IN SUPERVISION (CASE 1.4)

Barbara is an example of another grain of sand caught in the turmoil of her bosses' seemingly unethical behavior and resulting organizational change. However, she was able to be true to her loyalties and take positive actions that may have saved her job as well as her employer's livelihood:

Barbara is a 47-year-old woman, married, with two grown children. Her administrative job of 12 years was disrupted when the senior partner in the medical practice became ill. *The other partners and professional personnel changed the office routines and eventually split the practice and moved out on their own. Barbara and several colleagues stayed loyal to the senior partner, who eventually returned to pick up the pieces. This staff of diehards worked with little compensation to keep patients until the senior partner returned to pick up the pieces of his practice.*

ANOTHER CASE OF DOWNSIZING (CASE 1.5)

This case is an example of framebreaking change—a job loss that came from out of the blue. It describes how poor insight results in an initial shock when the axe falls.

Bob is a 48-year-old male, married with two sons in their early 20s. With a BS in accounting, he held a series of controller positions. The focus of the case is his last position with a printing firm where he had worked for 3 years. The company ran into financial troubles as a result of poor investment decisions by the owner. To help cut costs, Bob recommended firing two people who were deadweight. Unfortunately, he did not foresee that his boss would do the same with him. This was a shock. After 21 weeks of looking, he found another CFO job.

Bob's coping strategy was to go all out to find another position. He sent out 1,500 resumes with a 7% response rate, proving that finding a job is partly a numbers game (as is selling anything). His philosophy was that he was highly qualified and that eventually he would find someone who was looking for the experience and expertise he had to offer. He did, but at a slightly lower salary, a much longer commute, and after about 5 months on unemployment.

II

How People React to Career Barriers

2

The Pain of Failure

In the last chapter, I suggested that career barriers are more traumatic when they occur suddenly for no clear reason, they are costly in terms of their effects on a one's life, and they cannot be reversed easily. This chapter examines people's emotional reactions to career barriers and how they think about (make sense of) career barriers. Feelings and thoughts are related. Our emotions affect how we interpret or make sense of events. Moreover, our interpretation of events may lead us to draw conclusions about how we feel about them. Our feelings may even be the result of hearing what others who are similarly affected said about the same situation.

This chapter starts by considering how emotions arise from negative events and change over time as the situation evolves. Next, thought processes resulting from career barriers are considered by examining how negative situations are viewed—that is, how we notice, categorize, and reach conclusions about the reasons for events and their likely effects. I then cover the linkages between emotions and thoughts as a basis for understanding how people cope with career failure.

First consider two cases of people who faced situations that were hard for them to interpret at first, yet had lasting effects on their careers and lives.

STRUGGLING TO UNDERSTAND
TOUGH SITUATIONS (CASE 2.1)

Carl was a law barrister in a Caribbean country whose career dead-ended after refusing to accept a bribe. He was blamed for the situation and could not overcome the accusation of collusion. He was initially bewildered by the accusations that he was a partner in crime, not a victim; he was not sure what he could have done to clear his name. Because he was never formally charged, he had no formal opportunity to defend himself. Even if he had been found innocent in a court of law, his reputation was irretrievably damaged. Once he fully understood the political underpinnings of his situation, he decided that his only alternative was to leave the country. He continued to practice as well as he could while being shunned by his colleagues. He reacted calmly, biding his time until it was possible for him to relocate to the United States. He did so, but settled for a less prestigious position that did not utilize his education and experience.

Whether a more insightful and creative individual could have found a more constructive response is uncertain. Of course, the situation may have presented a convenient excuse for immigrating. In any case, Carl suffered a severe loss in self-esteem and reputation that he will never completely recover. This case shows how bad luck, unsavory acquaintances, and a slow response can stymie a career. Carl did not recognize what was happening to him until it was too late. Although he did the right thing, his only recourse was to withdraw—from his prestigious job and the country.

JEALOUSY AND UNFAIR TREATMENT
(CASE 2.2)

This case focuses on Carol, a medical technologist, who had worked in her profession for 9 years and had been with her current employer, a major medical laboratory, for the last 7. The problem deals with the effects of coworkers perceiving a close working relationship developing between Carol and the department director—Carol's boss' boss.

Carol's boss began to find problems with her work. This escalated to verbal and written warnings about her job performance. Eventually, Carol's personal affairs and work record began to be the subject of gossip. The department head felt there was nothing he could do without making things worse. After about a year of this, the chief administrator reassigned Carol to another department under the guise that her shift was no longer necessary. Unfortunately, the new department was not as prestigious and did not have as interesting work as the first department. Carol felt powerless. The reassignment was humiliating, and as such was not exactly a fresh start. However, at least she did not have to face the same people anymore day in and day out.

This is an example of another situation that was difficult for the individual to interpret. As in Carl's predicament, Carol's career barrier was brought on by others when a positive relationship with the department head seemed to make others jealous, souring the situation for Carol.

REACTIONS TO JOB LOSS

Both Carl and Carol faced humiliating and emotionally debilitating situations. Carl decided to make a major career and life change because of it.

Chapter 1 described some emotionally devastating career barriers, such as discrimination. The cases of Abe and Bernie, described at the outset of chapter 1, dealt with job losses late in their careers. Our knowledge of feelings and thoughts that accompany career barriers stems primarily from studies of job loss. As I mentioned in the first chapter, Leana and Feldman (1992) studied how people responded to losing their jobs. Specifically, they studied 163 employees associated with the aerospace industry in and around Brevard County, FL, following the Challenger disaster in January 1986, and 198 steelworkers from U.S. Steel's Homestead plant in the Monongahela Valley outside of Pittsburgh in 1986. Following is a summary of their findings.

Perceptual Changes

Perceptual changes refer to trying to make sense of the job loss—for example, appraising why it happened and what it says about the individual and future opportunities. For many the job loss was perceived as intense, causing severe stress and disruption in their lives. They saw the situation as almost irreversible and expressed having feelings of hopelessness. Moreover, they blamed themselves. The longer they were out of work, the longer they began to feel that nothing they could do could alter the situation. This is the phenomenon of "learned helplessness" (Abramson, Seligman, & Teasdale, 1978).

Emotional Changes

Job loss can result in a variety of negative emotions, such as depression, loneliness, apathy, passivity, resignation, and overwhelming pessimism. On the other hand, some people respond to job loss by enhanced motivation to restore personal control to their lives (Wanberg & Marchese, 1994). This is most likely for those individuals who maintained their belief that they had the freedom to engage in behaviors that would produce positive outcomes, that this was important to them, and that it was worth fighting to avoid losing this freedom. Leana and Feldman (1992) found in their two samples that depression and apathy were strongest during the first 6 months of unemployment. Depression lessened a bit for those out of work 7 to 9 months, and then increased again for those unemployed over 9 months. Once money from unemployment insurance ran out (after the first 6 months), those still unemployed responded by trying to gain control. After that, they sank into depression and learned helplessness.

Physiological Distress

Job loss has been linked to negative effects on the immune system (the individual's ability to combat illness; Zakowski, Hall, & Baum, 1992). Leana and Feldman (1992) found high levels of physiological distress in their samples, but these symptoms were not related to stages per se. With this as background, let us now look more deeply into emotional and thought processes.

EMOTIONS

Emotions are subjective experiences that arise from a situation, stem from characteristics of the individual, or both. An emotional *state* refers to feelings about a particular situation. As a result of the situation you feel mad, angry, irritated, annoyed, resentful, and so forth (Frijda, 1988). An emotional trait is an enduring personality characteristic. For instance, you have a fiery temper, or generally feel depressed, anxious, or sad. Some emotions that might result from career barriers include humiliation, depression, sadness, disappointment, apathy, hurt, anger, fear, worry, insult, insecurity, disgust, resignation, resentment, grief (feelings of loss), guilt, self-deprecation, self-pity, and victimization. Both Carl and Carol experienced many of these feelings (hurt, anger, humiliation) as they tried to interpret their situations and determine what to do.

Our feelings generally reflect what has happened and guide later actions. In this sense, emotions are the bridge between the past and the future (Weiner & Graham, 1989). Emotions help people direct their attention to certain goals and the methods they use to achieve them (Schwarz, 1990). This applies to how employees make choices about what specific job behaviors to engage in and how much initial effort to exert and to how employees regulate their behavior once they are engaged in a chosen task (Kanfer, 1990).

Feelings and Moods

Feelings are less intense than emotions, and are commonly referred to as moods. Moods generally do not interrupt ongoing thought processes and behaviors, but they can influence them. Thus, emotions can interrupt thought processes and behaviors while moods provide the context for thought processes and behaviors. An individual can become used to an emotion and his or her ongoing behavior is influenced by the less intense, although prevailing, mood.

There are, of course, positive and negative moods. Positive moods include feeling attentive, interested, alert, excited, enthusiastic, and proud. Negative moods include feeling afraid, guilty, hostile, or distressed (Burke, Brief, George, Roberson, & Webster, 1989).

Moods have internal and external causes. Internal roots include personality. External roots include situational conditions. Context affects motivation through mood (George & Brief, 1995). Moods are not just individually based. Work groups and organizational climate can generate moods, such as general enthusiasm or distress, that affect the individuals in these groups or organizations.

Feelings and How We View Ourselves

Situations that elicit feelings may influence what we think about ourselves. For instance, research indicates that recalling a positive or negative achievement experience for which people take personal responsibility influences their judgments of how competent they are when trying to achieve a goal (Levine, Wyer, & Schwarz, 1994). Forming judgments about oneself and others is not simply a calm, rational process. It involves feeling emotions in ourselves, feeling emotions as we observe others, and making inferences about the emotions others are feeling (empathy; London, 1995a).

Evidence of Emotions

Emotions and associated personality characteristics, such as arrogance, agreeableness, and gregariousness, are evident from nonverbal as well as verbal behavior. There may be a set of basic emotions that we use to structure our perceptions of others and ourselves. This set of emotions is likely to include happiness, sadness, anger, fear, and disgust (Johnson-Laird & Oatley, 1989). However, the set may be much larger, including such emotions as (in alphabetical order) anger, awe, contempt, disgust, embarrassment, enjoyment (which encompasses amusement, contentment, relief, and accomplishment), excitement, fear, guilt, interest, sadness, shame, and surprise (Ekman, 1992).

THOUGHT PROCESSES

In earlier work, I argued that how we see ourselves and others arises from the way we process information (London, 1995a). Information that can be categorized into our current view of ourselves is processed automatically or mindlessly (Beach & Mitchell, 1990; Langer, 1975). Information that is startling in some way, such as the sudden realization of a career barrier, results in mindful thought processing. That is, the individual has to give the event and its implications some thought. However, mindful processing might still result in categorizing the information into our current self-perception. As such, the information fails to deliver a new message and does not change behavior or perceptions of oneself or others.

If the information cannot be readily categorized or interpreted, the individual must decide the reason for the event and its likely effects. This is called a *causal attribution*. The attribution may change how the individual sees him- or herself, the work environment, and future career directions and opportunities. This is the development of career insight. Accurate attributions are likely to result in functional coping strategies, as long as the individual has the capability to behave in new ways to remove or overcome the career barrier. Inaccurate attributions may be defense mechanisms that protect the individual in the short run from having to deal with the situation.

Consider some examples of how these thought processes evolve. Suppose an employee receives negative performance feedback (a poor performance rating or a rejected project proposal). The employee may process the information automatically by believing "My boss never says anything good about anybody," or "Projects are never accepted the first time around." If the employee gives the information some attention, the employee may still arrive at the same conclusion, perhaps after collecting comparative information about how others were evaluated or faired on their proposals.

Alternatively, thinking about the information may not yield a convenient way to explain the behavior. The employee may attribute the evaluation to forces beyond his or her control in the form of a new category, possibly denying the negative impact of the evaluation (e.g., "Negative ratings do not mean anything anyway" or "No one cares whether my proposal is accepted or not—it does not have any implications for how much I make or what opportunities are open to me"). Another possibility is that the employee accurately attributes the negative information to an external cause, and internal cause, or both (e.g., "The boss speaks from experience, and can give me good advice about what to do now" or "I know I did not put my best work into the proposal, but now I have a chance to revise it").

Some events are difficult to process carelessly. They hit with such force or are so puzzling or surprising that they cannot be denied or ignored. Losing one's job is a good example; however, an inaccurate attribution can still result as a way to protect one's self-concept. Thus the displaced employee may attribute the reason to external causes such as a corporate merger, blaming the job loss on the company or luck ("It was just chance that I was not chosen to stay with the firm"). This may be functional in helping the employee feel better about him or herself, but will not contribute to learning new, more effective behaviors. It may even give rise to a fatalistic approach to job search ("It is all luck. All I can do is send out my resume and wait for a bite.") On the other hand, the individual may recognize the factors in him- or herself and the situational that led to the job loss, and take constructive actions to find another job.

Explanations of How People Process Information

Several perspectives help explain how people think about career barriers. These include social information processing, control theory, and social comparison theory.

Social Information Processing.   Social information (for instance, one's boss' opinions) affects our perceptions, attitudes, and behaviors (Salancik & Pfeffer, 1978). Social information will affect an employee's perception of the job or task characteristics (Zalesny & Ford, 1990). These perceptions in turn affect the employee's job attitudes.

Control.   People seek to control the information about themselves that they recognize so that the information matches internally held standards (Carver & Scheier, 1981, 1982, 1990; Nelson, 1993; Powers, 1973a, 1973b). When they recognize a deviation from a particular standard, they may be motivated to change the environment so that the information they receive about themselves matches their standard (Conlon & Ross, 1993; Kernan & Lord, 1991; Nelson, 1993). Therefore, perceived discrepancies may be the basis for goal improvement. Performance feedback or information about how others performed establish standards for comparison, which in turn can become goals for doing better.

Control theory holds that people engage in a continual process of matching their behavior to a goal. Discrepant feedback causes them to reduce the discrepancies (Ashford, 1989; Carver & Scheier, 1981). Therefore, employees set standards, obtain feedback, detect discrepancies, and attempt to reduce discrepancies. They consider whether the standards they have chosen can be accomplished. Furthermore, they evaluate their own behavior in a manner consistent with how others perceive and evaluate it (Ashford, 1989).

Social Comparison.   People evaluate their opinions and abilities by comparisons with others, especially others who are similar to themselves (Brewer & Weber, 1994; Festinger, 1954). People particularly want to make such comparisons when they are uncertain about the level of their ability or the correctness of their opinions. People compare themselves with others who they perceive to be similar to themselves (Berger, 1977; Goethals & Darley, 1977). In addition to using social comparisons to gain accurate information, people use social comparisons to cope with threats to their self-esteem, for instance, by comparing themselves to others against whom they look good (Gibbons & Gerrard, 1991). Although this makes them feel better about themselves, the comparisons neither provide a constructive direction for improvement nor motivate improvement. Another dysfunctional comparison is comparing oneself to others who are so advantaged that they set standards one cannot possibly attain.

Barriers to Insight

Accurate attributions may not occur because of judgment biases. Examples include overconfidence (interpreting information in a way that confirms expectations and making an inaccurate judgment to avoid admitting a mistake; Russo & Schoemaker, 1992). These biases can be self-perpetuating in that they allow us to continue to have an inaccurate view of ourselves (Hill, Lewicki, Czyzewska, & Boss, 1989). The biases operate as we perceive and interpret information; as a result, some thoughts we take to be insights are not.

LINKAGES BETWEEN THOUGHTS
AND FEELINGS

Emotions and thought processes are inextricably linked. Emotions themselves do not require much thought processing in that minimal information may produce a strong emotional reaction (e.g., hearing a rumor of an impending layoff; Murphy & Zajonc, 1993). Also, negative emotions may cause us to avoid thinking about what happened as a way to prevent further pain (Heatherton, Polivy, Herman, & Baumeister, 1993). On the other hand, emotions may cause thought in the sense that feelings such as anger or sadness cause a search for explanation or interpretation (Schachter, 1964; Sinclair, Hoffman, Mark, Martin, & Pickering, 1994). For example, happiness may cause one to think about ways of helping others. Failing to accomplish a goal may lead to disappointment and search for an explanation (Mandler, 1990).

Social psychologist Robert Zajonc (1980) argued that thought and feelings are separate systems, although feelings often precede thought. Generally, information is perceived more positively when people are happy than when they are sad (Forgas, 1994). As such, the new information becomes associated with the positive feeling.

Although emotions may affect thoughts, the reverse is also true (Fiske & Taylor, 1991). For instance, the perception or anticipation of an event may give rise to emotions (as when one meets a new boss for the first time and feels apprehensive).

Certain types of occurrences are likely to give rise to specific emotions (Weiner & Graham, 1989). Failure caused by lack of ability is presumed to evoke different feelings than failure attributed to factors beyond one's control. Similarly, success attributed to high effort should produce emotions distinct from those elicited by success interpreted as due to help from others.

Lazarus (1991; reprinted with permission) suggested how specific emotions arise from certain types of events:

> Anger—A demeaning offense against me and mine.
> Anxiety—Feeling uncertain, existential threat.
> Fright—Facing an immediate, concrete, and overwhelming physical danger.
> Guilt—Having transgressed a moral imperative.
> Shame—Having failed to live up to an ego ideal.
> Sadness—Having experienced an irrevocable loss.
> Envy—Wanting what someone else has.
> Disgust—Taking in or being too close to an indigestible object or idea.
> Pride—Enhancement of one's ego identity by taking credit for a valued object or achievement.
> Relief—A distressing goal-incongruent condition that has changed for the better or gone away.
> Hope—Fearing the worst but yearning for better.
> Love—Desiring or participating in affection, usually but not necessarily reciprocated.
> Compassion—Being moved by another's suffering and wanting to help.
> Pride—Feeling good about oneself because of some accomplishment. (p. 122)

Other feelings are shame, humiliation, and embarrassment. These happen when the cause of a negative event is internal but uncontrollable.

Emotions may also be influenced by our personal characteristics. For instance, compassion increases as one ages. Pity and helping increase throughout the life span, whereas anger decreases. This was found in a study of people ranging in age from 5 to 95 (Weiner & Graham, 1989). This suggests that emotional reactions to negative events may differ depending on age. Older individuals, perhaps because they have a greater under-standing of the perils of life, are more compassionate and understanding, less prone to anger, and more prone to pity and helping. The converse suggests that younger people are more likely to be angered and perhaps deal less constructively with negative events.

Emotions color our judgments. For instance, people who feel sad are more likely to report health problems and be pessimistic about future health (National Advisory Mental Health Council Behavioral Science Task Force, 1995). Training may help people suppress sad or depressing thoughts that in turn encourage more thought processing and constructive responses.

GRASPING THE SITUATION: HOW WE INTERPRET CAREER BARRIERS

Now that we have covered some of the basics about thoughts and feelings, we can consider more deeply how people put their thoughts and feelings together to make sense of career barriers. The way we interpret a career barrier influences our ability to adapt to the barrier and treat it as a challenge (McAuliffe, 1993). We appraise career barriers by reasoning why they oc-curred and who was to blame, determining their likely effects, and judging whether the situation is really going to happen and whether it can be changed. The appraisal of a career barrier involves subjective, intuitive assessments of the discrepancy between the way things are and they way things should be from the individual's vantage point. The tendency to avoid such a discrepancy may lead to the distortion of information or interpretation that protects and motivates the individual. So an optimistic person may interpret job loss as a challenge in order to cope cognitively with the discrep-ancy—for example, "an opportunity to show what I can do" (Lazarus, 1991).

People can put up with a lot as they interpret the situation. Consider some more case examples. The following case describes a young man who with-stood a stressful job for 6 years until his was finally laid off when the firm went bankrupt. The next case describes another young person who stayed with a sinking ship and delayed facing a job search until she was unemployed.

DELAYING ACTION (CASE 2.3)

Ed, now 36 years old, is currently employed as a shop supervisor by a manufacturer of ultrasonic cleaning equipment. He is a high school graduate, is married, and has two children. He has worked for his present employer for 1 year. Prior to that he had worked for five different manufacturing firms. His last job lasted 6 years. Although this last job became increasingly stressful, Ed stuck with it until the firm went bankrupt and he lost his job. As the owners of the firm invested less of the profits in the business, Ed experienced fewer opportunities to grow professionally. Tuition assistance and training were cut. Also, he was expected to produce more with lower quality standards. The firm's reputation declined, and so did Ed's motivation and commitment. His creativity decreased, and he was not able to keep up with new technology because the firm did not update its equipment. Ultimately, the firm was forced to downsize and file for Chapter 11 and Ed lost his job. With the help of his family, the interviewee attended a technical institute, learned new skills, and found a new job.

An open question is why Ed did not act sooner, because he had a history of moving to new and better jobs every few years. Maybe his life stage and desire for job stability made him stay for as long as he did. Ed demonstrates that some people stick with a negative situation for a long time, and may not act until they have to. Either they have trouble appraising the situation for what it is, or they feel locked in by the job and their life stage. Ed faced an incremental career barrier—one arising during the course of 6 years of job stress. Eventually, he took positive action, including training in a new area.

GOING DOWN WITH A SINKING SHIP
(CASE 2.4)

Ellen is 29 years old and single with a BS in accounting. A staff accountant for what turned out to be a declining business, she was able to stay in her job until the office closed. Although she could have been transferred to another office, she did not want to commute. Her boss advised her to stay until she was laid off. Ellen received little information about the impending layoffs and office closing other than the rumors and job moves; she just let the situation evolve. Ellen's skills were general enough to be applicable to a variety of other organizations. However, as the layoff approached, she was upset about having little or no work to do and realizing she was "outta there." At the time of the interview, she had been unemployed for about 2 weeks with no prospects in sight.

People have trouble understanding what is happening to their employers. This may be especially likely for inexperienced people, such as Ellen, who feel they had little control over the job situation. Rather than take control by looking for another job, they stay with a sinking ship. This was also Ed's situation. However, he was more experienced than Ellen and should have known better. He had a history of poor job choices, and maybe this is what led him to avoid taking action for as long as possible even as his commitment and motivation declined.

Consider the effects of unemployment on emotions. Job loss frequently results in an initial grief-like response, which, not surprisingly, is more likely for people who felt strongly attached to their jobs before being laid off (Archer & Rhodes, 1993). Psychosocial symptoms are highest in the first year of unemployment (J. Jones, 1991–1992). The symptoms are highest on notification of job loss and 6 months after job loss. This may be because unemployment benefits diminish the blow until they run out. Psychosocial symptoms lessen and stabilize in the second year. Unfortunately, change may be difficult to bring about because people get mired in negative emotions (Beiser et al., 1993). There is a reciprocal relationship between unemployment and depression. Job loss results in increased risk of depression, and depression makes it more difficult to stay employed after finding work.

Emotions and the Interpretation of Events

As I indicated earlier, moods influence how people judge events. Individuals in a positive mood tend to see things in a positive light and be optimistic about the future (George & Brief, 1995). Mood affects how favorably we view the value of possible behaviors and outcomes and our optimism about our chances of achieving them. Moreover, people in a positive mood are likely to recall positive material from memory. So, for instance, they will remember the positive features of previously difficult situations (e.g., how good it felt to overcomes an obstacle, such as a boss who said no to an idea) and not recall the negative aspects of these situations (e.g., how much sleep was lost agonizing over how to convince the boss otherwise).

In addition, mood affects attributions. People in a negative mood make more internal and stable attributions for failures than for successes, whereas people in a positive mood make more internal and stable attributions for successes than for failures (Forgas, Bower, & Moylan, 1990). Negative mood and self-blame may have been why Ed and Ellen did not take action sooner to help themselves as their employers failed. Conversely, people in positive moods make more internal attributions for successes than failures both for themselves and others, whereas people in negative moods make more internal attributions for their own failures but not for the failures of others.

Being in a state of crisis influences feelings and judgments about why things happen. For example, people experiencing occupational crisis emphasize stable external and recurrent external attributions to negative events (Merja, 1995). Experiencing a crisis makes one consistently focus on external causes (e.g., blaming others) for the negative events. (By the way, this is not necessarily dysfunctional. For example, people who attribute their unemployment to external causes display higher self-esteem and less hopelessness than those who attribute their unemployment to internal causes; Winefield, Tiggermann, & Winefield, 1992.) Those not in crisis use nonrecurrent attributions combined with internal, unstable, and controllable attributions. That is, they tend to process the situation more mindfully, avoid automatic categorizations and attributions, and arrive at a reason, often an internal one, for the event.

We know that how people appraise an event—for instance, its perceived fairness—influences how they feel about it. For instance, the perceived fairness of the decision for who is laid off affects the extent to which the layoff experience is perceived negatively. One study included 218 people who were layoff victims, 150 employees who survived a layoff that occurred 5 to 7 months earlier, and 147 people who were scheduled to be laid off were recent layoff survivors (Brockner, Konovsky, Cooper-Schneider, & Folger, 1994). Perceptions of unfair treatment were associated with more adverse negative reactions.

Our beliefs about why something happened influence our emotions. Being laid off leads to lower levels of distress than being fired. A study of 1,016 working-class men between the ages of 20 and 45 who were recently unemployed found that men who were laid off attribute their job loss to external factors, such as the economy, whereas those who were fired attribute their job loss to unfair treatment by employers (Miller & Hoppe, 1994). Laid off workers who attributed the job loss to unfair treatment were as emotionally distressed as those who were fired, suggesting that the person's emotional reaction stemmed from perceived reasons (attributions) for the job loss.

Cognitive activity is important to emotion in determining how meaning is achieved and changed in an adaptational encounter (Lazarus, 1991). A *primary appraisal* involves reacting to the situation in which one has a personal stake. A *secondary appraisal* (what might be termed *hypothesis generation*) involves determining whether any given action might prevent harm, ameliorate it, or produce additional harm or benefit. It is an evaluation of a person's options, identification of resources for coping with the situation, and assessment of the likely success of the coping options.

Once accomplished, the appraisal is not static. It is a process, even for relatively stable beliefs and motives. We continuously engage in a struggle to understand what is happening to us. Moreover, we try to achieve an understanding that is consistent with our existing beliefs and psychological structures that we have established over the course of our lives. Also, we revise our goals and commitments that no longer make sense.

Appraisal Styles

People develop fairly stable appraisal styles—dispositions for appraising environmental conditions. We apply these styles especially to ambiguous situations. For example, some people are fundamentally optimists and others are pessimists. Such belief systems, also called schemas or scripts, consist of generalized knowledge about a concept or an experience. They can be thought of as a personal theory guiding what we tend to notice and recall and how we interpret new events and unfamiliar experiences (Epstein, 1980). Although a pattern of styles may dominate how an individual interprets events, this pattern may be changed and another style may emerge as a result of deliberate cognitive effort, trauma, psychotherapy, or some conversion experience.

Determining How People Appraise a Career Barrier

Lazarus (1991; reprinted with permission) offered the following questions that can be asked to determine how people evaluate a stressful situation:

- How important was the event to you?
- Think about what you didn't want in this situation. To what extent were these undesirable elements present in the situation?
- Think about what you did want in this situation. To what extent were these desirable elements present in the situation?
- To what extent did you consider yourself responsible for this situation?
- To what extent did you consider someone else responsible for this situation?
- Think about what you wanted and didn't want in this situation. How certain were you that you would be able to influence things to make (or keep) the situation the way you want it?
- How certain were you that you would, or would not, be able to deal emotionally with what was happening in this situation however it turned out?
- Think about how you wanted this situation to turn out. When you were in this situation, how consistent with these wishes (for any reason) did you expect this situation to become (or stay)?

Further, Lazarus showed how various conclusions about a stressful situation are related to different emotions. Here's the list of emotions and associated conclusions:

Blaming others—Anger

I have been cheated or wronged.

Someone else is to blame for the bad situation I am in.

I have been dealt with shabbily.

Some asshole is interfering with my goals.

Some jerk is trying to take advantage of me.

This bad thing would have been prevented if the other person had been worthy of respect.

Blaming oneself—Guilt

I have done something bad.

Things are bad because of me.

I am to blame for this bad situation.

Danger/Threat—Anxiety

I feel threatened by an uncertain danger.

I am in danger and might not be able to handle it.

I do not know whether I can handle what is about to happen.

Loss/Harm—Sadness/Resignation

I feel a sense of loss.

Something I cared about is gone.

Something important to me has been destroyed.

Harm

I feel helpless.

I do not see anything I can do to improve this bad situation.

Just now I seem to be powerless to make things right in this situation.

Nothing can ever be done to fix this bad situation.

This situation is hopeless.

This bad situation is never going to improve.

Optimism—Hope and Challenge

Somehow things might work out in this situation.

In the end there is a chance that everything will be OK.

I feel that things are going to get better in this situation.

If I try hard enough I can get what I want in this situation.

With some effort I can make things better in this situation.

I can handle this difficult task.

Relevance—Interest
  Something important to me is happening in this situation.
  This situation touches on my personal concerns.
  There are important things to think about here.
Removal of Threat—Relief
  A burden has been lifted from my mind.
  Things have worked out after all.
  A threat or harm has been removed from the situation.
Success—Happiness
  Things turned out great.
  I have gotten what I wanted in this situation.
  Things have gone wonderfully well in this situation.
Concern for Another—Sympathy
  I feel sorry for this (other) person.
  It bothers me that this (other) person is in trouble.
  This (other) person needs help.
Irrelevance—Boredom
  This situation is totally irrelevant to my concerns.
  I do not care at all about what is happening here.
  What is happening here is a total waste of time. (pp. 447–448)

Thus, how we think and feel about a stressful situation are linked together. We can ask people questions to determine how they interpret a situation and the conclusions they reached about how and why the situation occurred. The answers tell us something about their inner feelings—emotions they may not readily share if asked directly. Now we need to understand how thoughts and feelings affect how people cope with career barriers. This is the subject of the next chapter.

SUMMARY

This chapter focused on how thoughts and feelings interact in response to tough life situations such as career barriers. Not surprisingly, emotions arise from negative events and characteristics of the individual. Moreover, emotions change over time as the situation evolves. People struggle to understand negative events such as job loss. They develop rationales for themselves about why the event occurred and what it says about them and their future. In doing so, they go through a variety of emotional changes, such as depression, loneliness, and apathy. We also know from other research that emotional distress has physical consequences, such as negative effects of stress on the immune system. Feelings not only reflect what has happened but also provide guides for later actions. Strong emotions interrupt our ongoing thought processes and behaviors influencing the extent to which people can rationally interpret a career barrier and determine a constructive course of action. Moods are weaker than emotions and generally do not constrict or interrupt ongoing thought process and behaviors, but they can influence them.

We process information about career barriers as we try to make sense of them. Information that fits our predetermined beliefs about the world is categorized automatically. We do not learn anything new about from them about ourselves. However, a career barrier is not the type of event that fits our predetermined scheme of the way things should be. As a result, it can be a wake-up call that forces attention to information about the event and requires making conscious (mindful) attributions about the cause of the event and determining possible courses of action. Unfortunately, biases and strong emotions may get in the way of making realistic attributions, changing how we view ourselves, and arriving at constructive coping strategies. Having standards for comparison or watching others who are going through the same experience helps put things in perspective and formulate reasonable and effective responses.

When people confront a career barrier, they essentially appraise the discrepancy between the way things are and they way they would like them to be. Of course, people do not welcome such a discrepancy, and they distort information or develop an interpretation that protects them and maintains their motivation—at least for a while. Their emotional response to the career barrier leads to meaning and actions. Strong emotional responses are likely when the career barrier is recognized as important and possibly avoidable at one time (e.g, "If I only had gone back to school when I had the chance..."). Having a positive frame of reference can allay negative emotions. For instance, people take comfort in believing that they are still in control and can do something about the situation. Unfortunately, once strong negative emotions arise, they are hard to shirk. How people assess a career barrier can influence how they feel about it. For instance, the same barrier will elicit a stronger negative emotion if the barrier is perceived as unfair.

How people appraise a career barrier and respond to it emotionally can be determined. To determine how people appraised a career barrier, we could ask about how important the career goal was to them, the extent to which they did not want the barrier to occur, the extent to which they blame themselves or others, their belief that the situation can be changed in a positive direction, the extent to which they believe they can cope emotionally, and how they expect things to turn out. We can also ask how they feel about the situation (e.g., feel guilty, feel sad, believe the situation is hopeless, etc.).

Now that I have covered how people interpret career barriers and respond to them emotionally, I turn in the next chapter to what they do about them. First, however, here are some additional case examples.

FROM THE CASE FILE

Several of our case examples show how people make sense of situations that are emotionally trying and difficult to understand. Carl's situation described at the start of the chapter showed how someone can be victimized, leaving the victim little choice but to escape. Carol demonstrated how someone's jealously can create an intolerable situation with few obvious courses of action.

Here are several more cases. In the first one (Case 2.5), new technology was the excuse that sparked the individual to flee a dead-end position and learn a new profession. In Case 2.6, an increasingly difficult work schedule incited a young professional to explore opportunities for being her own boss. The next case (2.7) describes a person who had a history of working for employers who went out of business. The individual worried that others would blame him for the business failures, or at least for his bad job choices. Discovering that one's job or career has limited prospects can be disappointing. Case 2.8 describes someone who made a major transition in his twenties to find a more satisfying career direction. The following case (2.9) demonstrates that organizational change can cause people to evaluate and take steps to protect what is most important to them. The case describes a middle-aged woman who had been in the same job for 14 years and took a downgrade to a more secure job when the organization started to downsize. Finally, in Case 2.10, a person had to recognize the limitations of his own performance.

FACING NEW TECHNOLOGY (CASE 2.5)

Donna, a divorced woman in her mid thirties, had worked as a paralegal in a law office for the past 15 months. Prior to that she had been a waitress for 8 years, a real estate broker for 3 years, and a proofreader for 6 years—her last position before becoming a paralegal. The case describes why she made the career transition from proofreader to paralegal.
Donna's job in publishing was affected by new technology. With the advent of

computers, fewer proofreaders were needed. She and her coworkers were given a year's notice about the transition. Donna felt that she and the other employees affected by the change were resigned to losing their jobs. She had not been happy with the job itself. It was boring and going nowhere. She was relieved to get out of this dead end, but well-paying, job. However, she panicked about 4 months before her job ended. It helped to have others in the same boat. She was a single mother in a relationship that fell apart during this transition ("extra stress that I didn't need."). Donna stayed with her firm until "the end," and then began full-time paralegal training. Six months later, she found a job with a law firm where she had been an intern during her training. Now after 15 months she is making more money than she did on her previous job.

Donna learned that she can land on her feet. The career transition was scary, but she handled it in stride as a part of life's ups and downs. It is somewhat surprising that Donna stayed in her prior job as proofreader as long as it lasted without taking some action to prepare herself for another job. She could have gone to school part-time (although parenting responsibilities and her boyfriend may have made that difficult). She was smart to take the 6 months of full-time training, and it apparently worked out well.

FEELING OVERBURDENED (CASE 2.6)

This case shows how someone can struggle to evaluate changing circumstances (increased job demands) and formulate a career strategy:

Darlene is a 31-year-old occupational therapist who is experiencing job stress and would like to go into partnership with someone to start her own practice. After a year on her current job, which was initially rewarding and challenging, she and her peers now feel overburdened by the need to do more with less (caused by a paring down of state budgets). She has to handle an increased case load and do more paperwork, which she can finish only by taking it home, with no prospect of making more money. At present, Darlene is exploring other career opportunities in her profession. In particular, she would like to open a private practice that will include water therapy (e.g., swimming, use of whirlpools, and such). This requires capital. She is considering working with a partner, but the partner does not have much money to invest either. Darlene feels the burden of being stretched so thin in her current job (and as a result not providing the level of service her clients need) and the excitement of starting a new enterprise. In the little free time she has, she is learning more about how to start the new business and about the latest technical aspects of the profession. However, she has an underlying dread that she will not get the funds she needs to open her own practice. This would mean being stuck in her current, increasingly stressful job. She could look for something else, but has not reached that point yet.

WORRYING ABOUT WHAT OTHERS THINK OF
YOU (CASE 2.7)

This case shows how someone can get mired in worrying about what others think as he faces changing organizational conditions beyond his control. The interviewee hesitated to take action to find other employment. When he found another job, he got himself into the same situation:

> *Dan, a 41-year-old project manager, worked for a construction company for 12 years and was fired one week before Christmas a little over a year ago. He was not given any notice, and was told to leave the same day with no severance pay. The firm was a tightly held family business with about 100 employees. Dan was one of five project managers. The firm's owner gambled, and Dan had received several calls from the firm's creditors about overdue accounts. Dan thought something was amiss but did not think it would affect his job. He was devastated and embarrassed by his dismissal and took pains to explain to everyone that it was the company's fault, not his. He waited until after the holidays to start searching for a new job, and in the interim sought professional help in writing a resume.*
>
> *Dan found another job as a project manager for a start-up construction firm. He had to take a steep cut in pay, but was promised a raise after the first project was completed. He worked day and night, finished the project early, and was fired a week later. Apparently, the firm needed someone with his expertise for the project, but they had no intention keeping him. Again devastated, his principal concern was how others would see him. He worried that his family, friends, and prospective employers would question his abilities, even though he knew that his predicament was the result of being in bad situations. Feeling that next time he was not going to settle for the first job that comes along, he worked for a friend's marine repair business during the summer season. His wife felt they needed his previously higher salary, and she was tired of working full time to bring in more money. She felt he should be looking for a job in his field. However, he enjoyed working for his friend, despite the low salary. He considered a partnership with his friend, but the deal soured. By the end of the summer, a neighbor put in a good word for him with his employer—another construction firm. Dan was working again, and his wife went back to her part-time work schedule. It was unclear whether Dan learned anything about the value of investigating his employers before starting a new job, although working in any small firm, especially in the construction business, can mean uncertain job security.*

CREATING NEW CAREER OPPORTUNITIES
(CASE 2.8)

Whereas some people delay reactions to a career barrier, other people assess their career situation and make a move. Of course, this is easier for someone in early career. Following is the case of someone who made an early career change from engineer to attorney. As he made the career change he was naturally apprehensive about the stress and high expectations but he was obviously talented enough to accept them as challenges. His hard work paid off in being accepted to law school, doing well in his studies, and finding an excellent first job:

Earl, a married man, now 30 years old, graduated 9 years ago with a degree in mechanical engineering. He worked in the defense industry for several years. Although the work was fulfilling, he realized that the company was downsizing and his job was dispensable. After considerable thought, he decided to pursue a career in law which would utilize his engineering and technical experience. Earl left his firm and enrolled in a local law school as a full-time student. He considered several specialty areas, such as intellectual property and product liability, and eventually began practicing patent law. The transition took four years from the time he started law school to his present position as an associate with a law firm. He finds the work challenging, although it is stressful due to the constant pressure to excel.

FACING ORGANIZATION CHANGE (CASE 2.9)

Seeing the handwriting on the wall and taking action may be easier for someone who is seasoned:

Flora is 50 years old with an associates degree in paralegal studies. She is married and has three children, two of whom are in college. She has been employed as an administrative assistant at a university for 15 years and has been in her present title for 14 years. When she realized that the university was cutting back staff, she took a downgrade to gain civil service status and job security. Essentially, Flora prevented the career barrier from occurring, but simultaneously limited her income. After 14 years in the same job, job security was her principal concern.

POOR JOB PERFORMANCE (CASE 2.10)

People who work for a difficult boss are unsure what that means for their careers. The case show how people can misjudge their performance—sometimes because they get inaccurate or incomplete information. In this case, the interviewee was left on his own to figure things out.

Fred is under 30 years of age and recently married. He and his wife are expecting their first child. He is an educational administrator in a local government office where he has worked for the last year and a half. Fred felt he deserved a higher level job beyond his trainee status, and requested a promotion. Although Fred received

favorable information from other supervisors about his performance and promota-
bility, these supervisors apparently did not say the same things to Fred's immediate
supervisor. Meanwhile, Fred's home environment was stressful, largely due to
financial problems of a new house and a baby on the way. Fred "failed" to get the
promotion, and his wife "relentlessly persecutes" him about it. Recently his boss
imposed a performance plan for improvement that will be reviewed at the next
quarterly performance discussion.

Fred went from feeling that his job performance was excellent to having
a performance problem. He is tempted to attribute the problem to a boss
who just does not like him. He could easily believe the other supervisors
who told him he is ready to move ahead, but the fact is that his immediate
supervisor does not support that view. Fred is learning the hard way about
organizational politics, communication, and family pressures. Fred's boss
took the time to work out a plan to help him improve. However, the plan
puts him at risk. If he does not make the grade within 3 months, his boss
has the documentation to dismiss him. Fred also has to deal with his
pregnant spouse, who cannot understand why he is not advancing faster
and making more money.

3

Coping Strategies

Coping behaviors may be functional, leading to positive outcomes. Alternatively, they may be dysfunctional, perhaps relieving immediate anxieties but not solving the problem in the long run. Examples of dysfunctional coping are denying the problem or blaming others rather than taking action to resolve the problem. Coping behaviors may even be destructive—for instance, arguing with others in a way that increases the barrier. Whether our coping is functional or dysfunction may depend on our appraisal of the situation. In this chapter, I examine the relationships between our perceptions of the situation and how we cope. In the process I describe a variety of coping strategies.

ESCAPING A DESPERATE SITUATION

The cases I chose for this chapter show different ways people cope with career barriers; I start with one case here and present two more at the end of the chapter. In the first case, a person on a stressful job, the stress being caused in part by a poor job match, found her performance plummeting. The situation was difficult for her to understand, let alone how to cope with. Ultimately, she took a leave of absence and then quit.

STYMIED BY TOUGH JOB DEMANDS (CASE 3.1)

Geraldine is a single woman in her early 30s. She has an MBA degree and speaks several languages fluently. She worked as an administrator in a college financial aid office where she had to cope with being harassed by students and their families who did not like her decisions or did not understand how to comply with the application requirements. In one incident, Geraldine told her boss she would not deal with a particularly irate student, but her boss indicated that this was not her decision to make. A subsequent altercation with the student led Geraldine to call the campus police.

In general, Geraldine did not like the work she was doing, and a gap was developing between her and her boss. Work overload was making the problem worse. Over time, Geraldine realized that her performance was declining, and she thought about leaving the university. A subsequent incident with an aggressive student led her to take some time off; she returned only to submit her resignation. At the time of the interview, she had not been able to find another job and had run out of unemployment insurance.

TURNING LEMONS INTO LEMONADE: MAINTAINING A POSITIVE OUTLOOK

Threat or trauma limits the degree to which an individual is likely to risk taking action. Geraldine is a good example of someone who felt beleaguered. Such an individual may hunker down and avoid taking positive steps to find a better job or new career direction. On the other hand, challenge and positive feelings can lead to a free-flowing use of intellectual resources (Lazarus, 1991). A positive mood enhances motivation by facilitating initial involvement, interest, and enthusiasm (George & Brief, 1995). Once a person is performing a task, positive mood enhances motivation—for instance, by encouraging persistence. Thus a positive mood is especially important in a negative work environment or under unpleasant conditions. For example, an assistant professor who was distraught over not receiving tenure immersed himself in his research. This proved to be the best medicine emotionally and functionally, leading to increased productivity, more professional contacts, and job offers.

People are motivated to maintain positive mood states. This facilitates employees to evaluate their ongoing tasks favorably and progress toward their goals (George & Brief, 1995). Happy, optimistic employees are less likely to believe that they have failed to make reasonable progress towards their goals. As a result, they persist in trying to achieve these goals, and they are likely to set even higher goals for themselves.

Laws Guiding Emotion and Coping

Frijda (1988) outlined several "laws" governing how emotion affects persistence:

- Emotional events maintain their power to generate emotions indefinitely unless they are counteracted by repeated exposures that allow extinction or habituation of the emotional response. Although the emotional impact of traumatic events may never wane, it can be overwritten by other events. As time passes and new events intervene, one forgets about the effects of a long-ago traumatic event unless reminded by someone or something (e.g., coming across a layoff notice). The old feelings then may return as strong as ever. On the other hand, a person can become pre-occupied with a negative event and not let other events or forces intervene. As an example, a young faculty member who was denied tenure set out to devote his life to write about the unfairness of the tenure approving process instead of dedicating himself to his field.

- Feelings are absolute. They are what they are to that individual regardless of how others see the situation. The absoluteness of feelings is reflected in how people act. The readiness to act is primary at the time the emotion occurs and tends to override other concerns or goals. This captures the involuntary nature of emotional impulse or urge. However, this is tempered by the law of care for consequence.
- Every emotional urge generates a secondary urge that tends to modify it in recognition of its possible consequences. Thus, the impulse to act gives way to restraint in recognition of the potential negative consequences. If the consequences of satisfying the impulse to act are not seen as negative (or not recognized), then restraint does not kick in and the impulse may be satisfied, possibly to the detriment of the individual, not to mention those around him or her.
- People develop their own personal meaning for a situation. Emotions that result from a situation depend on how it is interpreted. People interpret negative events in ways that decrease emotional intensity, prevent occurrence of emotion, or make events seem more tolerable or pleasing. That is, when possible, situations are interpreted in ways that minimize the negative emotional load. As a result, defense mechanisms are common—for instance, denial and avoidance or admitting lack of control when confronted by negative situations.
- Whenever possible, people try to interpret a situation to maximize the emotional gain. Even negative emotions and associated actions are done to give rise to positive gain—as when a person acts depressed to gain sympathy and attention.

Problem-Focused and Emotion-Focused Coping

Coping strategies may focus on the appraisal of the event—that is, an effort to understand and find meaning in a crisis. *Problem-focused coping* attempts to deal with the reality and consequences of the crisis and create a better situation. *Emotion- (or symptom)-focused coping* attempts to handle the feelings provoked by the crisis (Leana & Feldman, 1992).

Coping can be viewed in terms of our relationship to the stressful situation (Perrez & Reicherts, 1992). This includes whether we can influence the stressful component directly, avoid the situation, omit actions, hesitate, or wait. Also, we can change how we think about the situation. We can do this by ignoring information or searching for new information—perhaps information that confirms a prior belief about ourselves.

Lazarus (1991) outlined some ways of coping with stress that apply to career barriers. I list my adaptation of them in the following types of coping strategy. Think about a career barrier, failure, or disappointing situation you faced and see if any of these statements describe your reactions:

Confrontive
   I tried to get the person responsible to change his or her mind.
   I expressed anger to the person(s) who caused the problem.
Distancing
   I went on as if nothing had happened.
   I did not let it get to me. I refused to think about it too much.
Self-controlling
   I tried to keep my feelings to myself.
   I tried not to act too hastily or follow my first hunch.
Seeking social support
   I talked to someone to find out more about the situation.
   I asked a relative or friend I respected for advice.
Accepting responsibility
   I criticized or lectured myself.
   I apologized or did something to make up.
Escape–avoidance
   I hoped a miracle would happen.
   I avoided being with people in general.
Planful problem solving
   I made a plan of action and followed it.
   I just concentrated on what I had to do next—the next step.
Positive reappraisal
   I changed or grew as a person in a good way.
   I rediscovered what is important in life.

Thus, coping can be problem-focused dealing with the reality and consequences of the crisis and creating a better situation, or it can be emotion or symptom-focused dealing with the feelings provoked by the crisis. Constructive ways of coping with stress also apply to career barriers. Now consider how negative emotions provoke dysfunctional coping.

NEGATIVE EMOTIONS AND THE IMPAIRMENT OF PERFORMANCE

Negative emotions can facilitate performance, or at least have a benign effect on performance as when feelings of unhappiness and disappointment stimulate positive action to change the situation. However, negative emotions may give rise to destructive behaviors—as when anger results in taking retribution in some way (e.g., getting others in trouble; Lazarus, 1991). Having a warning to an upcoming harmful or negative event can be an important adaptational tool. It allows people to anticipate the event and ways to cope with it. The individual can prepare or possibly prevent or ameliorate the negative event. Frame of mind also matters. Positive expectations may increase the chances of disappointment and with it sadness and anger. Negative expectations may make a negative outcome seem positive (e.g., "It could have been worse").

Interpreting events in a way that protects our self-esteem can have negative effects. For instance, consider the concept of *self-handicapping*. This is when we protect our self-esteem by making things so difficult that we fail, but we are able to blame the failure on factors beyond our control. Our failure then can be rationalized (for example, "No one could have done better under these circumstances"). Thus our failure says nothing about our competence. If we happen to succeed, which is unlikely, we can conveniently say that this shows our ability to overcome severe obstacles (Kelly, 1972). Another self-protective mechanism that is self-defeating is saying "I just do not care what happens to me." This may result from anxiety, fear, anger, and embarrassment. Self-defeating behaviors produce short-term relief but may do long-term harm (Baumeister & Scher, 1988).

Another type of self-defeating coping strategy is counterproductive behavior in which an individual seeks a positive goal in ways that impair chances for success (Baumeister & Scher, 1988). Examples are perseverance, choking under pressure, and ineffective ingratiation of another person. Here is what I mean by each of these:

Persistence is sticking with a task or goal long after it would have been better to have quit. Persistence is generally admired in Western cultures, and it is assumed to increase the chances of success. Therefore, people need to decide when persistence will pay off and when it will be useless or possibly self-defeating.

Choking under pressure happens when our efforts to succeed paradoxically lead to failure because we are inwardly preoccupied by trying to achieve the highest standards.

Ingratiation is humbling ourselves before others in hopes of seeking their approval and avoiding their rejection. Although most people want to be liked, and they behave in ways that they hope will win others' approval, this can generate dislike and rejection when the other person interprets the behavior as what it is—a ploy to win approval or affection. We generally overestimate our chances that others will respond positively to our ingratiation attempts.

COPING WITH NEGATIVE FEEDBACK
AND JOB LOSS

In order to understand constructive and destructive coping strategies, I now turn to how people cope with two common career barriers: negative performance feedback and job loss.

Dealing With Negative Feedback

Tsui, Ashford, and their colleagues considered how people cope with negative feedback—information about their performance that is discrepant from what they expected (Tsui, Ashford, St. Clair, & Xin, 1995). Constructive ways to reduce discrepancies between one's self-expectations and others' expectations include:

- *Exerting extra effort:*   I alter my behavior to be more consistent with what others expect of me. This involves exerting extra effort or changing actions with a multitude of small or large adjustments.
- *Influencing expectations:*   I try to convince others to recognize the downside of their expectations—for instance, telling the boss how others have tried and failed to do something the boss now wants me to do. A related approach is to influence the other person's opinions or evaluations of my performance or behavior.
- *Explaining actions:*   I offer an explanation or rationale for the actions taken (or to be taken).

Dysfunctional strategies that may even be destructive are indirect responses. They do not alter discrepancies between what someone expects from me (or I expect from myself) and what actually happened, but they may protect me by reducing the discrepancies in my mind. These may seem adaptive from my viewpoint but may not change evaluations of me by others.

- *Distortion:* I distort available feedback so that it confirms my success. This reduces the discrepancy cognitively without actually changing others' evaluations. A similar strategy is to distort information that conveys incompatibility. The problem is that my behavior does not adapt to my constituents' expectations.
- *Changing reference points:* I lower my standards so that expectations are consistent with outcomes. Not trying to please everyone, or believing that achieving a certain standard is not really important, reduces a discrepancy in my mind but does not address the actual gap between what happened and my own or others' expectations. Hence, it is not adaptive.
- *Disengagement and avoidance:* I avoid dealing with or thinking about a problem, avoid the feedback, or avoid thinking about the problem. Another approach is to withdraw from the situation—change jobs or change constituency set (i.e., "I don't care what my boss says as long as the VP is happy"). Geraldine from the case at the start of the chapter opted out of her job altogether as a means of escape. She understood that her job performance had suffered. She just could not cope with the job demands, and her boss' attitude just made things worse.

Strategies of extra effort, influencing expectations, and explanation are more effective than distortion, changing reference points, or disengagement and avoidance. The strategies of extra effort and explanation are positively associated with overall effectiveness from the perspectives of supervisors, peers, and subordinates evaluating managers in private and public sector samples (Tsui et al., 1995). Influencing expectations and avoidance are negatively associated with effectiveness ratings.

Coping With Job Loss

Based on his research with professionals who had lost their jobs, Kaufman (1982) outlined a four-stage model of responses to unemployment that mixes emotions and coping strategies: (a) feeling shock, relief, and relaxation; (b) making a concerted effort to find a new job; (c) if the initial job search is unsuccessful, feeling vacillation, self-doubt, and anger; and (d) feeling resignation and withdrawal. Kaufman found that professionals moved through these stages in only 5 to 7 months.

Job seeking behaviors refer to such activities as reading the newspaper and other publications for job opportunities, checking with an employment agency, and completing job application forms (Wanberg, Watt, & Rumsey,

1996). Three career-specific predispositions are confidence in job seeking, employment commitment, and conscientiousness. Job-seeking self-efficacy is the person's confidence in his or her ability to successfully engage in a variety of job-seeking activities. This deals with how competent people feel about completing a job application and writing a resume. Employee commitment is the importance of work to an individual. Someone who is high in employee commitment would be likely to continue working even after they won a great deal of money in the lottery—or at least say they would. Conscientiousness is the extent to which the individual acts in a way that is purposeful, determined, and well-organized rather than impulsive, undependable, and lazy. Unemployed people who are high in conscientiousness are more assertive at job hunting than those who are low in conscientiousness (Schmit, Amel, & Ryan, 1993).

As stated earlier, problem-focused strategies are behaviors to change the environment by eliminating the source of stress itself. For instance, problem-focused strategies for coping with job loss include seeking a new job or getting retraining in a new career field. Symptom-focused strategies are behaviors that decrease the depression or other negative feelings associated with the stress. Symptom-focused coping strategies for coping with job loss include joining social support groups. Leana and Feldman (1992)[1] identified the following coping strategies and associated items in response to job loss:

Job search activity
- I followed up on "help-wanted" notices.
- I tried to get a job through a government agency.
- I used community job bank services.

Seeking retraining
- I took courses at a college or university.
- I participated in a technical training program.
- I took steps to learn a new trade/profession.

Seeking to relocate
- I looked for a job in a different city.
- I made plans to move to a new community.
- I looked for job opportunities outside the community.

Community activism
- I became active in community effort to aid the unemployed.
- I became active in community efforts to stop unemployment.

- • I went to a support group for the unemployed.

Seeking financial assistance
- • I asked for financial assistance from friends or relatives.
- • I applied for aid in utility payments.
- • I applied for food stamps.

Seeking social support (symptom-focused)
- • I talked to your spouse about your feelings.
- • I kept in touch with people on the old job.
- • I talked to friends about problems with being unemployed.

In their sample of 198 steelworkers in Pittsburgh and 163 aerospace workers in Florida who had lost their jobs, Leana and Feldman (1992) found that nearly all participants in the study engaged in some sort of self-initiated job search activity, most frequently, following up on help-wanted notices. Few of the employees were offered training opportunities by their companies or sought further education themselves, although younger workers were more willing to get retrained. About half of the participants sought job opportunities in other communities; however, less than one fourth of them made plans to actually relocate. About one fourth of the employees became active in community groups to help the unemployed or to try to stop further unemployment. (This was most likely in the Pittsburgh area where there were long-standing community groups to provide such services.) The most frequently used symptom-focused coping mechanism was seeking social support—turning to spouses, friends, and former coworkers to express their anxieties and apprehension. Few of the laid-off workers applied for financial assistance other than unemployment benefits. Not surprisingly, actual reemployment was higher for those who engaged in active coping strategies, especially relocating and job search, although seeking social support was also important to landing another job. Whereas Leana and Feldman found that women engage in less job-seeking behavior than men, another study of more than 300 unemployed people found that women are more likely to have future intentions of looking for work (Wanberg et al., 1996).

In general, Leana and Feldman (1992) found reactions to job loss were related to coping strategies. Active coping (especially job search and geographic relocation) was higher for individuals who experienced less negative arousal and physiological distress. However, reactions to job loss did not matter for symptom-focused coping, in that just about everyone in their samples sought social support in one way or another. Other research found that the pervasive negative emotional effects of job loss handicap coping, creating a vicious cycle. Job loss can lead to lowered self-esteem, depression, and minor psychiatric illness, which in turn handicap job search and make continuing unemployment more likely (Hutchings & Gower, 1993). Attributions affect coping with job loss. In a study of 79 manufacturing employees, those who attributed their impending job loss (measured one month before the layoff) to their own deficiencies—deficiencies that are stable and not easily corrected—had more trouble finding reemployment 17 months after losing their jobs (Prussia, Kinicki, & Bracker, 1993).

Psychological Processes Underlying Coping With Job Loss.   Latack et al. (1995) considered the process through which people cope and ultimately adapt to job loss. They viewed reactions to job loss as the process though which people try to maintain balance in various facets of their lives (economic, psychological, social, physiological).

Job loss creates an imbalance between existing and desired states that causes various coping strategies. Feedback allows adjusting the strategy to maximally reduce the imbalance over time. Behavioral and cognitive changes are ways to attain balance. Coping is distorted by anything that impairs feedback perception; thus, for example, depression may cause a person to focus on the negative aspects of coping which can reduce motivation and persistence at tasks that could reduce the discrepancy. People who have positive perceptions of themselves or their control over the environment can encode information in a positive way. To the extent to which these perceptions are illusions, they may be maladaptive. Positive illusions can be adaptive or they may lead to misguided coping strategies and poor outcomes. The outcome depends on the purpose of the coping strategy. If the person's purpose is psychological bolstering of self-image without having to worry about economic security (as someone with a pension and social security might not have to), then a self-delusion might be fine. Thus, employment status is not the only relevant coping outcome. Coping continues until balance along multiple relevant dimensions is reached.

Job loss sets the coping in motion (Latack et al., 1995). After job loss, the individual appraises the situation by comparing his or her status to four life facets found to be relevant to the job loss—economic, psychological, psychological, and social—with a referent goal or standard. The next step is a discrepancy appraisal—an assessment of the extent to which the discrepancies are perceived as harm/loss or threat. This includes a primary appraisal ("How bad is it?") and a secondary appraisal ("What can I do about it?"). The individual then sets a coping goal. This is the individual's overall desired end result. The person's perceptions of coping efficacy (the individual's beliefs about successfully enacting a variety of coping strategies) affects the relationship between the discrepancy appraisal and the desired end state. People use a variety of coping strategies that may be mutually supporting. Coping resources also influence coping strategy—personal and environmental factors that are available to deal with life-facet discrepancies (e.g., AT&T's outplacement center for displaced employees). Coping resources determine the discrepancy appraisal, the coping goals, and the coping strategies. Three coping strategies include control (proactive strategies aimed at resolving the situation), escape, and seeking social support.

Voluntarily Leaving a Job

Voluntarily leaving a job can be a proactive coping strategy in reaction to perceived career barriers. For instance, a study of why managers changed jobs surveyed 255 males registered with a private employment agency for managerial personnel (Krausz & Reshef, 1992). The most important reasons given for wanting to change jobs were dissatisfaction with the present workplace, the need for personal change, and dissatisfaction with the specific job within the organization. Hoping for advancement (a higher level position and more money in another organization) was the most desired overall goal. Most of the respondents felt it was no longer fruitful to take actions to pursue their career goals within their current organization.

SUMMARY

How we appraise a career barrier influences whether we will cope in a constructive or destructive way. Constructive coping is likely when we evaluate information thoroughly and realistically, whereas dysfunctional coping is likely when we deny or ignore information or the barrier itself. Indeed this appraisal becomes a dysfunctional coping strategy. Career barriers maintain their power to generate emotions indefinitely, unless they are counteracted by other events. However, strong emotions can dominate our lives, especially soon after the negative event, and they tend to guide behaviors and actions and override other considerations or attention to other events. Fortunately, our immediate emotional urge generates a secondary urge that tends to modify it in recognition of possible consequences. We interpret events in ways that decrease emotional intensity because we generally want to avoid unpleasant feelings. Defense mechanisms are a convenient way to do this, even though they may not be the best way to cope in the long run.

Problem-focused coping, such as searching for a new job, deals with the reality and consequences of the crisis and tries to create a better situation. Symptom-focused coping, such as seeking emotional support from others, focuses on ways to handle the feelings provoked by the career barrier. Self-defeating approaches include interpreting the situation to protect our self-image and behaving in a way that ensures failure (a process called *self-handicapping*). Such responses to career barriers generate short-term relief but may do long-term harm. Other examples are perseverance when it is clearly too late, choking under pressure, and ingratiation.

The next chapter begins a discussion of individual characteristics that influence reactions to career barriers. In particular, I suggest how our career resilience, insight, and identity support our resistance to dysfunctional or destructive impulses and perseverance in identifying and pursuing constructive ways to overcome career barriers.

FROM THE CASE FILES

The following two cases are two more examples of coping strategies. The first describes an individual who sought better advancement prospects carefully surveyed alternatives before taking action. In the next case, a person who moved from job to job hoping for the best realized he could do more for his career by being proactive.

SEEKING WAYS TO EXPAND
CAREER OPPORTUNITIES (CASE 3.2)

Incremental changes, even when recognized, do not present immediate solutions. This case is about a person who faced developing performance problems, in part due to poor supervision and lack of support for development. Eventually, he left his position as a practicing clinician to move into sales:

> Gerry is a 39-year-old married man with three children. He has a BS degree in cardiorespiratory sciences and a MS in health sciences and is currently employed by a biomedical products firm in their marketing and sales division. His job is to educate practitioners about the company's products. He had had this job for about 3 months at the time of the interview. Prior to this, he had worked for 12 years as a respiratory therapist in a large metropolitan teaching hospital. He was repeatedly denied promotions and merit raises despite his feeling that he was well qualified compared to others who were rewarded with raises and promotions. Finally, after 9 years, he received a promotion; however, the department was closed a year later.

He returned to his former lower level position only to face continued frustration at his lack of advancement. Perceiving little support from management and not receiving constructive performance feedback, Gerry's morale declined. Others in the department felt similarly oppressed by the one-way (top-down) communication and generally poor management. Confronting managers did not work, so he stopped trying. However, his complaining to coworkers led to managers expressing their anger in loud confrontations.

Gerry felt depressed in a job that offered no direction and opportunities. Looking around at other medical facilities, the situation seemed to be similar. Increasing cost controls made the work more demanding and frustrating. Professionals in his field were being cut back in favor of lower paid people with less training. Therefore, after 12 years with the same institution he began a new career in medical sales. He got the job through acquaintances in the firm whom he had known for many years. Although the company did not train him in selling, the job is working out so far. His new managers support his ideas and seem to be pleased with his performance.

OVERCOMING LOW MOTIVATION (CASE 3.3)

Some people flounder from job to job. They work hard, but things do not work out as expected. In this case, the individual slowly recognized that more aggressive career planning and action would have helped him, but he has yet to do anything about it:

Rory is 44 years old with a wife and three children. After 3 years of college, he had a series of low-paying management jobs (managing a fast food restaurant, a tennis club, a drug store, and toy store). Eight years ago, a boyhood friend offered him a job in his construction company. After working for low pay as a project supervisor, his hopes of working his way up to become a partner did not pan out when the business was bought out and his friend was dismissed. Wholesale sales did not work out either. Now, after being unemployed for several months, Rory is working as a low-paid account representative. It is a fairly secure job in that he services the firm's steady customers and does not have to search for new business. Rory has worked hard and tried new initiatives that he hoped would be more satisfying and lucrative, such as sales, but he found it tough to be successful in these competitive areas that are influenced by so many factors within and beyond his control. Nevertheless, he feels that he was not aggressive enough in planning and taking action to be more successful.

4

Career Motivation: Resilience, Insight, and Identity*

There are three parts to career motivation: resilience, insight, and identity. Career resilience keeps people going and allows them to overcome career barriers. It helps people to stick with, and conquer, tough situations. Career insight is understanding oneself and the work environment. It gives people a clear and accurate view of their strengths and weaknesses and factors in the environment that support or hinder performance. Insight is the spark that energizes people to act, whereas resilience keeps the spark alive. Career identity directs one's energy and behavior toward a specific set of career goals. Overall, resilience creates the foundation that allows meaningful career insight to development. Insight, in turn, allows selecting a career direction that uses one's abilities to the fullest.

In this chapter, I explain career motivation and describe how it works when people confront career barriers. Career motivation can help prevent career barriers. When barriers arise, individuals may be suddenly confused about what is happening and whether they have the ability to meet the demands of the situation. As a result, they may need to change their career identity and insight (beliefs about their career goals and personal strengths and weaknesses). The chapter examines patterns of resilience, insight, and identity and suggests how these components can be enhanced to help people overcome career barriers. As in the previous chapter, I begin with several case examples.

I chose cases for this chapter that demonstrate the three elements of career motivation. I open the chapter with a case that has a happy ending; it describes someone who decided to accept a transfer and relocation rather than lose his job. Overcoming some tough situations, he eventually was

---

*Portions of this chapter were adapted from London and Noe (1997).

promoted. Later cases are less positive and show what happens to people who lose their way and cannot seem to get back on track.

ACCEPTING A JOB TRANSFER (CASE 4.1)

Herman is a 48-year-old divorced man with one college-aged child. He has an associates degree and worked as an avionics electrical tester for a defense industry contractor in the northeast for 25 years. He had the same title for most of his tenure in the company, and was assigned increasing supervisory responsibilities over the years. During the last several years, the company lost government contracts and many employees were laid off. Eventually the firm was bought out and all northeast operations were closed.

Although he predicted the downsizing years earlier, he stuck it out with the firm waiting to see what would happen. Herman was offered a transfer to Florida with a 15% pay cut. Seeing few other job possibilities and not having worked for any other company before, he accepted the transfer. After relocating to Florida, he applied for, and received, a promotion to another technical area—something he had been trying to do for years. Although the new job and the lower cost of living worked out for him, he lamented that many people were laid off with little if any severance. He also resented the initial animosity he and other transferees faced from their Florida colleagues because the transferees made more money even with the pay cut.

Herman's case suggests how resilience works in the face of organizational change and growing threat to job security. It also shows the importance of having insight about what is happening. Rather than taking action to find another job, Herman waited to see if he would be retained by the company. He found the prospect of starting a new career in midlife daunting. The case demonstrates that waiting it out and being adaptable can work, at least for a highly competent person with valuable work experience.

Now, in order to understand motivation underlying people's responses to potential and actual career barriers, I turn to my model of career motivation.

THE CONCEPT OF CAREER MOTIVATION

Since I first outlined my model of career motivation in 1983, there has been a fair amount of research examining the content, antecedents, and consequences of career motivation (London, 1983, 1985). Also, the model has been applied to the design of career development programs, often in changing organizations (London & Mone, 1987). Here I consider the evolution of the model, evidence for its validity, and its continued value for application.

While working as researchers at AT&T, Douglas Bray and I originally developed the model to answer a research question: What motivates managers to lead? Research during the mid- to late 1970s showed that young managers were not as motivated to attain leadership positions as those a generation earlier (Howard & Bray, 1981). The career motivation model began by listing and organizing needs, interests, and personality variables that could be important to the construct of career motivation. This led to the conceptualization of the central dimensions of career motivation that could then be used to design an assessment center to measure them. As such, the model was intended to be an integrative, organizing framework for existing variables. As the content of the model was developed and refined, processes were proposed to consider how the components of career motivation are influenced positively and negatively by situational conditions.

As indicated earlier, the career motivation variables are organized into three domains (London, 1985). Career resilience is the ability to adapt to changing circumstances, even when the circumstances are discouraging or disruptive. It consists of belief in oneself, need for achievement, willingness to take risks, and working independently or cooperatively as needed. People who are high in resilience are likely to respond positively to the following items:

I am able to adapt to changing circumstances.
I am willing to take risks.
I welcome job and organizational changes.
I can handle any work problem.
I look forward to working with new and different people.

Career insight is the ability to be realistic about oneself and one's career and to put these perceptions to use in establishing goals. It consists of establishing career goals, and knowing one's strengths and weaknesses. People who are high in insight are likely to say the following about themselves:

I have clear career goals.
I have realistic career goals.
I know my strengths (the things I do well).
I know my weaknesses (the things I am not good at).
I recognize what I can do well and cannot do well.

Career identity is the extent to which one defines oneself by work. It consists of job, organizational, and professional involvement; and the needs for advancement, recognition, and a leadership role. People who are high in career identity are likely to indicate the following about themselves:

- I define myself by my work.
- I work as hard as I can, even if it means frequently working long days and weekends.
- I am involved in my job.
- I am proud to work for my employer.
- I believe that my success depends on the success of my employer.
- I am loyal to my employer.
- I see myself as a professional, technical expert, or both (London, 1993a).

Edgar Schein (1978, 1990), a professor at MIT and well-known writer and researcher on careers, argued that although a person's initial career choice is based primarily on his or her interests, a stable career identity is formed by young adults over time through the integration of an individual's interests with his or her abilities and values. This happens as they gain a more accurate and stable view of their career identity. People in the same occupation may differ in their career identity and hence the goals they wish to achieve and the career track they pursue. Career anchors may be based on talents and abilities, needs and desires, or attitudes and values.

In his study of young managers, Schein identified seven career anchors on which people may focus their career identity. These are (a) the technical aspects of the work; (b) the managerial aspects of the work, such as the opportunity to analyze and solve problems and help people work together effectively; (c) job security and long-term attachment to the organization; (d) the need to build or create an enterprise (this applies to entrepreneurs); (e) being independent of organizational constraints (e.g., setting one's own schedule and pace of work); (f) challenges, such as overcoming major obstacles; and (g) balancing career and lifestyle, such as spending time with family or friends. Schein believed that a single anchor dominates each person's career identity, and people feel successful when they can develop their career anchor. However, others have hypothesized that people have multiple career anchors, and that some career anchors complement one another (for instance, focusing on entrepreneurship and autonomy or on autonomy and lifestyle, or challenge and technical competence; Feldman & Bolino, 1996).

Career identity is the direction of motivation, insight is the energizing or arousal component, and career resilience is the maintenance or persistence component (Noe, Noe, & Bachhuber, 1990). Career barriers cause people to question their career identity and reformulate their career insight. However, this is largely dependent on being resilient. Resilience helps people accurately appraise a career barrier and arrive at constructive coping strategies to match the situation.

Resilience, insight, and identity have strong links to existing career theory. Resilience is linked to Holland's (1985) notion that career decisions are influenced by the ability to face barriers, the need for information and reassurance and vocational identity. Also, career resilience can be tied to the concepts of hardiness self-efficacy and achievement motivation. The concept of human agency—being assertive, instrumental, and interpersonal facile—can be linked to resilience (R. N. Williams, 1992). Career maturity is a related concept. People who are high in career maturity make career decisions in a way that demonstrates involvement, decisiveness, independence, task orientation, and willingness to compromise between needs and reality (Crites, 1978). Resilience is also conceptually tied to the idea of flexibility and adjustment (Dawis & Lofquist, 1984). Work adjustment depends on the congruence between individual abilities and the requirements of the job and the congruence between individual needs and reinforcers in the environment. People who are high in work adjustment are characteristically high in perseverance, flexibility, and reactiveness (taking action to overcome barriers).

Career insight is conceptually related to Super's (1957, 1963) vocational self-concept, "crystallization." Career identity is conceptually tied to work commitment, organizational commitment, and organizational citizenship (Organ, 1988). Also, career identity is associated with Blau's (Blau, 1985, 1988, 1989; Blau, Paul, & St. John, 1993) concept of career commitment. Hall's (1976, 1987) model of career identification proposes that the importance of career to an individual depends on awareness of one's inclinations (sic. career insight) and being successful (which enhances self-confidence, part of career resilience).

Behavioral and Situational Linkages

In my model, the individual difference components of career motivation were linked to behaviors and situational conditions. Behaviors associated with career resilience include showing belief in oneself (e.g., requesting difficult assignments), striving for autonomy, demonstrating adaptability in face of changing demands or learning requirements, taking control, or seeking development. Behaviors associated with career insight include seeking feedback, establishing career goals, establishing a career path for goal achievement, changing goals, and responsiveness to social conditions (e.g., altering one's behavior to fit the situation). Behaviors associated with career identity include demonstrating job involvement (e.g., working long hours), professional behavior (e.g., describing oneself as a professional in a particular field), improving one's skills, striving for advancement (e.g., requesting to be considered for a promotion), seeking recognition, trying to lead, and striving for money.

The career motivation model predicts that situational conditions influence motivation (Katzell & Thompson, 1990). Situational characteristics associated with career resilience are positive reinforcement and constructive performance feedback, encouragement of autonomy, organizational change, opportunities for individual control and discretion (e.g., chance for input into work methods), opportunities to demonstrate achievement, support for creativity, demands for quality, support for learning, and skill development. For instance, the favorability and amount of job feedback received is strongly related to job satisfaction and self-perceptions of competence (K. J. Williams, Williams, & Ryer, 1990). People are more satisfied when they see themselves improving at work and receive positive appraisals from others.

Situational characteristics associated with career insight are structure for goal setting (e.g., existence of career alternatives, procedures, and assistance for setting career goals), path goal structure (e.g., standard career paths to various organization levels or positions), organizational flexibility, opportunity for change, and visibility of organizational processes (e.g., methods for appraisal and personnel decisions are explicit, observable, and veridical). Situational characteristics associated with career identity include encouragement of professionalism, press for organizational commitment (e.g., value of inducements such as salary and pension, for good performance and loyalty), advancement opportunities, potential for recognition (e.g., reward programs), leadership opportunities, and potential for monetary gain.

Individual characteristics will have a greater effect on career decisions and behavior when the characteristics are stable and integrated into the individual's self-concept (London, 1983). Situational characteristics will have a greater effect on career decisions and behaviors the more the situation controls or limits possible decisions and behaviors, defines what decisions and behaviors are socially acceptable, and requires individuals to justify their decisions and behaviors. Career decisions and behaviors will be more effective (i.e., have more positive outcomes for the individual and organization) the higher the congruence or match between the individual and the situational characteristics (e.g., a young manager wants to advance and the situation offers an early career management development program for high-potential managers).

Retrospective rationality processes indicate that the situation and decisions and behavior affect how people view themselves and what is important to them. They look back at their behaviors and the situation to make judgments about themselves. Prior career decisions and behaviors will have a greater effect on individual characteristics associated with career motivation the more they decisions and behaviors have positive or negative consequences and the longer the consequences last. Situational characteristics will have a greater effect on the individual characteristics the more the situation is viewed as positive or negative, the more recently positive or negative events occurred, and the more they control possible career decisions and behaviors. Individual characteristics will affect how the situation is perceived the more the situation initially is ambiguous, uncertain, cognitively inconsistent, or a combination of both.

Feedback Seeking.   Career insight stems in large part from information about one's performance. Some people may actively seek this feedback by monitoring the environment or asking others in order to guide their own development and improve their performance. They also may seek feedback to protect their self-image and control how they appear to others (Ashford & Cummings, 1983; Morrison & Bies, 1991). Individual difference characteristics that are part of resilience, such as self-esteem, influence feedback-seeking behavior. Although feedback is valuable, asking for it is risky because it might be negative and highlight one's weaknesses (Fedor, Rensvold, & Adams, 1992). Therefore, people who need feedback the most because they need improvement may be least likely to seek it (Karl & Kopf, 1993). When they do ask for feedback, they may try to lessen the negative information to protect their self-esteem (Larson, 1988). People who are high in self-esteem and need for achievement select sources of feedback who are expert and with whom they have a good working relationship. People with high performance expectations for themselves select sources who can provide valued rewards. However, people low in self-esteem and self-efficacy tend not to seek feedback from anyone (Vancouver & Morrison, 1995).

In general, people are less likely to seek feedback when they think that others will know about it because they are concerned about how they appear to others. People who are less self-conscious in public and high on social anxiety are less likely to seek feedback because information about themselves is not very important to them and focusing on the self results in high feelings of anxiety. High-self-esteem individuals are likely to avoid feedback seeking when they realize that the feedback is public because they need to protect their ego (Levy, Albright, Cawley, & Williams, 1995).

Career Barriers and Patterns of Career Motivation

In my view, resilience variables develop from reinforcement contingencies in the environment as one is growing up. As such, employees' career resilience should be well developed by early adulthood, although it can be strengthened or weakened over extended periods of time. Insight and identity develop through information processing; as such, they are easier to affect through career development processes. Career resilience, insight, and identity are independent across a sample at a single point in time. However, over time, for a given individual, resilience should contribute to developing accurate insight that in turn should contribute to meaningful identity. In general, the support people receive from others and the successes they experience bring about changes in their career motivation. Social comparison, information processing, and the existence of opportunities are important to career motivation (Schneider, Gunnarson, & Wheeler, 1992).

Together, an individual's career resilience, insight, and identity form a pattern that describe the individual's career motivation. Working with Mone (London & Mone, 1987), I identified four patterns of career development:

1. *Healthy development:* People start their careers with reasonably high resilience. They experienced successs as they were raised. Their resilience helps them use information about themselves and professional opportunities which in turn sparks an identity that can be fulfilled. These individuals are high in career resilience, insight, and identity.

2. *Redirection:* Some people make adjustments in their careers because of the barriers they face or even before the barriers arise. They explore alternatives and try one or more. Their high resilience and insight serve them well as their career identity shifts.

Diane Sirois is a good example of a resilient individual with foresight. She is a 39-year-old factory worker at the Stanley Works, a hand-tool manufacturer in New Britain, CT (Uchitelle & Kleinfield, 1996). She now works a complex machine that assembles retractable tape measures. Having kept an eye out for jobs that were unlikely to be cut, she bid for the position, believing that this machinery would be one of the last to be shut down. Under the union rules, during a layoff, a worker cannot be bumped by someone else with more seniority unless the more senior worker can learn the job in a week. It took Diane 3 months to learn to operate the machine. She explained, "There are people here who have gotten used to sitting on their tails and repeating the same small task hour after hour, and they don't want to change, even to save their jobs" (p. 29).

In contrast, some people do not seem to be motivated to avert tough situations. Maybe they do not have the insight needed to foresee likely events; maybe they do not have the sense of self-confidence or control which suggests to them that they can affect events to avoid potentially negative situations and create positive occurrences.

3.   *Intervening self-doubt:*   Other people experience failure, but the negative feedback is so severe that they question their ability. Their foundation of resilience is solid, wavering only temporarily. They may make a change that restores their belief in themselves. However, some individuals in this situation become mired in self-doubt and depression. These individuals lack insight into their abilities and what they could accomplish in the right setting.

4.   *Breaking away from an ineffective patterns:*   Some people have unrealistic goals (overly ambitious or so meager that they are meaningless). This pattern of self-doubt can be reversed over considerable time as these individuals achieve small successes. Over time, they may establish new, realistic goals.

The first pattern, healthy development, may take different directions—essentially different identities. Some people are *enlargers*—advancement-orientated individuals who want the status, power, influence, and money that go with advancement and being in a leadership role. Others are *enfolders*—people whose prime concern is a well-balanced life; their family is as important as work, and they try to do the best job possible recognizing their limited goals.

People who experience redirection in their career motivation or intervening self-doubt may be enlargers who lose support (they are passed over for promotion, their mentor retires, or they lose their jobs). They become *runners-up*. If they have high resilience and insight, they are likely to recoup quickly. Those who are not resilient or who do not know their environments well are likely to behave in a destructive way by losing their self-confidence, taking their anger out on others, panicking, avoiding future risks, becoming defensive, blaming others, or denying their problems.

People who maintain misguided identities are misfits. This is likely to happen because they lack accurate insight. However, they may have the resilience to keep persevering despite repeated failures. They attribute failure to others or the situation, and they continue to look for better opportunities. However, misfits with low resilience blame their failure on themselves, yet their lack of insight prevents them from making constructive changes; consequently, they repeat the same mistakes. They are frozen in a dysfunctional pattern. Over time, resilience may be built through sparks of positive reinforcement and new goals may be established by redefining the meaning of success. Failure and rejection become seasoning experiences. They find new sources of rewards by finding new situations that value their talents and abilities or by changing their views of what is important to achieve.

WHAT WE KNOW ABOUT CAREER MOTIVATION

In the early 1980s, Bray and I studied 24 managers in each of two companies (London, 1985). The companies were in the same industry and approximately the same region of the country. The managers were all recent college graduates hired within the last year at the time of the assessment and were followed for a year and a half after the assessment with interviews with their bosses and follow-up interviews. Managers in one company scored significantly higher on measures reflecting a leadership career identity (e.g., need for advancement, need for recognition, and importance of advancement). They were also higher on commitment to managerial work, personality measures of enterprising and ascendance, and assessment center ratings of goal flexibility and need for change and lower on measures of nurturing, friendliness, and authoritarianism). Those in the other company were higher on authoritarianism and need abasement, meaning that they were more likely to adhere to conventional values.

The fact that the managers in the two small samples were initially equivalent on a variety of background characteristics suggested that the situation (organizational policies and support for career development) was instrumental in maintaining and strengthening young managers' career motivation. This suggested the importance of organizational conditions and policies for management development. The company with advancement-oriented managers had programs that rewarded desire for advancement. For instance, these managers were on a fast-track advancement program. They were reassigned periodically to jobs that would enhance their development. Supervisors participated in the program by helping the managers formulate career goals and obtain experiences that would further those goals. In the other company, the focus was on getting the work done. Job assignments were made solely to meet immediate work needs, not for the development of the managers. Supervisors rarely spent time with subordinates to provide career counseling, let alone make assignments or encourage job moves for developmental purposes.

In another of my studies, self-ratings of career insight and identity from 183 employees were positively related to supervisor ratings of the degree to which the subordinate is empowered and receives support for career development (London, 1993a). A second sample of 59 employees and their supervisors with data collected at two points in time 3½ months apart showed low relationships between supervisor and self-ratings of the same dimension of career motivation suggesting that employees do not always see their career motivation in the same way that supervisors see it.

Wolf, Casey, Pufahl, and I recently studied the career motivation of 72 displaced engineers engaged in a semester-long training program in technology management (Wolf, Casey, Pufahl, & London, 1995; Wolf, London, Casey, & Pufahl, 1995). We found that for highly motivated individuals, prior job experience was positively related to engaging in productive training behaviors. However, for those with low career motivation, prior job experience seemed to prevent productive training behaviors—perhaps because these individuals were wedded to their past careers and found it difficult to change career directions.

In another study, I found that older workers showed as much career motivation as younger workers, and that some elements of career motivation increased with age (London, 1993b). I studied a sample of mid- and late-career workers (mean age = 57.8 year) from a variety of backgrounds. Career resilience increased with age across the sample. However, for men, full-time workers were lower on career resilience than part-time workers who had to adapt to changing work schedules and responsibilities. A second sample of 96 employees with a wide age range found high levels of career insight for older workers. Career identity was not affected by age or working full- or part-time.

IMPLICATIONS FOR CAREER DEVELOPMENT PROGRAMS IN COMPANIES

Career development programs vary on the extent to which they support career resilience, insight, and identity. For instance, self-assessment workshops or workbooks and career counseling may focus on promoting insight. A career motivation assessment center may promote insight through feedback and resilience through rewards for high achievement on the tasks. Supervisory training may promote identity and insight. Working for a boss who is a good role model and encourages subordinates' development can be a source of all three.

Business conditions result in different levels of support for career motivation (London, 1988). For instance, in a declining business environment, career motivation is generally diminished by layoffs and a focus on closing down rather than turning around the business. However, career motivation can be supported by communicating openly, discussing alternative career opportunities, counseling, and employee participation in organizational redesign and searching for new direction. In the case of mergers and acquisitions, career motivation is diminished when little information is revealed, decisions are made at the top, and employees are terminated involuntarily. However, career motivation can be supported during a merger or acquisition by employee involvement in planning, evaluation of organizational design and job skill requirements, and incentives for voluntary terminations.

CAREER CHANGE AND CAREER MOTIVATION

Howard and Bray's (1988) AT&T longitudinal study of managerial careers found that personality characteristics associated with career motivation change as a person ages, in part due to changing career experiences. This is an incremental process as career changes unfold in the normal course of events. In particular, managers' work involvement, optimism about their future, job satisfaction, and identification with management declined over time. Those at higher organizational levels in mid- to late career were less family- and community-oriented, more involved in their jobs, and more concerned with self-development than those at lower organizational levels. Not surprisingly, higher level managers had a more varied, stimulating, and stressful career history, with more job changes and relocations.

Now consider framebreaking career changes: Sudden and unexpected career changes are times when people are most receptive to new insights about themselves and the environment. These transitions are times for renewed self-confidence, increased awareness of one's capabilities, and establishing new career goals. Framebreaking changes can come from within the individual (endogenous) or from the work environment (exogenous). Life stresses may cause people to question the meaning of their goals and the extent of their capabilities, in turn leading to career shifts. Some people never overcome mid- or late career crises, whereas others are able to overcome their self-doubt and commit themselves to new career and life goals. Externally caused framebreaking career changes include losing one's job, being turned down for a key promotion, facing a changing organizational culture after a merger, or having to adapt to a new technology. Framebreaking changes can destroy one's career identity and confuse career insight. However, for people with strong resilience and environmental support, framebreaking career changes can be positive transitions, or at least have positive outcomes.

SUMMARY

This chapter described career resilience, insight, and identity. Resilience sets the foundation for developing clear insight into oneself and the work environment. This in turn contributes to establishing a meaningful career identity—career goals that can be accomplished. I discussed elements in the environment that reinforce resilience and provide information that leads to insight and identity.

Career barriers test a person's career motivation because they lead people to question their career identity and reformulate their career insight. This process is not likely to be effective or constructive if their resilience is weak. Individuals who are initially high in career resilience, insight, and identity are often able to maintain their career motivation in the face of career barriers; they may, however, need to revise their view of the environment and their strengths and weaknesses. Also, they may change their career identity—committing themselves to new goals and career directions. Others suffer intervening self-doubt—their resilience wavers as they question their self-confidence and desire to achieve. Unfortunately, without a supportive environment that bolsters their self-confidence, they may become mired in this self-doubt. Their insight becomes cloudy and they lack career direction. These individuals need to break away from the ineffective pattern of career motivation rising from the career barrier. An environment that supports resilience is the key—there must then be sufficient information for individuals to learn about their capabilities and new career opportunities. Because it is the foundation of career motivation and critical to coping with career barriers effectively, I devote the next chapter to a closer look at resilience.

FROM THE CASE FILES

I close the chapter with two cases that show how resilience, insight, and identity work together. Unlike Herman, who was described in the case at the start of this chapter, the following case describes someone who had little career direction and could not seem to get back on track. The next case describes someone in an occupation that had fluctuating work opportunities. He recognized his difficulties, but his identity was tied to his occupation and he saw no way out.

WHEN MOTIVATION HAS A
SHAKY FOUNDATION (CASE 4.2)

This case shows what happens when a career derails in early adulthood, and the individual does not have a foundation of resilience, insight, or identity to move ahead. He becomes stymied by an unsupportive environment at home and living in a depressed rural area:

> Jake is a young man in a blue-collar job in upstate New York. At age 25, he is already divorced and remarried, and is responsible for two young stepchildren. He has a high school diploma and a technical training certificate from a community college.
> He had worked on the assembly line in a small electronics manufacturing firm in upstate New York, yet he lost his job when the firm was bought out and relocated to the west coast. That was 3 years ago. Since then, Jake has had a few temporary jobs, such as substitute school custodian and auto mechanic. He tried contacting companies recommended by his former employer and made some contacts on his own, but there were few opportunities in this economically depressed area. His wife did not want to relocate away from her parents, with whom Jake and his family are now living. At this point, Jake is resigned to not getting permanent employment anytime in the near future. The strain of the situation has taken its toll on his marriage, he has moved out of the house several times.

MIRED IN A DEAD END (CASE 4.3)

This case shows how someone can get stuck in a dead-end situation with little idea of how to change. The individual has been plagued by poor economic conditions for most of his career. As in the last example, this case shows how a poor economy can affect job stability. Learning a trade and being a union member does not provide the security it once did; it may mean a career of continuous cycles of employment and unemployment.

Kevin is a 51-year-old plumber, is married, and has two sons in their twenties who live at home. He became a union plumber in the construction business 25 years ago. His union assigns him to jobs as they come in, and jobs may last several months or even a year or more. When a job is finished, he goes on unemployment until another work request comes into the union hall. This was a secure situation for the first 10 years or so, during which time there were many construction projects in the region. There were fewer projects in the early 1980s, and Kevin experienced one layoff after another. In 1982 he took a job in a neighboring state that lasted a year and a half. The pay was good with as much overtime as he wanted, but he had to live away from home during the week.

Emotionally and spiritually, the uncertain employment and long stretches of idleness have taken their toll. Kevin's wife works full-time. His two sons work and attend college. Meanwhile, Kevin is often home working on the house, fixing his car, cooking, and cleaning. He tries to maintain a positive attitude, but seems jealous and somewhat resentful of his family's independence. Several months ago, Kevin landed a job at a sewer reconstruction project about 30 miles away. He is the foreman of a four-person crew, and the work should last for a year—then Kevin will be laid off again. In the meantime, he will be traveling an hour each way to work, working hard, and not exploring any career alternatives. He could set up a private plumbing business, but there is lots of competition and he would lose his union benefits. He believes that it is too late for him to change his occupation despite the limited future. He feels trapped by outside forces (the changing economic climate) and sees little way to change his future.

5

Resilience and Hardiness: The Basis for Inner Strength

Because this book is about overcoming career barriers, I want to provide a deeper explanation of the concept of career resilience. Career resilience is the foundation for developing accurate self-insight and a meaningful career identity. It is also the source of inner strength that helps us overcome career barriers.

In chapter 3, I mentioned some predispositions that influence persistence and success in finding a job, specifically confidence in job seeking, employment commitment, and conscientiousness (Wanberg et al., 1996). People who are high in conscientiousness are purposeful, determined, and well-organized in response to a career barrier (Schmit et al., 1993). Another predisposition that readily comes to mind in thinking about responses to changing situations is adaptability (J. Jones, 1991–1992). Such predispositions as adaptability and conscientiousness reflect individual fortitude. To some extent, these characteristics may be innate. However, to a large extent, they can be acquired—developed, reinforced, and enhanced over time. Alternatively, they can be diminished or weakened if a person is beaten down by continued failure. Predispositions work along with external sources of support to affect how people appraise and cope with career barriers (Lyons, 1991).

In the last chapter, I introduced career resilience as the foundation of insight and identity. Here I concentrate on resilience, and a related concept, hardiness. These are the source of inner strength that gives people the motivation to overcome career barriers. Although they stem from two separate literatures, they have similar meaning and effects. Hardiness and resilience are umbrella concepts that encompass personality dimensions, needs, and interests that help individuals overcome career barriers. First, here are two brief examples of how resilience pays off.

Overcoming a career barrier can take chutzpa. Sometimes being bold and perhaps brazen pays off. I do not mean this in a negative way; sticking to your guns may be the only way to survive in some situations. Here is a case that shows how aggressively maintaining your ground can pay off when fighting the political machine. The next case then shows a different kind of fighter—one who perseveres despite job loss and a debilitating illness.

FIGHTING CITY HALL (CASE 5.1)

Lorna, a 60-plus-year-old woman, was employed as the director of a major city government agency in a large metropolitan city. She is a highly accomplished and experienced woman in a responsible position facing political attempts to oust her. She fought hard to attain her high position, but the political system almost won out. The new department commissioner nearly forced her to retire, arguing for the need to downsize and cut costs. Lorna was able to keep her position by using all her political contacts, including support from her employees' union. She is a fighter who can contend with the most vicious political situation.

FACING JOB LOSS AND CANCER (CASE 5.2)

Job loss is bad enough, but it is worse when a major physical illness occurs at the same time. However, a positive attitude and knowing how hard it is to find another job can keep people motivated during the job search. This is a success story.

Larry is 53 years old and has been married for more than 30 years. He and his wife, an administrator with a local corporation have two grown children. Larry does not have a college degree. A manufacturing manager in an electronics firm, Larry lost his position after the firm announced that it would be moving its manufacturing facilities to another State. This was the second time Larry lost his job in the past 5 years. Whereas the first lay off happened without warning, Larry was able to see this one coming. Business had decreased and his immediate boss had been relocated. Although Larry had about 9 months to prepare, he was diagnosed with cancer several months prior to the layoff. His illness was treatable, but he realized he would be out of work for at least 6 months during treatment. When the treatment ended successfully, he began a job search and found another position 6 weeks later.

Larry had plenty of time to prepare psychologically for looking for another job. Overcoming his illness was his priority, and not having a job seemed less important. His previous experience with a lay off helped him prepare for the "roller coaster" of sending out resumes and being rejected. His manufacturing experience in the electronics industry served him well despite the lack of education. His illness did not appear to be a problem in finding another job.

Resilience implies being able to face tough situations and bounce back. We apply the term to people who have overcome adversity, grown emotionally, and increased their productivity. Lorna and Larry are two prime examples. There are plenty of others—some of whom are public figures. President Franklin Delano Roosevelt certainly comes to mind. A less-well-known individual who recently received critical acclaim is the writer Andre Dubus (Gussow, 1996). Before a devastating accident, he was a little known writer of short stories. In 1986, he was struck by a car as he attempted to help a motorist stopped by the side of a road. He had to have one leg amputated at the knee and lost the use of the other, dooming him to life in a wheelchair. After enduring a dozen operations, he was overcome with depression. His third marriage dissolved, and he stopped writing for 4 years. However, discovering the world of disability and misfortune and supported by a MacArthur award in 1988, he is now on his tenth book. His specialty is stories about quiet lives interrupted by violence.

Someone else who has been in the news lately is the actor Christopher Reeve, who was paralyzed after falling from a horse and is now embarking on a career of public speaking and directing movies. We may know someone personally who seems to have risen above a calamity to remarkable accomplishments under severe conditions. Such extreme situations are not predictable, and previous experience does not prepare us for them. They impose increased strain and pressure that may are likely to lead to dysfunctional behavior. For instance, perhaps not surprisingly, alcohol abuse is greater among those who have been laid off than among those who have not (Catalano, Dooley, Wilson, & Hough, 1993).

DEFINING RESILIENCE

Career resilience is the ability to adapt to changing circumstances, even when they are discouraging or disruptive. It consists of such dimensions as belief in oneself, need for achievement, willingness to take risks, and the need to evaluate events and circumstances. Resilience reflects the powerful interaction among a person's inner psychological life, his or her relationship to the surrounding world, and his or her emerging functional capacities (Fine, 1991). Psychological resources that support constructive responses to career transitions include readiness, confidence, perceived support, control, and decision independence (Heppner, Multon, & Johnston, 1994).

Researchers have turned to personality variables to understand why some people find a career barrier such as job loss to be devastating, whereas others take it as a challenge. Low trait anxiety buffers feelings of stress from job failure, whereas high-anxiety people who experience failure are more likely to suffer dramatic increases in feelings of threat and loss (Jerusalem, 1990). Leana and Feldman (1992) found that laid-off workers who were high in Type-A predisposition (aggressive, ambitious, and driven) were more likely to actively search for new jobs, investigate geographical relocation, apply for financial aid, and become involved in community activities. Internal locus of control (the predisposition to view important events in ones life as under ones control) was not associated with coping in Leana and Feldman's study, probably because most laid-off workers accurately attributed the cause of their job loss to external factors. Self-esteem was positively related to active job search. All the laid-off workers faced an objectively poor job market, but those with low self-esteem also had to overcome self-defeating perceptions that they did not deserve another job.

Predispositions influence survivor as well as victim reactions. Consider employees who "survive" organizational downsizing. One study surveyed 200 unionized technicians in the telecommunications industry who had recently avoided a workforce reduction (Armstrong-Stassen, 1994). Survivors who were high in optimism and had a strong sense of self-efficacy were more likely to engage in control-oriented coping in response to the threat of job loss. Those who had a higher sense of powerlessness were less likely to engage in control coping. Those with low optimism and self-efficacy and a higher sense of powerless were more likely to engage in escape strategies.

Resilience related variables promote constructive coping and earlier reemployment after job loss. Holmes and Werbel (1992) found in a sample of 186 laid-off workers aged 19 to 64 that those who found jobs within 3 months of losing their jobs were more "internal" in locus of control, had greater self-efficacy, and possessed better problem-solving skills than those who remained unemployed.

Predispositions may be important to general job satisfaction as well as to reactions to career barriers. In a recent study, 82 university employees (aged 20 to 67 years) completed scales measuring emotional traits at two points in time 9 to 39 months apart (Watson & Slack, 1993). The second survey also measured job change and satisfaction. Emotional temperament at time 1 significantly predicted job satisfaction at time 2. This suggests that some people are predisposed to being satisfied. The tendency toward positive mood should be a factor that contributes to resilience when the going gets tough.

Resilience is "the process of, capacity for, or outcome of successful adaptation despite challenging or threatening circumstances" (Masten, Best, & Garmezy, 1990, p. 425). Resilience is evident from (a) good outcomes in high-risk people/situations, (b) sustained competence under stress, and (c) recovery from a traumatic event. Resilience is a capacity that develops over time in the context of person–environment interactions (Egeland, Carlson, & Stroufe, 1993). As people get older, they allocate more energy to resilience-related processes rather than growth or adding new capabilities. Resilience refers to the maintenance of functioning and recovery from dysfunction (Staudinger, Marsiske, & Baltes, 1993).

Factors related to risk and resilience in people who face major barriers (such as learning disabilities) include (Spekman, Goldberg, & Herman, 1993):

- Type of problem.
- Multiplicity of barrier-related difficulties.
- Severity of the barrier or event.
- Age at identification of the barrier or problem.
- Chronicity of the barrier or problem.
- Offsetting contributions of internal and environmental protective factors. (Spekman, Goldberg, & Herman, 1993)

How Resilience Works

Resilience involves the psychosocial capacities of competence, coping, creativity, and confidence (Fine, 1991). Coping skills demonstrating resilience do not come all at once; they grow through a process of selecting from available alternatives and reinforcement of constructive behaviors. Resilience is important because (a) personal attributes compensate for loss of competence during stress (b) personal attributes protect the individual against perceptions of harm, and (c) stress is perceived as a challenge.

Career barriers situations compromise opportunities for commitment, control, and challenge. Cognitive and behavioral coping mechanisms and efforts to recruit social support find expression through:

- Hope and the will to overcome.
- Affiliation and the recruitment of social support (acquiring a sense of belonging to a social group or, for that matter, to all of life).
- Finding meaning and purpose (the identification of purpose, or finding meaning in an ordeal).
- The capacity to step back (oneself and one's trouble become the object of introspection from which one might generalize).
- Stressing one's assets rather than deficits.

- Novel applications of problem-solving strategies (the ability to turn a familiar way of solving problems into a novel application—such as using musical rhythm to overcome a physically painful situation).
- Transforming barriers into adaptive behavior (e.g., through humor as a defense mechanism; Fine, 1991).

Phase-specific attributes of resilience include (a) the acute phase—energy is directed at minimizing the impact of the career barrier (b) the reorganization phase—a new reality is faced and accepted in part or in whole, and (c) the rest of one's life (Fine, 1991).

The National Institutes for Mental Health identified resilience and its opposite, vulnerability, as priority research areas to aid in understanding, treating, and preventing mental and behavioral disorders (National Advisory Mental Health Council Behavioral Science Task Force, 1995). They suggested that the resilience of an individual's self-concept depends on genetic predispositions and environmental experience. Stable temperamental traits and personality patterns developed early in life are precursors and predictors of later problem behavior, such as depression. Interventions in adulthood can change some of these patterns—for instance, through behavioral counseling.

Effects of Resilience

Studies of resilience to diseases and physical hazards show that resilience does not derive from avoidance of risks, but from controlled exposure (Rutter, 1993). Also, turning points in people's lives are important to recognize. People set on a maladaptive life trajectory may turn onto a more adaptive path. Other factors that may affect resilience include experience of success, early sensitizing experiences, temperament characteristics, how people judge their own situations, and the influence of psychological and environmental protective mechanisms.

Resilience and Learning From Experience. McCall (1994) considered how ability to learn from experience (that is, taking advantage of developmental experiences) can be used to predict an executive's potential to succeed in an international environment. Variables that can be used to identify managers who can learn from experience include curiosity about how people and things work, accepting responsibility for learning and change, seeking and using feedback, a sense of adventure, readiness/hardiness, a bias toward action, respecting differences, and consistent growth.

HARDINESS

A similar concept to resilience is hardiness. Kobasa, Maddi, and Kahn (1982; see also Kobasa, 1979) defined hardiness as a constellation of personality characteristics that serve as a resistance resource in the face of stressful events. Hardiness consists of three personality dispositions: commitment, control, and challenge.

Commitment is a tendency to involve oneself in tough situations rather than isolate oneself. In terms of cognitive appraisal, committed people have a sense of purpose that allows them to identify with, and find meaning in, their environments. This investment in themselves and the social situation makes giving up under pressure difficult for them. Coping responses include action and approach rather than passivity and withdrawal.

Control is a tendency to feel and act as if one is influential in the face of tough situations rather than helpless. The individual who is high in control is realistic about what he or she can affect. Nevertheless, the individual recognizes that he or she has the knowledge, skill, and imagination to influence events and people. This enhances resistance to tough situations by increasing the likelihood that difficult situations will be seen as controllable, not foreign, unexpected, or overwhelming experiences. As a result, the individual copes by taking actions to transform events into constructive outcomes that are consistent with an ongoing life plan, not jarring, threatening experiences.

Challenge is the belief that change rather than stability is normal in life. Changes are viewed as interesting incentives to growth instead of threats to security. Difficult situations are appraised as stimulating rather than harmful just because they require readjustment. Coping behaviors are attempts to transform oneself rather than protect what one can of the status quo. Challenge fosters openness and flexibility, which in turn encourage constructive responses to highly incongruent events.

Further, elements of deep cognitive structures associated with hardiness include self-concept, self-attribution, preferences for self-relevant feedback, and positivity bias toward self (Compton, Seeman, & Norris, 1991).

Hardiness and Coping With Stress

The basic premise of Kobasa's (1979) theory is that hardiness moderates the relationship between stress and mental and physical health by affecting situational appraisal and coping. Hardiness and self-esteem (a major part of resilience) are important components of overall quality of life (Evan, Pellizzari, Culbert, & Metzen, 1993). Psychological characteristics predispose people to illness. Such variables include thoughts and beliefs that foster hopeless and helpless feelings, a loss of control, hostility, a lack of commitment and little enthusiasm about life's challenges, and social isolation (Sperry, 1992). People tend to be healthier and happier when they are generally optimistic, have high levels of hardiness, have basic trust in other people, and have close satisfying relationships (Maddi & Khoshaba, 1994).

People who feel high levels of stress but remain healthy have a different personality structure than those who become ill under stress. This has been supported by considerable research. In a survey of 259 upper- and middle-level male managers (mean age = 48 years), hardiness decresed symptoms of illness for those under stress (Kobasa et al., 1982). In another study, hardiness and locus of control buffered the effects of stress on illness in a 5-year follow-up of 32 women (aged 27 to 64 at the time of follow-up; Lawler & Schmied, 1992).

Another study examined 326 officer candidates (most between 19 and 21 years old) in the Israel Defense Forces who completed self-report stress surveys during four critical course events and a hardiness measure at the start and end of the course (Westman, 1990). Hardiness was negatively related to experienced stress. Moreover, hardiness was positively related to objectively assessed performance throughout the course and in the subsequent course and to the first on-the-job performance appraisal a year later. Further, hardiness buffered the cadets from the detrimental effects of stress on performance.

In a study of 276 Israeli military recruits, measures of hardiness, mental health, cognitive appraisal, and ways of coping were collected at the start and end of a demanding, 4-month combat training period (Florian, Mikulincer, & Taubman, 1995). Two elements of hardiness—commitment and control—measured at the beginning of the training predicted mental health at the end by affecting situational appraisal and coping. In particular, commitment improved mental health by reducing the appraisal of threat and the use of emotion-focused strategies. Control improved mental health by reducing the appraisal of threat and by increasing problem-solving and support-seeking strategies. Studying 18 adults awaiting dental surgery and 32 people who had already undergone the surgery, they found that individuals with less anxiety and high hardiness displayed a reduced physiological response when encountering this stressful situation (Solcova & Sykora, 1995).

Hardiness and Reactions to Discrimination.   Another study found that the relationship between experiencing discrimination and psychological symptoms was stronger for people who were low in hardiness—found in a study of 184 members (aged 18 years and older) of Toronto's Chinese community (Dion, Dion, & Pak, 1992).

Hardiness and Athletic Performance. Hardiness was found to improve athletic performance. For instance, team members' hardiness scores collected before a basketball season were correlated with a composite measure of team performance throughout the season in a study of 37 male high school basketball players (Maddi & Hess, 1992).

Hardiness and Physical Illness. An avoidance coping style predicts physical illness. For instance, in a study of 95 professional employees (aged 24 to 57 years), those who were lower on hardy appraisals of work/life and were higher on Type A behavior reported significantly more fatigue and exhaustion 1 year later (Nowack, 1991). Those who perceived less stress and expressed more cognitive hardiness reported significantly greater work/life satisfaction.

Hardiness Related to Stress and Job Satisfaction. A study of 163 female nurses aged 21 to 64 found that those who reported less stress and low work pressure tended to report less illness and more job satisfaction (Neubauer, 1992). Those with high absenteeism rates tended to be older, work evening shifts, have less experience, and rate their work environment high in stress and low in control. For those with a hardy personality, illness was unrelated to absenteeism, suggesting they were able to cope with a work environment that was high in work pressure and low in control without withdrawing through high absenteeism.

Hardiness's Effects on Responding to an Evaluative Threat Task. When confronted by a task on which a person will be evaluated, hardiness was positively associated with more frustration tolerance, viewing the task as less threatening, and responding to the task with more positive and less negative emotion (Wiebe, 1991).

Hardiness and Pressure From the Demands for Change. Another study examined the effects of pressures for change perceived by 325 senior-level employees in the public sector (different state government agencies) and the possible ways in which employees' psychological hardiness affects feelings of and reactions to stress (Ruch, Schoel, & Barnard, 1995). The demands for change were positively related to feelings of stress, subsequent dissatisfaction, and intentions to withdraw. People low in hardiness felt the stress more and were more dissatisfied than those high in hardiness. They concluded that hardiness may be an important counterforce to the effects of pressure for change on employees' intentions to leave the public-sector workforce.

Assessing Hardiness

Kobasa et al. (1982)[1] drew from different preexisting scales to measure the components of hardiness. In particular, people low in hardiness would respond affirmatively to items such as the following:

- The attempt to know yourself is a waste of effort.
- Life is empty and has no meaning in it for me.
- I long for a simple life in which decisions do not have to be made.
- I find it difficult to imagine enthusiasm for work.
- I find it hard to believe people who actually feel that the work they perform is of value to society.
- I wonder why I work at all.

DEVELOPING RESILIENCE AND HARDINESS

People can learn to be resilient and hardy. One way to do this is to take advantage of naturally occurring events. Although I do not recommend creating a hardship in order to learn endurance and persistence, people can turn tough work situations into developmental experiences. These include early work experiences, job rotations, project task forces, leading new efforts, and working with bosses. Hardships may include career setbacks, changing jobs, business mistakes, and subordinate performance problems. The favorability and amount of job feedback received is strongly related to job satisfaction and self-perceptions of competence. People are more satisfied when they see themselves improving at work and receive positive appraisals from others (K. J. Williams et al., 1990). McCall, et al. (1988) who studied how executives learn from experience and wrote:

> Any developmental event creates a tension between where a person is and where the person wants to be. This tension triggers some sort of adaptive response. Because of this, nearly all development events involve a confrontation with adverse circum-

---

[1]Copyright © 1982 by the American Psychological Association, Adapted with permission.

stances—intractable people or troublesome business problems—obstacles that must be overcome…. A failed assignment emphasizes lessons different from those of a challenge successfully met. When faced with their own failure, executives who learned from it did not reflect only on externalities. Instead, they turned inward and took a hard look at themselves. (p. 87)

McCall et al. (1988) argued that learning from hardships is more difficult than learning from other types of experiences. It is so easy and tempting to distance oneself from the event, blame others, be cynical or fatalistic, or withdraw. Learning from trauma requires "absorbing the suffering rather than reacting against it" (p. 91). Failures can be powerful reminders of our limitations.

Some of the managers interviewed by McCall et al. (1988), although successful, had experienced career barriers. For instance, a few had missed expected promotions, had been demoted, had been transferred to undesirable jobs, or had been fired. These executives "were forced to confront the truth about themselves. They were forced to recognize that they had flaws and that these flaws made a difference" (p. 97). They could not continue advancing in their careers until they learned how to reduce their deficiencies. For instance, an accountant on the fast track who had been passed over for an early promotion resigned in anger. After considerable reflection, he realized that the firm was right. He did not have the maturity or seasoning. He recognized that the career targets he set for himself were not absolute and needed to be tempered with realism. Managers who learned from career setbacks faced their limitations and scaled down their unrealistic expectations. They learned what sorts of jobs they liked and did not like, learned about how their organizations worked—for instance, who to sell their ideas to and how—and the need for patience and a long-term view.

Executives who learned from business mistakes recognized that they failed to take proper account of other people. They learned the importance of persistence even when the odds for success seem slight. They also learned humility. Executives who learned from managing problem subordinates learned not to act impulsively but also not to procrastinate. They learned to invest time and energy to confront the situation, but most of all, to do so with empathy.

Executives who learned from experience learned to correct weaknesses where possible and to live with the others by compensating for them. McCall et al. (1988) offered several examples:

- An executive who knows she in inattentive to detail could hire staff who relish detail.

- Someone who is inarticulate at presenting could keep speeches short, use professional graphics, and share or delegate presentations.
- A person who recognizes he has difficulty resolving conflict can avoid settings where conflict is likely and find someone else to handle the problem.
- An executive who has a proclivity to overmanage subordinates could take a vacation at a critical time or establish a reporting mechanism to satisfy compulsion to know what is going on without hands-on intervention.

SUMMARY

Resilience is the foundation for insight and identity and the set of personality characteristics that most contributes to overcoming career barriers. People who are high in resilience believe in themselves, need to achieve, are willing to take reasonable risks, and need to evaluate events and circumstances. Resilient individuals are competent, resourceful, and creative. Hardiness is a similar concept to resilience that serves as a resistance resource in the face of stress. Hardiness consists of commitment (the tendency to involve oneself in tough situations), control (the tendency to feel and act as if one is influential in the face of tough situations rather than helpless), and challenge (the belief that change rather than stability is normal in life). People who are hardy appraise stress in a positive light and cope with it constructively. People can learn to be resilient and hardy, and some learn by experiencing and overcoming adversity. They turn tough work situations into developmental experiences.

FROM THE CASE FILE

Similar to the cases at the outset of this chapter, the following case shows the value of resilience and perseverance. It describes a woman with a physical handicap who faced an increasing work load.

STAMINA TO KEEP GOING (CASE 5.3)

Perhaps the most resilient individuals are those who earn a living while suffering an increasingly debilitating physical handicap:

Mona is a 59-year-old woman, divorced, with one son. For the past 14 years she has worked as a receptionist for a State agency that provides vocational training and placement for disabled people. Mona is herself disabled, having developed multiple sclerosis almost 28 years ago. She is confined to a wheelchair and needs regular treatment from several different medical specialists. Her husband was unable to cope with the situation and left her years ago.

Mona says that her job is highly stressful. She has to handle numerous calls from a variety of constituencies as well as deal with visitors to the agency. The progress of her disease is unpredictable, and her physical condition continues to deteriorate. However, she maintains a positive attitude, and tries to help herself whenever and wherever she can.

III

*Ways to Help People Overcome
Career Barriers*

6

Sources of Support

The last two chapters outlined the components of career motivation and suggested that they can be developed and strengthened by the right environmental conditions. These conditions form a positive environment for continuous learning and development. Such an environment serves employees well when they need to make a transition to avoid or overcome a career barrier. In this chapter, I describe the importance of a supportive environment in mediating the effects of a career barrier. I outline the situational conditions that support career resilience, insight, and identity, describe factors that constitute a continuous learning culture, and conclude by considering ways to support older workers who face career decline.

DEALING WITH JOB STRESS

I start this chapter with the case of a young woman who faced poor supervision and a demanding work environment. She continued her education, but did not seem to learn how to cope with job stress.

MANAGING A BAD BOSS (CASE 6.1)

Mary is 28 years old. She has been married for just under a year and has no children. She earned a BA in business administration and is now working part-time toward an MA in liberal studies. After graduation from college, Mary was unable to find a job. She felt that her degree provided her with general business knowledge, but that she wasn't prepared to do anything specific. After a few months of a fruitless job search, she began a 6-month training program to become a paralegal. Her first job in a law firm was demanding. She worked at a fast pace and did whatever was necessary to meet one deadline after another. After about a year, she was promoted to a supervisory position. Being in a position to supervise several office staff members who had become her friends made life more difficult for Mary. Working harder than ever, the firm refused to hire more staff, and Mary felt that the firm was controlling its costs at her expense. An illness, possibly brought on in part by the stressful job, led her to quit the firm.

After staying home and resting for a year, Mary thought she would start something new. She entered a semester-long training program in medical technology and took some additional management classes. This led to some temporary positions in her new field and further education. Ultimately, she found an excellent full-time position that allowed her to use her old and new skills. Although coworkers were congenial, her supervisor was abusive, underqualified, disrespectful, and generally unprofessional. She continued her education and returned to one of the temporary part-time positions she had earlier.

Mary's case shows the troubles many people face as a result of poor management. It demonstrates how a person can enter a new field that builds on existing skills and experiences through continuing education and getting job experience in different temporary jobs. However, the case also shows how someone can develop a tendency to fall back on something that is comfortable—in Mary's situation, going back to school, not for advanced education but for training in a new occupational area. For someone relatively young, this is a way to explore new career avenues. However, it is not a way to learn how to cope with a stressful work environment.

SUPPORTIVE SITUATIONAL CONDITIONS

The discussion in chapter 2 of how people react to career barriers indicates that reactions are likely to be more constructive when the environment provides support to soften the blow. Mary's situation may have been very different if she had received the training and support she needed to manage in her new supervisory role. In general, reactions to a career barrier depend on the larger situation or circumstances at the time. For instance, in evaluating employees' reactions to job loss, Leana and Feldman (1992) found that financial circumstances, labor market conditions, and attachment to the job prior to layoff influenced how people reacted to losing their jobs.

Unless an individual has other sources of income (a spouse earning a high salary, or a pension), job loss results in a drastically reduced standard of living. Leana and Feldman (1992) found that the greater the financial strain, the greater the intensity of the job loss experience, the higher the feelings of distress and depression, and the more negative physiological reactions, such as illness. In another study, financial concerns increased stress symptoms in a sample of 41 unemployed workers in the timber industry (Mallinckrodt & Bennett, 1992).

Naturally, the higher the unemployment rates, or the fewer the job openings people perceive in their area of expertise, the more pessimistic they are. Leana and Feldman (1992) found that the higher the unemployment rate, the more intense the job loss experience but the less the feelings of internal blame. They also found that people who reported higher job involvement in their previous jobs perceived the job loss as more intense, more distressful, and less reversible.

Consider the following additional findings from other research on support systems:

- For unemployed people who are married, the spouse and family provide a strong support system that has protective effects on mental health (Caplan, Vinokur, Price, & van Ryan, 1989).
- Characteristics of career alternatives can influence career decisions. For instance, a study of 66 employees of a research and development laboratory faced with the decision to relocate with the lab or lose their jobs identified variables that predicted the decision to relocate (Turban, Campion, & Eyring, 1992). Relocation was more likely for employees who had positive perceptions of the new job's attributes, positive attitude toward work and the location, and positive perceptions of the relocation policy. Employees with high-school-age children were more likely to relocate than those without high-school-age children probably because they did not want to face job loss when their children were close to college.
- Communication that reduces uncertainty facilitates the adjustment of employees who transfer to new locations in the same organization (Kramer, 1993a, 1993b). Communication from coworkers and supervisors about one's role and performance can clarify expectations and improve feelings of comfort. Moreover, such communication serves as a buffer against unmet expectations.
- Support from significant others for job seeking is of particular importance for successful reemployment (Wanberg et al., 1996). This support refers to having a spouse or other important people who think they should try hard to get a job.

SUPPORT FOR CAREER MOTIVATION

My research on career motivation, summarized in chapter 4, showed that young managers' career motivation is higher in organizations that treat them as a resource for the future by offering continued training and varied job assignments (e.g., management development programs). This is in contrast to organizations that treat young managers merely as resources for meeting immediate business needs and do little to enhance their career development. The components of career motivation (the variables that comprise career resilience, insight, and identity) suggest ways to support career motivation. In particular, the following summary is based on London and Mone (1987):

> *To support career resilience:* Provide positive reinforcement for a job well done, generate opportunities for achievement, and create an environment that is conducive to risk taking by rewarding innovation and reducing the negative consequences of failure. Also, show concern for others and encourage group cohesiveness and collaborative working relationships. Positive reinforcement is likely to develop self-confidence. Opportunities for achievement and risk taking contribute to a need for achievement and a willingness to take risks. Supportive work climates promote cooperation or independent action, depending on which is needed.

> *To support career insight:* Encourage goal setting and give career information and performance feedback. Encouraging goal setting, giving feedback on performance, and providing information about career opportunities foster the establishment of career plans and knowledge of oneself and the environment.

> *To support career identity:* Encourage involvement with work through job challenges and chances for professional growth, provide opportunities for leadership and advancement, and offer rewards such as recognition and bonuses. Job challenges, encouragement of professional activities, and opportunities for leadership and advancement result in job involvement and a desire to advance.

In general, there are many supportive management strategies. Managers who are coaches and developers of people give performance feedback, give reinforcement for positive performance, provide resources for training and development, and are role models of positive performance (including supportive management). Organizations support the manager's role as coach and developer by human resource programs that measure and reward managers on these activities, provide resources for training (including training programs), and training managers on systems for measuring performance and giving feedback.

Managers who are not fortunate enough to have such supportive organizational systems can still be effective coaches and developers. They buck the system and, solely on their own initiative, become known in the organization as good bosses—bosses that care about their subordinates' development. As a result, they are able to attract the best and brightest employees to their department. Of course, there are some managers who are not developmental even when the organization provides supportive systems. These managers have difficulty giving feedback, rewarding performance, investing departmental resources in training, and promoting or rotating employees to other departments for their learning and advancement. What is needed is a holistic environment with managers and systems that support employee growth and development. In the next section, I consider what such an environment is like and how to develop it.

TOWARD A CONTINUOUS
LEARNING CULTURE

The work environment influences the extent to which newly trained employees are able to apply on the job the skills they learned in training. (I also covered this material in my paper on continuous learning coauthored by Mone; London & Mone, in press). A study of 505 supermarket managers from 52 stores found that support for the specific skills learned and, more generally, an environment that supports continuous learning, improved the transfer of supervisory skills from training to the job (Tracey, Tannenbaum, & Kavanagh, 1995). Employees who reported more environmental support were viewed by the supervisors as having changed their behavior in accord with the goals of the course.

Some firms provide training for employees to acquire multiple skills that will increase their value to the firm and enhance their employment security. However, when the company provides the enabling resources, the employees must be willing to take advantage of them. A good example is the Intel corporation, the computer chip manufacturer (Sanger & Lohr, 1996). It invests $120 million a year on training, or about $3,000 per employee on average. This is more than double the national average. Although the firm is highly profitable and can afford the cost, it views training as a matter of survival. The semiconductor business endures considerable technological change, and its employees need a new set of skills every 2 or 3 years to match the latest generation of microprocessor. Training is a way to reprogram employees as fast as the chips. When redeployment is necessary, workers are given 4 months to find new jobs in the firm. Participating in training rests with the workers who are responsible for gaining new skills so they can continue to be employable inside the firm or in another company.

Andy Linn is an example of someone who has taken advantage of the training to move into higher skilled, higher earning positions at Intel's plant in Portland, OR. Starting in 1988 at age 25 as a $15,000-a-year technician monitoring acid baths in which silicon wafers are dipped, he found one job after another at Intel on his own initiative. Earning $30,000 eight years later, Intel paid for his continual training and education. This included tuition at a community college and four-year university. He is now a skilled "concept engineer" responsible for scouting new product ideas at universities.

Tracey et al. (1995) defined continuous learning as "an organizationwide concern, value, belief, and expectation that general knowledge acquisition and application is important" (p. 242). This is reflected by a pattern of shared meaning linked to multiple methods for acquiring and applying new knowledge. Employees learn from a variety of sources, not just formal training programs. Support for continuous learning is evident by the policies that emphasize employee development, and by norms that encourage quality improvement, innovation, and competitiveness:

> A continuous learning culture encourages and promotes the acquisition, application, and sharing of knowledge, behaviors, and skills from a variety of sources. Continuous learning may be encouraged through supervisor and peer support for learning, diverse and challenging task assignments, and organizational systems and structures that facilitate efforts to be progressive, innovative, and competitive. (p. 242)

Further, Tracey et al. (1995) outlined four components of a continuous learning work environment building on the work of Dubin (1990), Noe and Ford (1992), and Rosow and Zager (1988):

1. Knowledge and skill acquisition are essential responsibilities of every employee's job. Thus jobs must be designed to be sufficiently challenging to promote personal development. Learning is integrated into all the jobs in the firm. Everybody understands and accepts this.
2. Knowledge and skill acquisition are supported by social interaction and work relationships. An interactive work environment gives employees an understanding of each other's tasks and how they are interrelated. Teamwork within units and cooperative alliances between units are encouraged.
3. Formal systems reinforce achievement and offer chances for personal development. The organization provides employees with the resources and oppor-

tunities they need to acquire and apply valuable knowledge and skills. Policies inform organization members about the importance of continuous learning, and employees are evaluated and rewarded on their learning and application of that learning to performance improvement.

4. Innovation and competition are expected and rewarded. Employees ascribe to the highest performance standards, and they expect as much from each other. Concurrently, the organization strives to be the best in its industry.

As a result of these four attributes, employees in a continuous learning environment share perceptions and expectations that learning is an essential part of the way the organization or institution does business. "These perceptions and expectations constitute an organizational value or belief and are influenced by a variety of factors, including challenging jobs; supportive social, reward, and development systems; and an innovative and competitive work setting" (Tracey et al., 1995, p. 241). As such, continuous learning becomes part of the organization's culture.

Tracey et al. (1995) developed three scales to measure a continuous learning culture:

Social support: The extent to which supervisors and coworkers encourage the acquisition and use of any new relevant skills and behaviors (e.g., coworkers encourage each other to use new knowledge and skills on the job).

Continuous innovation: The extent to which an organization promotes ongoing efforts to be innovative and progressive (e.g., the organization expects continuing technical excellence and competence).

Competition: The extent to which an organization promotes an image of being the best in its field through high levels of individual performance (e.g., the organization strives to be better than its competition). (p. 246)

Here are the items they used to measure a continuous learning culture. They can be used to assess the support in your own work environment (Tracey et al., 1995):

In your work location (or department):

1. Job assignments are challenges that stretch managers' knowledge to the limit.

2. Supervisors give recognition and credit to those who apply new knowledge and skill to their work.
3. Coworkers are able to provide reliable information about ways to improve job performance.
4. There is a performance appraisal system that ties financial rewards to technical competence.
5. Job assignments consistently expose managers to new technical information.
6. Supervisors match an associate's need for personal and professional development with opportunities to attend training.
7. Coworkers tell each other about new information that can be used to increase job performance.
8. There is excellent on-the-job training.
9. Job assignments are made in the manager's area of interest and designed to promote personal development.
10. Independent and innovative thinking are encouraged by supervisors.
11. Coworkers consistently suggest new approaches to solving problems based o their own experiences.
12. Associates are provided with equipment and facilities to acquire and apply new knowledge and skills.
13. Job assignments include free time to explore new, advanced ideas and methods for improving performance.
14. Supervisors ask for ideas about how to solve technical work-related problems.
15. Coworkers are willing to listen to new ideas.
16. There is a job rotation program to give its managers diverse job assignments during the first years of employment.
17. Job assignments continually require the evaluation of alternative solutions to problems.
18. Supervisors openly express their support of continuous learning.
19. Coworkers encourage each other to use new knowledge and skills on the job.

This corporation (or institution):

20. Is highly innovative.
21. Expects continuing technical excellence and competence.
22. Has a progressive atmosphere.
23. Attempts to be better than its competitors.
24. Expects high levels of work performance.

Transfer of Training Climate

Tracey et al. (1995) distinguished between continuous learning culture and transfer of training climate. The former is a general concept reflecting the overall atmosphere (social support, innovation, and standards of excellence for continuous learning), whereas the latter is a specific concept reflecting characteristics of the environment that support and reinforce applying what was learned in training on the job. These are reminders for trainees to use the training after they return to the job (Rouiller & Goldstein, 1993).

A study of 102 management trainees and their supervisors in addition to 297 managerial coworkers in 102 restaurants from a large chain of fast-food franchises found that coworkers' perceptions of transfer climate in the restaurants were related to posttraining behavior of the trainees (Rouiller & Goldstein, 1993). (Managerial coworkers rated transfer climate, supervisors and subordinates rated the trainees' behaviors several weeks after the arrival of the management trainee.) Two aspects of transfer of training climate—situational cues and consequences—were equally important predictors of learning transfer. An example of a situational cue is a goal set by the supervisor for the employee to use a newly learned skill. An example of a consequence is a supervisor's giving the subordinate positive feedback and public recognition for using the learned skill. Although this was a study of new managers, Tracey et al.'s (1995) research found that both transfer of training climate and continuous learning culture are important to the transfer of training of experienced employees who attend training and then return to work.

Tracey et al. (1995) outlined the following components of transfer of training climate:

> *Social and goal cues:*   The extent to which supervisors and coworkers encourage and set goals for trainees to use new skills and behaviors acquired in training (e.g., newly trained managers discuss how to apply their training on the job with their supervisors and other managers).

> *Task cues:*   The extent to which characteristics of a trainee's job prompt or remind him or her to use new skills and behaviors acquired in training (e.g., the job of a newly trained manager is designed in such a way as to allow them to use the skills taught in training).

> *No-feedback consequences:*   The extent to which supervisors neither support nor discourage the application of new skills and behaviors acquired in training (e.g., supervisors do not notice newly trained managers who use their training). (negative)

Punishment consequences: The extent to which trainees are openly discouraged from using new skills and behaviors acquired in training (e.g., newly trained managers fail to use their training, and they can expect to be reprimanded). (negative)

Extrinsic reinforcement consequences: The extent to which trainees receive extrinsic rewards for using new trained skills and behaviors acquired in training (e.g., newly trained managers who successfully use their training will receive a salary increase).

Intrinsic reinforcement consequences: The extent to which trainees receive intrinsic rewards for using new trained skills and behaviors acquired in training (e.g., supervisors and other managers appreciate newly trained managers who perform their job as taught in training). (p. 246)

SOURCES OF SUPPORT FOR
OLDER WORKERS' CAREER MOTIVATION

Trying hard to find another job is not enough for older workers. A study of variables that predict job-seeking behavior found that older people who engaged in frequent job seeking were less likely to find work than younger people who engaged in frequent job seeking (Wanberg et al., 1996). Frequent behavior does not necessarily translate into the right behavior. Older people are less likely to be assertive enough in seeking employment compared to younger people.

Sources of support for career motivation stem from the work one does, the nature of supervision (e.g., performance evaluation and feedback), the policies of the organization, and the career opportunities available (London, 1990). Support for career motivation is critical at late career when opportunities for the future maybe cut off abruptly, prematurely, and inappropriately. If we apply the variables that support career resilience, insight, and identity described earlier to older workers, the goal is to use current older workers more fully and, in the case of employment cutbacks, ensure that older workers have opportunities for continued career satisfaction.

One key motivating opportunity is to enhance resilience through involvement. Older workers should be involved in designing programs and processes for enhancing their own contribution to the organization. This may include designing training or retraining programs, deciding on the components of retirement-planning workshops, or establishing and implementing ways to enhance the quality of the firm's operations.

Organizations undergoing mergers and acquisitions have successfully used interfirm committees to design new organizational structures and self-select who will stay and who will go. Such involvement reinforces self-confidence and achievements valued by the organization. In addition to increasing older workers' involvement, they should be kept informed as much as possible about events that are likely to affect their jobs and careers. Information is the cornerstone for career insight. This should include information about impending organizational changes and feedback about the individual's competitiveness in the organization. When cutbacks are needed, supervisors may be required to rank employees or "band" them into categories. Individuals in high bands are "protected," whereas those in low bands are at risk. Employees will want to know where they stand and what options are available to them. They will also want to be assured of the fairness of these decisions, and the extent to which they can influence the outcome. In such cases, information about decision processes and available alternatives before the decisions are made may prompt individuals to self-select for early retirement, relocation, or transfer to a new function or department.

Older workers should have career choices that allow them to match their needs with available options. This includes choosing different types of work and different work schedules and locations. Unfortunately, age discrimination can limit career choices—for instance, able older individuals who are seeking part-time work to supplement retirement income may find few opportunities commensurate with their skill and experience level. Choice of career options is likely to enhance feelings of resilience and identity.

The sources of support for career motivation reviewed earlier suggest ways that organizations can soften the blow of framebreaking career change. Interventions should reinforce good performance and effective use of skills. Job offers should include the potential for continued achievement and respect—albeit indifferent directions and for different reasons. Feedback is needed to provide evidence of competence. The employee's role should be a source of continued or new career identity.

A number of career options are possible for creating a motivating environment. Given that career derailment is likely to cause an older worker to question long-established insights and self-confidence, most individuals (even those with initially high resilience) are likely to need this support. Only a few individuals will have the psychological strength to seek new opportunities for achievement in an unreceptive environment. The following are some suggestions for organizational interventions to support the career motivation of employees in late career. The discussion shows the potential value of the interventions by describing how they might influence career resilience, insight, and identity.

Career motivation can be enhanced in the wake of framebreaking change. It is possible to soften the blow of major changes by interventions that reinforce good performance and effective use of skills. Job offers, even at lower organizational levels and at lower levels of pay, should include the possibility for continued achievement and development, albeit possibly in different career directions. A motivating environment can be created in a number of different ways. For instance, here are some ways to bolster career motivation for employees who are older, have experienced a career plateau, or both:

- Reward workers for mentoring younger employees.
- Redesign organizational structures to make them flatter, thereby giving all employees more responsibility.
- Rehire retirees for temporary full- or part-time work.
- Provide stress-coping workshops.
- Expect employees to be sources of quality control and ideas for quality improvement.
- Provide self-assessment methods and workbooks to help employees think about their career objectives in relation to other life concerns.
- Transfer older workers between departments.
- Provide training to enhance employees' marketability outside as well as inside the firm.
- Implement phased retirement jobs—positions that allow older workers to reduce the number of hours worked as they approach retirement.
- Offer financial incentives to encourage retirement or job change.
- Join a consortium of firms and local government to hold job fairs that match individuals to available positions.
- Provide career-end management support to help people cope with advancing age.

Older employees who are high in self-insight may be quick to realize the extent to which they have continued work opportunities or how they may continue their work interests in partial retirement. They may also seek ways to expand their involvement in, and identification with, activities outside work. The same types of support that foster career continuity may encourage a shift in career motivation from the job to nonwork pursuits—for example, mentor programs that pair a person who is planning retirement with someone who has made a successful adjustment after retirement.

SUMMARY

The effects of a career barrier depend not only on the individual's resilience (covered in the last two chapters), but also the nature of the environment. A supportive environment softens the blow of a career barrier and helps create a constructive response. Also, a supportive environment may prevent barriers from occurring. Not surprisingly, people find coping with job loss easier when they have a financial cushion, when other jobs are available, and when they were not especially attached to the job they lost.

This chapter reviewed the environmental elements that support the major components of career motivation. For instance, to support career resilience, provide positive reinforcement for a job well done, generate opportunities for achievement, and create an environment that is conducive to risk taking by rewarding innovation and reducing the negative consequences of failure. To support career insight, encourage goal setting and give career information and performance feedback. To support career identity, encourage involvement with work through job challenges and encouragement of professional growth, provide opportunities for leadership and advancement, and offer rewards such as recognition and bonuses. An environment that supports continuous learning is one in which there is a belief throughout the organization that general knowledge acquisition and application is important. This means that knowledge and skill acquisition are essential responsibilities of every employee's job, knowledge and skill acquisition are supported by social interaction and work relationships, formal systems reinforce achievement and offer chances for personal development, and innovation and competition are expected and rewarded. Continuous learning environments are particularly careful about supporting transfer of training—that is, being sure that employees have an opportunity to apply on the job what they learning in training programs.

Finally, I examined how older workers' career motivation can be enhanced in the wake of framebreaking change or facing a career plateau. Steps include rewarding workers for mentoring younger employees, rehiring retirees for temporary full- or part-time work, providing stress-coping workshops, providing training to enhance employees' marketability outside as well as inside the firm, and implementing positions that allow older workers to reduce the number of hours worked as they approach retirement (phased retirement).

In the next chapter, I continue this discussion of situational support for facing and managing career barriers by describing programmatic interventions. These are tools and techniques for organizations to adopt to help employees cope constructively when career changes are in the offing.

FROM THE CASE FILE

Poor supervision, a boring job, and job stress can create major career barriers. In the next case, a man stayed in a dull job and took several years to explore career alternatives, got some training, and embarked on a new career direction. In the subsequent case, job stress and a clash with a supervisor forced a person to quit and seek career counseling. The last case in this chapter describes a hard-working young woman whose bosses took advantage of her competence and career motivation.

WHEN CAREER OPPORTUNITIES
ARE LIMITED (6.2)

Not surprisingly, people are put off by jobs that do not offer what they want—for instance, a chance to use their imagination and creativity. This is especially a problem for someone locked into a family business. Sometimes it takes self-initiative to create your own supportive work environment. It helps, of course, to have financial backing:

> *Mack is a 49-year-old married man with two children from a previous marriage. He made a career transition from a mundane position in his father's manufacturing firm to a job offering the creative opportunities for which he yearned. The transition took about two years, during which Mack explored various career options and took courses in graphic arts and design while working for his father. As it turned out, advanced planning paid off. His father's company began to do poorly, and Mack would have had to find another job anyway. Having financial support from his wife helped make the transition. Mack found a job as a graphic artist. After about a year, his wife had an opportunity to relocate to Florida, and Mack was happy to follow. He found a position as an interior designer for a local firm. When his wife relocated next to Santa Fe, NM, Mack again followed. With his wife's financial and emotional support, he opened his own firm.*

STRUGGLING TO FIND A NICHE (CASE 6.3)

Job stress coupled with lack of career identity can cause a person to flounder. Following is a case of someone who is uncertain about continuing in her profession and has trouble dealing with her bosses' job demands and lack of support:

> *Nancy, age 33, has been married for a year and a half. She has no children and is currently unemployed. She left her most recent position in public relations 2 months ago. Before this job, she had several prior positions in public relations. Her last job*

was with her college alma mater, where she had taken a position with considerable hope and excitement. She cared deeply about the college and looked forward to serving it in a professional capacity. She also hoped the position would give her more time with her family. During her 5 months on the job, Nancy felt increasing stress from the constant deadlines and demands and had less time than ever for her family. She quit suddenly after a blowup with her boss.

Nancy is now working with a career counselor, and is considering learning about a new field. She believes this has increased her self-insight. She is clearer about her priorities (especially the importance of personal and family time).

MORE BOSS TROUBLE (CASE 6.4)

This is another case of bad supervision and unkept promises for career advancement. The case describes an overworked young woman who rose from the ranks to quite a responsible position, but confronted age or sex discrimination along the way.

Olive had worked for a company for 8 years, starting when she was 19 years old. The company was a chain of furniture stores, and Olive worked in a large store as a shipping clerk, then as a manager in the customer service office. She reached a point where she was working 70 hour weeks with no overtime pay, and had to face verbal abuse by her manager. She had no time even to look for another job. While she was out with pneumonia, her boss demanded that she come to work. Overhearing the telephone conversation, her father insisted that she quit on the spot.

Olive's next position was not much better. Through connections, she quickly landed a job with a bank where she thought she would be assistant to one of the vice presidents. She was told she would be trained by rotating through a series of jobs. However, her first assignment as a customer service representative continued without change. She eventually realized that she landed the job because the bank wanted to keep her uncle, an important customer, happy. Now she is worried that her position as a customer service clerk will be a barrier to finding a more responsible job elsewhere, despite her considerable experience with her former employer. Compounding the problem is that her boss is condescending to her. Olive is proficient at her job, and thinks her boss might be worried that she will take his job. Meanwhile, the VP who hired Olive barely speaks to her.

Olive's situation shows that a career barrier can be a series of events and unexpected turns that seem to have no end or solution. Olive apparently gets frustrated but is not a quitter. Her reluctance to be more proactive in seeking new opportunities or be more vocal in her current situation seems to lead others to take advantage of her. She fears that exerting more control will only lead to more problems and could use some constructive ways to seek more from her firm (maybe by talking to someone in the human resources department) or looking for another job.

7

Interventions for Constructive Appraisal and Coping

The factors that affect how people react to career barriers described here so far are the foundation for creating methods to help people cope. This chapter describes and evaluates a number of approaches people can seek to help them manage career barriers. Some interventions are one-on-one between the affected employee and his or her supervisor or a counselor. Other interventions are self-management techniques that people can learn so they are prepared to cope with career barriers when they arise. Still other interventions are training programs to teach people skills to cope with specific barriers and take positive actions.

These interventions attempt to enhance individuals' self-esteem and show them ways to take constructive action and practice new behaviors. A typical example of constructive action is teaching unemployed people job search skills and self-management (Magnusson & Redekopp, 1992). Timely and meaningful interventions involve multiple therapeutic tasks, such as helping persons find meaning in their crises, helping them handle feelings provided by their situation, helping them with the reality and consequences of their condition, and fostering the functional skills and behaviors that they will need to fulfill their potential (Fine, 1991). Some people are their own best facilitators. They are able to set goals and manage their situations. Others need considerable help.

FACILITATING CAREER TRANSITIONS

Brown (1995) suggested a values-based approach to facilitating career transitions. The approach centers on identifying, clarifying, and prioritizing values as a way to understand and manage transitions. This is especially helpful for planned transitions that occur because of values clashes, for instance, because people are unable to engage in work they deem important or their values contradict those of their supervisors. In the case of unplanned transitions, negative emotions should be handled before reemployment to avoid future values clashes.

Timing is a critical ingredient when planning an intervention to help others experiencing a career barrier. Early intervention after unemployment is likely to be important in ameliorating the undesirable effects of job loss on psychological well-being (Osipow & Fitzgerald, 1993).

Another ingredient is understanding the individual's feelings, judgment, intentions, and actions at different points after a career barrier has occurred. Perrez and Reicherts (1992) developed a questionnaire that can be administered by paper and pencil or computer to measure such reactions to a stressful work situation. Here are some sample items:

I feel:
1. nervous/anxious 0 1 2 3 4 5 calm/composed
2. depressed/sad 0 1 2 3 4 5 cheerful/serene
3. angry/furious 0 1 2 3 4 5 gentle/peaceful

The following items are also rated on 0 (low) to 5 (high):

Judgments
4. The chances of this situation taking a turn for the better without effort on my part.
5. The chances that I can influence this situation for the better.
6. The overall amount of stress I feel.
7. I have experienced a similar situation before.

My intentions
8. To actively confront the situation.
9. To maintain a friendly atmosphere.
10. To remain calm and composed.
11. To maintain my self-esteem.

My actions
12. I fade out, stop paying attention, look for distractions.
13. I make clear to myself what is at stake and what I should do.
14. I get my emotions under control.
15. I blame myself.
16. I blame others.
17. I wait for something to happen.
18. I try to withdraw from the situation (e.g., by avoiding other people).
    (pp. 214–215)

When some time has elapsed, the situation has been resolved, or both, individuals can be asked to rate their feelings (as in the list) and their attributions for the outcome of the situation (...to my own behavior, ...to the behavior of others, ...to circumstances).

The results of such a questionnaire can be valuable to counselors working with clients to help them cope with career barriers. The questionnaire can also be a useful self-tracking mechanism. In the next sections, I outline methods for counseling, teaching self-management, supporting self-control, and teaching useful coping skills.

ONE-ON-ONE INTERVENTIONS

Career counselors can help people deal with unrealistic expectations, problems with financial pressures, and taking one step at a time rather than passively waiting or failing to communicate (Fry, 1991). A career counselor can help assess the way the individual implicitly interprets or makes sense of a career barrier (McAuliffe, 1993). Also, the counselor can challenge and support the clients in a way that might help them open up to new possibilities. Such counseling may benefit people making fairly minor career transitions (e.g., change of job within the same firm) in that this may be a time to shift the way they create meaning in the direction of discovering what they can learn from a career change. That is, a minor transition is the time to teach individuals to interpret events in terms of what they can learn rather than who they can blame.

A study of subjective aspects of career management among 132 midcareer senior executives attending a careers counseling program (Pemberton, Herriot, & Bates, 1994). Five areas of career management include knowledge, confidence, attribution, significance of signals of career progression, and expectations of the employing organization. Counseling increased career knowledge and confidence, self-assurance in regard to careers, the ability to negotiate career change, and attribution of career progress to their own personal qualities.

Focus on Personal Characteristics and Career

An eclectic career counseling model focuses on both personality and career development (Imbimbo, 1994). This model requires the counselor to alternate between the active and directive role of career counselor and the facilitative and exploratory role of the personal counselor. This requires the counselor to be expert in career and personal counseling. Another approach is to involve rehabilitation counselors.

Rehabilitation Counseling

An interesting thought is that rehabilitation counselors and occupational therapists who usually help people with disabilities have skills that can be valuable to people who suffer loss of income or job (Gregory, 1995). These counselors understand the severe loss in motivation and self-confidence suffered by people who face major career barriers, just as people who are injured or have physical handicaps often have trouble believing they can be productive. A rehabilitation model teaches clients job search skills, new job skills, how to work with others, and how to deal with their persistent negative feelings and defeatist attitudes (both the attitudes they have themselves and others have about them).

Computer-Based Counseling

Counseling implies an in-depth, one-on-one relationship between the counselor and client who is facing a career barrier. Another approach is computer-based counseling. This consists of self-assessment, score interpretations, outlines of possible career alternatives, solutions to career problems, and advice. In a study of 188 auto workers (aged 23 to 42) in career transition, workers were able to increase their level of career decidedness and make progress in their commitment to occupational choice through the use of a computer-based career counseling program (Marin & Splete, 1991). Computer-plus-counselor intervention was more effective than computer-only intervention.

Outplacement Counseling

Reemployment after job loss is more satisfying for people who reach emotional acceptance of being unemployed. A study of 516 involuntarily dismissed adult white-collar workers (12% female) found that new jobs were generally characterized as less financially rewarding yet more psychologically gratifying (Eby & Buch, 1994). People who had come to terms with the job loss emotionally (e.g., got over their anger, resentment, and fear) were more likely to view the new position as satisfying. Because reemployment after job loss is more satisfying for people who reach emotional acceptance of being unemployed, employment or outplacement counselors can ease the transition into satisfying new jobs by helping recently unemployed worker deal with the negative emotional trauma of job loss. The counselors can encourage active coping strategies and foster realistic job expectation, tailoring the counseling to meeting individual needs.

Outplacement counseling should include at least the following three goals: (a) increased awareness of personal assumptions about oneself, career opportunities, and job selection processes; (b) knowledge of relevant information—knowing what is important and how to acquire the information; and (c) skill in taking appropriate action (Pedersen, Goldberg, & Papalia, 1991).

Hot Lines

Hot lines are potentially valuable tools for helping to reach people who are suffering a variety of problems, including career barriers. For instance, a mental health hot line was established for Soviet immigrants in Israel (Mirsky & Barasch, 1993). Those with access to the hot line reported lower levels of distress determined by emotional factors, and were more concerned with objective problems related to immigration, such as finding a job.

SELF-MANAGEMENT TECHNIQUES

Knowing the possible effects of stress on performance can benefit adaptation and effectiveness (Walton, 1990). This includes teaching employees about the concepts of hardiness, cognition and coping, self-efficacy, and social support. Also, experiential training can be a form of stress inoculation. People participate in role-playing exercises that simulate the experiences they are likely to have on the job. For example, this is useful in helping people adapt to an overseas job assignment.

Learning to Look for Information

People can learn to be on the outlook for valuable career information —about career opportunities or about one's own performance and skill needs. Forces for career transition, such as changes in the organization, changes in job structure and design, and changes in the individual's psychophysiological makeup, are especially difficult for people at midcareer. Such individuals are concerned about maintaining work competency and managing change-related stress, as opposed to younger people who are still exploring career alternatives and older people who are approaching retirement. Midcareer employees can be taught and encouraged to scan the organization continuously for pertinent information, review self-perceptions, and consider individual/personal issues and concerns (Davis & Rodela, 1990). Continuously scanning the environment can enhance career insight and assist midcareer employees when it comes time to handle a career transition.

Writing as a Cathartic Experience

Writing about a negative experience may have a cathartic effect. One study examined this introspective intervention by randomly assigning 41 recently unemployed professionals to an experimental writing condition or to a control (no writing) condition (Spera, Buhrfeind, & Pennebaker, 1994). Those who wrote about the trauma of losing their jobs were more likely to find reemployment in the months following the study than the controls, even though those in the writing group did not receive more phone calls, make more contacts, or send out more letters than those in the control condition. This suggests that writing prompts clearer and more accurate insights that lead to better (i.e., more effective) job-search actions, perhaps because the act of venting one's emotions in writing promotes clarity of thought when it time to conduct the job search.

Rational-Emotive Therapy

Rational-emotive therapy (RET) is essentially learning the power of positive thinking. For instance, this therapy can challenge and change fired employees' ways of interpreting losing their jobs (Klarreich, 1993). Employees examine their strengths, capabilities, and opportunities for development with a career transition consultant. The process challenges employees' irrational beliefs so that they can turn a traumatic job loss into a career transition. Employees who dedicate themselves to this positive line of reasoning have more positive career outcomes.

Rational-emotive therapy, developed by Albert Ellis, attempts to help people turn a career barrier (for instance, a traumatic job loss) into a reasonably successful career transition (cf. Bernard & DiGiuseppe, 1994; D'Zurilla, 1986; Ellis & Harper, 1975). The technique teaches people how to challenge their thinking by questioning themselves and thinking positively. They are encouraged to think realistically, understanding and accepting such statements as, "I admit that my job/life is not always fair and just." "I recognize that job loss is unpredictable and can come at any time." "Many changes coming at once which include job termination can be uncomfortable and confusing yet I will try to organize life and deal with the most important problems first..." "I will handle this job loss to the best of my ability..." "It is not too late for me to manage this job transition in a different way" (Klarreich, 1993). Working with a "career transition consultant," the technique encourages displaced workers to consider their strengths, capabilities, and areas for development. As such, they design a marketing strategy for themselves, identify possible employers, and prepare for interviews.

A rational-emotive self-assessment questionnaire can help people understand the situation they are in at different points in time following the onset of a career barrier. The form would ask:

1. Describe the situation.
2. What are the consequences of the event in terms of my behaviors and in terms of my emotions?
3. What do I believe about myself and this situation?
4. Are these beliefs rational and sensible? Which ones are not? Why?
5. How would I like to behave and feel?
6. What are some key rational beliefs about myself and this situation? (Bernard & DiGuiseppe, 1994, p. 26; Reprinted with permission)

A portable computer may be used by people to respond to preprogrammed interview questions about coping. In this way, the individual can be encouraged to reflect at a moment close in time to an emotional encounter thereby minimizing memory problems and rationalization (Perrez & Reicherts, 1992).

Some confidence-building, anxiety-reducing rational attitude items are:

1. Just because things did not go well does not mean I have no hope.
2. While achievement and recognition are very desirable, I don't need them to survive.
3. Rejections and mistakes are inevitable. I can accept myself while hating my mistakes and setbacks.
4. Things are rarely as catastrophic as I imagine.
5. My work performance does not define my self-worth as a person.
6. I have done many things in my career successfully in the past, and I will succeed in the future.
7. I have enough intelligence and talent to learn what I need to do and how to do it to accomplish my goals.
8. I am confident that everything will turn out okay. I have my goals, I know what to do, and I am willing to work hard. (p. 27)

Problem-solving training based on rational-emotive therapy would include the following components (D'Zurilla, 1986): (a) introductory statements of goals and rationale, (b) efforts to increase sensitivity to problems of living and inadequate coping processes and styles, (c) examination of the role of emotions in problem solving, (d) exploration of particular problems with the goal of reevaluating what has been happening and setting realistic problem-solving goals, (e) generating alternative solutions, (f) evaluating the best solution, (g) implementing the solution and verifying its effectiveness, and (h) consolidating the effects of training, facilitating their maintenance, and generalizing what has been learned to other problems.

Stress-Reduction Techniques

Stress-management methods such as relaxation and cognitive stress reduction have health benefits by reducing the impact of stress on the immune system (Zakowski, Hall, & Baum, 1992). Resilience and flexibility are important for managers to utilize the value of creative pressure and tension needed at work while maintaining tolerable stress levels. To address this problem, stress-reducing Hatha Yoga techniques were demonstrated to managers in a British steel company (Heilbronn, 1992). These include breathing and meditative exercises to calm or energize, methods of relaxation to release destructive tensions, and postures that use creative muscle tension to promote physiological and psychological health.

Yet another approach is to simply get away for a while. Career barriers may lead to floundering in search of the "right" solution. A possible intervention is to suggest that the individual take a moratorium from a floundering search (Salomone & Mangicaro, 1991).

WAYS TO SUPPORT SELF-CONTROL

People who are high in self-control avoid inaccurate appraisals for the cause and effects of a career barrier. This is hard to do because inaccurate appraisals are reinforcing. For instance, consider the following rationalizations: "I had nothing to do with it," "I am sure this was all a mistake," "Next time, they will see the light," "It doesn't matter to me anyway," "There is nothing I can do about it." These provide self-protection against threats to our self-image. Moreover, they are immediate and do not require action. Accurate and rational cognitions may be hard to take emotionally, and they may portend a much longer wait, not to mention considerable effort, to be worthwhile. Therefore, it is easier to collect unemployment and hope something will come along than seek retraining in a new career.

The following ideas from Logue's (1995) suggestions for changing self-control may be useful to promote problem-centered coping strategies in dealing with career barriers:

1. *Recognize alternatives.* The individual must perceive that choices are available. It helps to know the value of these choices (e.g., job opportunities in a new career field) and the costs (effort) and probability of success (likelihood of finding a job after retraining).

2. *Shorten time for obtaining a positive outcome.* Impulsive thinking (cognitive defense mechanisms) are, as stated earlier, immediate. Reality-based cognitions and constructive actions pay off only in the long term. So anything that can be done to shorten the time span and highlight the value of constructive action should reduce impulsive thinking. Training may be shortened, for instance.

3. *Manipulate the perception that the outcomes are present.* A related approach to shortening the time span between activity and outcome is making the outcomes clearer and more salient. For instance, a study I was involved in at the State University of New York at Stony Brook (the Jobs Project discussed later) found that assigning displaced engineers to unpaid "internships" one day a week during a semester-long retraining program improved their morale and increased the chances for successful reemployment after the program. Being on a job, working on an important project, and being affiliated with a company made them feel useful and important. They could see how they could add value to the enterprise and why it was important for them to demonstrate their worth. Those who were not on such an internship continued to press for a new job assignment as if the program was an employment agency or would be similar to their prior employers, who would reassign them when a project was completed.

4. *Increase the size of the outcomes.* Perceiving that the outcomes are indeed worth the effort will increase constructive actions to obtain those outcomes. So Leana and Feldman (1992) found that unemployed workers who saw the potentially high benefits from relocation were more successful in finding employment sooner.

5. *Combine outcomes.* Combining negative outcomes or positive outcomes increases the weight given to the outcomes. Thus denial becomes less reinforcing when it is accompanied by some undesirable outcomes, such as lack of social support (less empathy and support from friends). The positive outcomes of relocation may be increased if there are other positive attributes about possible relocation sites in addition to a better job market, for instance, cheaper and better housing, lower taxes, excellent schools. Another example is that combining social support with a job search increases the value of participating in a jobs club.

6. *Encourage precommitment to constructive action or contracting.* If there is some advance warning or time before the career barrier actually arises, the individual can make some contingency plans that preclude an inaccurate attribution and dysfunctional coping. As rumors spread that the individual will not receive a long-hoped-for promotion, the individual can tell himself and

others, "Well, if I don't get it, I will try to move to another job" or "I will start working for an advanced degree in..." This is a way to save face and make plans. The organization can help by providing career planning mechanisms that require contingency planning or establishing several goals, rather than encouraging the employee to work toward a single job target that may never be achievable. Some companies offer funding to employees to seek retraining so they will have multiple skills of value to the firm or so they will maintain their competitiveness for other jobs internal to the firm or in other companies. Such efforts may even focus on the rewarding aspects of job loss (e.g., a second chance at success, new challenges, a chance to pursue other interests for which the individual never had time, do what you always wanted to do).

7. *Prompt recognition of contingencies.* Another useful way to increase self-control and constructive coping is to enhance the individual's awareness of what outcomes different responses will generate. An example is a job-search training program that teach unemployed participants to expect rejection, think about what it will feel like, and understand responses available to them when it happens. They can be taught to keep track of their own responses so they do not slump into a depression, focus on continued positive action, or use self-statements to remind themselves that this happens to everyone.

INTERVENTIONS AND TRAINING
FOR UNEMPLOYED WORKERS

Training can increase hardiness. Consider an employment preparation program developed to inculcate the achievement of greater responsibility, self-reliance, and independence. A study of such a program selected 136 clients with low self-esteem, low self-expectations, and little perceived control over life (Gosse, Sullivan, Rosse, & Simmonds, 1992). Forty-six percent of the 87 participants who completed the program found employment, whereas 26% continued on to secondary education. Participants increased significantly on assertiveness and self-esteem measures and on the commitment component of a measure of psychological hardiness.

A number of programs have been developed specifically for helping displaced workers find new employment. These programs are often joint efforts between local corporations, government agencies, and colleges or universities. The following sections present some examples (from London, 1996; see also London, 1995c, for more details about each project).

The Michigan JOBS Project

The JOBS Project at the University of Michigan was designed to help unemployed workers seek jobs, prepare for the rejection that most unemployed workers experience during the job search process, and overcome or limit their feelings of depression (Price & Vinokur, 1995; Vinokur, van Ryn, Gramlich, & Price, 1991). Such a program can be delivered by business groups, universities, or government agencies with participants recruited through unemployment offices or through corporate human resource departments. The program consists of five 4-hour sessions distributed over a period of 1 week to 2 weeks. It provides participants with social support and a positive learning environment to acquire job-search skills and simultaneously inoculate the participants from common setbacks that are part of the job seeking process. The goals are to prevent the deterioration in mental health (i.e., risk of depression) that often results from unemployment and to promote high-quality reemployment, thus contributing to individual growth.

The program focuses on problem strategies that prevent the emergence of symptoms. These include helping participants build trust in trainers, develop accurate self-assessments and appraisals of the job market (number and types of available jobs), identify methods to present job skills to prospective employers and understand the selection process from the employer's point of view, learn job search skills (e.g., how to prepare a resume, develop contacts, and secure an interview), and maintain motivation by planning reactions to setbacks and making decisions about offers. At the end of the program, participants report confidence in being able to handle rejections and reversals. Follow-ups of more than 300 participants 1 and 4 months and 2½ years after the program showed that the participants found jobs more quickly than their counterparts in a control group and that the jobs they found were better in terms of pay and stability.

Retraining for Displaced Engineers

Another effort, conducted at the State University of New York at Stony Brook, established a government-funded retraining program for displaced engineers from the defense industry (Wolf, Casey, et al., 1995; Wolf, London, et al., 1995). The program focused specifically on professional employees—those who had at least a bachelors degree and many years of experience as an engineer and a manager of engineers. Prospects were contacted from lists provided by major defense companies in the area that had laid off engineers in the preceding 6 months. Admissions seminars were conducted for groups of 10 to 20 applicants during which the project was outlined. Fifty-seven were admitted to the first class of the program and 15 to the second class for a total of 72. The mean age of the total group of entering students was 45.3 years old. They had spent a mean of 20.1 years in the defense industry and had held a mean of 4.1 jobs. Of the 72, 65 were men.

Each class participated in a semester-long program aimed at helping the participants to enhance their career behavior (e.g., job search), increase their knowledge in areas of technology management, and encourage them to do what they could to create jobs for themselves. The program began with a 3-week orientation course to address emotional issues, career goals, job-search methods, communication styles, and business development and strategy. At the end of this orientation, the participants selected a track for in-depth study. The tracks were formulated based on skill needs in industry and the availability of course offerings in the university. Tracks included the management of manufacturing, the management of information systems, the management of the environment and waste, and the management of materials. Throughout the semester, participants worked at least 8 hours a day taking courses, studying, engaging in discussion groups, and working on internships. The experience simulated a usual business day rather than the unstructured life of a typical college student.

The first group was exposed to a series of company representatives presenting costly problems faced by their firms. The purpose was to engage the participants in important, real-world issues that would allow them to demonstrate how they could add value to an enterprise. The second group conducted during the following semester engaged in unpaid internships in the firms working on problems the organizations needed to solve. Here again the focus was on helping the managers understand how they could contribute to the organization—the hope being that the added value would lead to job creation. Successful participants adopted an entrepreneurial mind-set that they could apply in making a contribution to new and existing enterprises, thereby creating employment opportunities for themselves.

Of course, all the participants in the program hoped, at least initially, to find full-time jobs. Of the 57 who started the first program, 43 finished the semester. Of these, four had jobs at the conclusion of the program, and 10 had consulting projects. Sixty-five percent of the 43 program graduates found employment 6 months later (17 had full-time jobs and 11 had part-time jobs). Of the 15 entering the second program, 8 completed the semester. Six of them had created jobs for themselves at the conclusion of their course work.

The displaced engineers varied considerably in their attitudes about the job-search process and their roles in job creation. Some expected to be handed a list of job opportunities and be placed in the assignment where they were needed. This was the model they had followed for years in the bureaucratic environments of large defense contractors. Other participants were willing from the outset to learn new skills and prove their value. Some were malleable in their willingness to learn new skills and experiment with new behaviors. Still others remained depressed and unable to risk new learning and new ventures.

The Center for Commercial Competitiveness

Another example of business, government, and university cooperation is the Center for Commercial Competitiveness was established at the State University of New York at Binghamton with funds from the U.S. Department of Labor and New York State (Last, Peterson, Rapaport, & Webb, 1995). The goal was to generate employment opportunities by creating new products and services. The heart of the program was an effort to work with displaced workers and regional industries to identify new commercial markets and products, and make teams of displaced workers, newly trained on the practice of working in self-directed teams and in the process of commercial development, available to work on the new enterprises. Project ideas were generated by industry sponsors or self-generated by the participating dislocated workers. The participants evaluated the project proposals themselves based on likely interest of sponsoring industry and availability of skills and resources. Self-directed teams were formed to develop projects deemed viable.

Displaced employees were accepted into the 9-month program based on an assessment of their creativity, entrepreneurial goals, drive, team orientation, technical experience, and motivation judged from their responses to application essay questions and an interview judged by six evaluators. Short courses focused on team building, business development, manufacturing systems, and corporate culture. Adult learning theory guided curriculum development with courses containing lectures and opportunities to practice new skills through hands on applications and participant interaction. Of the first 104 applicants, 69 were accepted, and 55 were enrolled. After the first run of the program, 86% of the participants were economically productive to varying degrees, a few in relatively low-income jobs. Thirty-four people completed the program, 20 of whom were working in a team or autonomous venture.

An Internal Contingent Workforce

Another innovative program is an internal contingent workforce consisting of displaced managers and professionals who can be assigned to temporary projects across a large company (Smither, 1995). Such an effort was established by AT&T's corporate headquarters. Called "Resource Link," the unit negotiates with project managers who need extra assistance but do not want, or are not ready, to hire permanent staff. The projects are usually 3 to 12 months in duration. This allows the firm to use its own employees, rather than temps from outside agencies. It increases the firm's staffing flexibility, and it offers potentially displaced employees a sense of employment stability. Resource Link matches employees' skills and experiences to the needs of the project. The initiative has become so popular that some employees have volunteered to be assigned to the unit because it offers employees exposure to different parts of the business as well as the variety and challenge of working on a new assignment, often in a new and growing area of the company. In mid-1994, more than 450 employees (called "associates") were on assignment from Resource Link in 27 units and divisions of AT&T. The company is considering expanding Resource Link by offering employees to other firms (noncompetitors) for temporary projects. No one became part of Resource Link involuntarily; employees had to apply and be accepted to participate. Of course, they might have preferred having a secure job that did not force them to consider this as an alternative. The Resource Link was not meant to solve all of the company's outplacement problems by any means. Rather, it is another employment option that allows the company to have the flexibility of an internal contingent workforce for special projects.

Entrepreneurship Training

New jobs in the 1990s have a different character than they did 30 years ago. Jobs in high technology, financial services, communications, information services, and personal services can be characterized by a focus on quality service and by the entrepreneurship that contributed to the growth of these firms. "An entrepreneur is someone who starts up or develops a business through providing a new product or service that adds incremental value to society. Entrepreneurial behavior is opportunity-seeking, value-adding, risk-accepting, creative activity where ideas result in organization birth, growth, and/or transformation" (Stumpf, 1992, p. 26; also see Bird, 1989). In contrast, nonentrepreneurs are adaptive, risk-averse, and focused on problem solving.

Entrepreneurial characteristics can be learned. Some people are ripe for entrepreneurship training. They have the basic characteristics already and just need to learn ways to harness or apply them—that is, they need to know the technical aspects of starting a business—everything from communicating an idea clearly to obtaining capital and developing a market. Others need a better understanding of their personality tendencies and their capabilities. They need to be reinforced for taking incremental risks and to be reassured that they are able to bring about positive outcomes. That is, they need to build up their resilience before they can benefit from insight about the environment and alternative directions for innovation. Those with a disposition to entrepreneurship learn best through experimentation and concrete experience (Kolb, 1984; Stumpf, 1992). Others may need to use their existing knowledge and skills to expand their risk-taking potential and relearn from their errors, rather than avoid errors. They can be guided to observe others' success stories and failures. Over time, they became less sensitive to feelings of failure, and more concerned about learning and development from trial and error.

The challenge is that the people in need of career transition are likely to be those who do not have entrepreneurial tendencies. They are likely to have had conventional, stable careers. They are less energetic than they are efficient; more conscientious than they are self-confident. They need affection and inclusion, whereas entrepreneurs need influence and control. Those in need of a career transition must learn what it means to be enterprising and create value.

Example of a Program in Entrepreneurship.   In light of changing opportunities in large businesses and not-for-profit institutions and the resulting fluidity of careers, many college graduates will be employed by small businesses or start their own business. Small-business development has traditionally been an avenue for individual career growth and community economic development. However, people are rarely prepared for the experience. They need to know how to add value and sell their ideas. They must recognize that their employment security depends on their making a continued contribution to the enterprise.

This is an idea for a summer program for students in entrepreneurship to help them understand the process of business creation, economic growth, and business survival and success. The goal is to foster a working knowledge of how to generate ideas for new enterprises (whether profit or not-for-profit), communicate these ideas, secure financial support, and produce and market a product or service.

The two-week program is for college students regardless of major. Although business majors are welcome, the program does not assume prior knowledge of business concepts. The program is ideal for students in such areas as science, engineering, health sciences, social sciences, social welfare, and the arts and humanities.

The program is for students who know they want to start their own business. It is also for students who may not have a current interest in starting their own business but who can benefit by recognizing that their career success in whatever field they choose depends on their adding value and contributing to economic growth.

Specifically, the program teaches:

- An understanding and appreciation of basic business skills.
- Entrepreneurship—how to start a business.
- "Intrapreneurship"—how to create opportunities for growth and development within fledgling or already successful enterprises.
- How to ensure your employment security by adding value to an enterprise.
- How to promote community development through job creation.

The program focuses on identifying market needs and niches, transferring technology, and using state-of-the-art computer technology. The program encourages the participants to be proactive in developing their ideas. Moreover, it inoculates them against failure by helping them expect and learn from it. The program fosters a "can-do" attitude that builds self-confidence and self-worth. Students visit with entrepreneurs and tour manufacturing facilities, laboratories, and fledgling companies operating in business incubators (offices, often made available at universities, that provide low-cost space and services to new technology businesses). Each student writes a business plans and revises it with input from entrepreneurs and other small business development experts.

Program components include:

- Career assessment (aptitude, interests, managerial strengths and areas for improvement).
- A workshop on the creative process.
- Workshops with entrepreneurs in areas of science and technological development, services, (financial, retail), and manufacturing including fledgling firms, small growing businesses, and large companies—three half-day site visits
- A workshop on the entrepreneurship process: The heart of the program is a daily (2 hours each morning) entrepreneurship workshop that takes the participants from idea generation to the business plan completion.
- Communication skills; four 2-hour workshops focusing on speaking skills, business writing, and multimedia presentation aids).
- Technology transfer (half-day seminar and half-day visit to a business incubator).

- Basic business skills covering financing, accounting, marketing, sales, personnel (selection, training, compensation, benefits), operational management, and information systems.
- Review of available resources, such as small business development centers, small business administration loans, and sources market information.

Sample Schedule

Day 1—Introduction
 Career assessment module
 The creative process and the meaning of risk taking
 Entrepreneurship module 1
  The entrepreneurship process
  Stages of business development
Day 2—Entrepreneurship module 2
  Components of a business plan
  Generating ideas for new ventures
  Testing ideas—idea incubation
 Career-assessment results
 Communications skills
 Workshop with minority entrepreneur
Day 3—Entrepreneurship module 3
  Settling on an idea for a business plan
  Initial business plan draft
 Finance and economic indictors
 Financial sources
 Communications skills
Day 4—Entrepreneurship module 4
  Researching the business plan
  Revising the draft
 Marketing
 Sales
 Workshop with minority entrepreneur

Day 5—Entrepreneurship module 5
  Review of business plan
  Each plan is presented to the class and a small-business
   development consultant, who discusses the proposal and
   makes suggestions for revision
 Site visit

Day 6—Entrepreneurship module 6
  Business plan revision
Accounting
Information systems
Communications skills
Day 7—Entrepreneurship module 7
  Implementation strategies
  One-on-one consultation and review
Personnel
Operations management
Workshop with minority entrepreneur
Day 8—Entrepreneurship module 8
  Further research and revision of business plan
  Draft final presentation
Site visit
Day 9—Entrepreneurship module 9
  Fine-tune plan and presentation
Technology transfer workshop and site visit
Day 10—Entrepreneurship module 10
  Final presentation to class and business consultants
Site visit
Concluding session

Business and Laboratory Incubators

As noted earlier, universities working with government economic development funds may often establish incubators to help new businesses get off the
ground. These are usually businesses that propose to develop markets for
new technologies (a process known as *technology transfer*). In Israel, the
government has extended this idea to incubator laboratories for immigrant
scientists whose earlier basic research could be developed into fruitful
applications. Scientists apply to the incubators to receive laboratory space
and several years of funding to develop their ideas. Rouvain Bension—a
chemist—and I proposed the following similar idea for chemists who have
been displaced by closings and downsizings of government and corporate
laboratories.

*A Proposal for Laboratory Incubators of New Chemical Products and
Processes.*   A 1995 survey of scientists receiving doctorates conducted by
Stanford University's Institute for Higher Education Research found a 1 in

4 chance of underemployment (Browne, 1995). From a societal perspective, we face a "brain power" problem. This is opposite of the "brain drain" experienced by underdeveloped countries. The challenge is to channel our excess brain power to expand economic development and growth. Executives and managers can join forces with institutions of higher education and government to promote economic growth that builds on underutilized human resources. Moreover, unemployed and underemployed professionals should realize that their employment security rests on their adding value to an enterprise or creating new ways to contribute to economic growth. Displaced workers will not be employable unless they can add value.

Recognizing the increase in underemployment and unemployment of its current or prospective members, professional societies have been taking a proactive role in retraining and creating job opportunities. To cite one example, the American Chemical Society appointed a task force to "investigate the feasibility, and propose the implementation, of actions that would alleviate the employment problems of chemists, with special concern for those who have been caught in 'downsizing'" (Bennett, 1995, p. 29). Their recommendations included creating and maintaining an online job database, expanding career services for graduate students by increasing the number of career planning workshops offered by the Society on university campuses throughout the country, developing a series of packaged programs on alternative careers in a variety of specialty areas, and implementing a 1-year experiment to offer short courses at no cost to unemployed members with no limit on the number of courses a member may take per year. Other ideas for professional societies would including linking would-be scientist entrepreneurs to underutilized lab space in corporations and universities and helping organizations with costly problems to find professionals who can solve them.

Our proposal is to provide laboratory space for displaced chemists with ideas for the development of potentially marketable products and processes. Chemists who have lost their jobs because of downsizing and organizational restructuring and recent graduates who have had trouble finding new employment would benefit from the opportunity to use laboratory space to work on their own ideas. Unlike some technical disciplines for which ideas can be developed with comparatively minimal resources (e.g., picture the electronics wizard or computer scientist working in a garage), today's regulatory environment and the complexity of chemical processes require sophisticated laboratory and fabricating equipment and bench space to conduct chemical experiments and trials. The "chemistry incubatory" would provide opportunities to individuals who meet criteria for participation in the program. Eligibility would include education (PhD in chemistry or related field), experience (prior work on new product development), and an idea with market potential. A panel of experts would evaluate a candidate's application. Successful applicants would receive minimal financial support, including a stipend to help with living expenses, a laboratory budget, and space for a specified duration. Funding would be sought from state and federal funds for economic development and redeployment of displaced workers from defense and other industries. Space for the project would come from unused or excess laboratory facilities from public and private firms or universities. A network of business, financial, and legal consultants would be established to provide support. The project would be evaluated based on successful new product/process development.

Job Clubs

Job clubs use a behavioral approach to teach and reinforce job search skills and competence. In addition, members are reinforced vicariously as they observe their fellow members finding employment. The "club" environment offers some emotional and social support that displaced workers might not have on their own. Consider one example of a job club for older, unemployed people (Rife & Belcher, 1994; see also Azrin, Besalel, Wisotek, McMurrow, & Bechtel, 1982). The club met two afternoons per week. Meetings were used to help participants set job-search goals, receive information about job seeking (e.g., interviewing, resume writing, completing applications), receive support and information on job leads from each other, and use telephones to call prospective employers. A study compared 26 randomly assigned older workers (age 50 and older) to the 12-week job club, and 26 to a control group receiving services normally available to unemployed citizens through government job services and community referral programs (Rife & Belcher, 1994).

Job-club participants were more likely to secure employment 12 weeks after the job club ended compared to the control group. In particular, 17 (65.4%) of the job-club group had obtained employment compared to only 7 (26.9%) of the control group ($p < .01$). Moreover, job-club members achieved a significantly higher continued employment rate and higher income and hours worked compared to the control group during the 12 weeks following the club's completion. Also, job-club members reported significantly lower depression immediately after the 12-week intervention compared with the control group. Despite the club members' success in obtaining and retaining employment, the jobs obtained by members of both groups were often part-time and relatively low paying. The researchers attributed this to the location (a small town of 40,000 people) and the sluggish economy. Most of the positions were service-oriented (clerk, customer service, food service).

Roles for Executives and Managers

In summary, here are some guidelines for executives and managers to follow to support the career motivation of displaced workers:

To build career resilience:
- Enhance and maintain value of current employees (continuous learning environment).
- Foster a culture of intrapreneurship by rewarding creative new ideas and self-management.
- Assign people to teams and work processes rather than to single, unifunctional jobs. Foster new, more cost effective and quality-oriented, customer-responsive work structures and prepare employees for this changing nature of jobs.
- Adopt continuous improvement programs based on employee participation.
- Partner with regional universities and colleges and government and community agencies (private industry councils) to develop support systems for displaced workers, train people in areas that create or add value through problem solving and support for new initiatives and joint ventures.

To build career insight
- Offer assessment and feedback processes to help people understand their strengths and weaknesses better.
- Provide problem-focused (in addition to symptom-focused) training to unemployed in job-search skills, entrepreneurship, and realistic expectations.
- Conduct human resource forecasting to inform and direct organizational initiatives. This entails conducting job analyses for positions that do not yet exist and communicating the results as input to individual and organizational planning. Moreover, scenarios of likely environmental trends and organizational strategies can be constructed as ways to envision different sorts of change and its implications.
- Assist federal and state programs for reemployment and coping that recognize individual (e.g., age, profession, malleability) and regional-economic factors.

To build career identity
- Fund and implement outside redeployment efforts stemming from restructuring (outplacement).
- Support the professional development of all functional specialties. Develop job families and career paths within specialty areas.

- Train employees in multiple skills and use these different skills in role assignments.
- Band together with other organizations and agencies in the community to create new economic opportunities (e.g., participate in job fairs).

SUMMARY

The chapter began by suggesting that identifying, clarifying, and prioritizing values is a way to understand and manage transitions. A way to measure reactions to career barriers and other stressful work situations was described. I then outlined methods for counseling, teaching self-management, supporting self-control, and learning useful coping skills. In addition, career counselors can help people deal with unrealistic expectations, problems with financial pressures, and taking one step at a time. One counseling model requires the counselor to alternate between the active and directive role of career counselor and the facilitative and exploratory role of the personal counselor. Other one-on-one interventions are rehabilitation counseling, computer-based counseling, outplacement counseling, and hotlines. Self-management techniques include learning to look for information, writing as a catharsis, and rational-emotive therapy (learning the power of positive thinking). Problem-solving training based on rational-emotive therapy includes ways to increase sensitivity to inadequate coping processes and styles and an examination of the role of emotions in problem solving. Stress reduction interventions include methods that support self-control, such as helping people recognize alternatives available to them. Examples of training programs for displaced workers often combine job-search skills and dealing with symptoms of job loss and rejection. A number of examples were described for job placement, entrepreneurship, and temporary placement.

IV

Ways to Avoid Career Barriers

8

Toward Multiple Careers and Continuous Learning

In this last chapter, I summarize the book and draw some implications. In the process, I examine how people are likely to have more than one career, how the changing nature of work is imposing new skill demands on almost everyone, and how people need to be continuous learners to prepare for the future in their present careers or in new careers. First, however, consider how the ideas presented in this book show how to analyze a career barrier. Here is a step-by-step summary:

1. Take into account emotions, thoughts, and their interaction. Identify emotions resulting from the barrier.
2. Distinguish between appraisal of the situation and strategies for coping with emotions and the situation. Track changes in the individual's appraisal and coping strategies over time as the situation evolves and as coping strategies have an effect.
3. Consider what thought processes are used to appraise the situation. Are they more mindless than mindful, or vice versa? What attributions are made for the causes of the situation—self, other, both? What are the likely effects of the barrier for the individual? What emotions (e.g., frustration vs. hope) and frame of reference (e.g., optimism vs. pessimism) influenced the attributions of the situation's cause and evaluation of its likely effects?
4. Focus on the coping strategies adopted. How did these coping strategies stem from the appraisal of the situation? What emotions accompanied these coping strategies? How did the emotions change over time as the coping strategies had an effect (positive or negative)?
5. Determine whether the coping strategies were revised over time depending on their success. How?
6. Consider how resilient the individual seemed to be before the barrier arose. Did resilience help the individual appraise the situation realistically and devise and revise coping strategies?

7. Pinpoint sources of support in the work environment for appraisal and coping. How did these elements of support work?
8. Determine whether resilience and environmental support led the individual to change his or her self-concept and view of the career environment. Did this increased self- and environmental insight affect subsequent career goals and commitments?

SUMMARY OF THE BOOK

In the Preface, I described the potentially devastating effects of career barriers. They arouse strong emotions, and people do not always understand why and how they happened. People differ in how they interpret a career barrier. Some people process information carefully, going beyond their disappointment, anger, and frustration. Others are overcome by their emotions. They lack direction and take a long time to bounce back, if they do at all. How people explain a career barrier to themselves and their understanding of possible actions and their consequences determines what they will do. For example, their feeling of control, their belief about whether the career barrier can be reversed, and the information they have about other available opportunities will influence how much initiative they take to overcome the career barrier.

Chapter 1 described characteristics of career barriers (for instance, their clarity and their emotional and financial cost). I proposed that career barriers are more traumatic when they occur with little or no warning, have pervasive effects on other parts of one's life, and cannot be changed or reversed. Career barriers can be split into the following types: (a) general trends in the economy or society; (b) specific conditions in the organization; (c) decisions that affect certain individuals; (d) general individual characteristics; (e) job-related individual characteristics, non-job-related individual characteristics; and (f) unfavorable life events that spill over to work. This chapter presents the methods used in my career barriers interview study and survey.

I described emotional and thought processes and their interaction in chapter 2. Negative emotions arise and evolve as the realization of the career barrier takes hold. People make sense of career barriers by developing rationales for themselves to explain why the barriers occurred and their likely consequences. Feelings influence later actions. I indicated that strong emotions interrupt ongoing thought processes and behaviors and make it difficult to interpret a career barrier rationally and determine a constructive course of action. Careless information processing may prevent people from recognizing a career barrier for what it is. In general, information that fits people's predetermined beliefs about themselves is processed automatically. On the other hand, a career barrier is not the type of event that fits preestablished beliefs of the way things should be, and they can startle a person into attention and action. However, negative emotions, or the desire to protect oneself from negative emotions, cause people to ignore or deny information. I suggested that having standards for comparison or watching others who are going through the same experience helps put things in perspective and formulate reasonable and effective responses. Having an optimistic attitude can limit negative, debilitating emotions, prevent distorting information, and promote construction action.

Appraisal leads to coping, the subject of chapter 3. I suggested that constructive coping is likely when the individual evaluates information thoroughly and realistically. Dysfunctional coping is likely when the individual denies or ignores information or the barrier itself. Career barriers can have long-term emotional impact, especially for individuals who have trouble getting back on track or remain derailed. However, most people recognize that they cannot act on their initially strong negative emotions. To do so would be counterproductive and lead to more problems. People who are laid off may want to vent their emotions and give their boss hell; hopefully, however, after a breather, they understand that burning their bridges could hurt them in the long run. People who engage in *problem-focused coping* appraise the situation realistically and try to improve the situation. People who engage in *symptom-focused coping* seek emotional support from others as a way to deal with negative feelings.

Chapter 4 showed how the components of career motivation (resilience, insight, and identity) affect reactions to career barriers. Career resilience sets the foundation for developing clear insight into oneself and the work environment which in turn contributes to establishing a meaningful career identity. Conditions in the organizational environment can reinforce resilience and provide information that leads to insight and identity. A career barrier causes people to question their career identity and restructure their views of themselves and the work environment. This process is more effective when resilience is strong.

Chapter 5 focused on career resilience and the complementary characteristic of hardiness. Resilience is the ability to overcome career barriers. People who are high in resilience believe in themselves, need to achieve, are willing to take reasonable risks, and need to evaluate events and circumstances. People who are high in hardiness are high in commitment (the tendency to involve oneself in tough situations), control (the tendency to feel and act as if one is influential in the face of tough situations rather than helpless), and challenge (the belief that change rather than stability is normal in life).

Chapter 6 delved into aspects of the work environment that support or destroy employees' career motivation. A supportive environment diminishes the negative impact of a career barrier and helps create a constructive reaction or prevent a career barrier altogether. Support for career resilience stems from positive reinforcement for a job well done, opportunities for achievement, and an environment that is conducive to risk taking by rewarding innovation and reducing the negative consequences of failure. Support for career insight stems from goal setting and giving employees career information and performance feedback. Support for career identity stems from job challenges, encouragement of professional growth, opportunities for leadership and advancement, and rewards such as recognition and bonuses. A continuous-learning work environment promotes employees' acquisition of general knowledge and helps it on the job. Knowledge and skill acquisition are essential responsibilities of every employee's job. Career motivation can be increased in the wake of a career barrier in several ways—for instance, by rewarding workers for mentoring younger employees, rehiring retirees for temporary full- or part-time work, and offering stress-coping workshops.

Chapter 7 described ways in which organizations help people cope with career barriers. Methods include counseling, teaching self-management, supporting self-control, and learning useful coping skills. People can be taught self-management techniques. In general, people can develop sensitivity to their emotions and how they affect their behavior.

The appendices include more case examples (Appendices A and B), case description forms completed by the interviewers and rating forms completed by the interviewees (Appendix C), and analyses of the forms and ratings (Appendix D). The results of analyses of the forms and ratings showed that job loss was far more traumatic than other career barriers and required support to alleviate the employee's anger and encourage the employee to see things realistically, be proactive, and cope constructively. Career barriers were easier to manage when people had advanced notice and clear explanations. Some people were better able to handle career barriers—women, workers with more education, and professionals and managers. Blue-collar workers had more trouble coping with career barriers than professional and managerial employees. A proactive strategy tended to be frustrating but less stressful than a reactive strategy. People needed an accurate view of why the barrier occurred and how they contributed to it to prompt them to consider what they could do themselves to alleviate the situation. Career motivation and support for career motivation contributed to constructive coping strategies.

DIRECTIONS FOR THE FUTURE

Today's work environment promises little job security. People need to worry more about their employment security—the extent to which their skills and talents are in demand in the labor market. The only way to avoid or quickly overcome career failure may be to know what abilities and knowledge will be required in the future and "Be Prepared," to invoke the Boy Scout motto. This means having to assess the environment, determine where the career opportunities are, and match oneself to those opportunities. The key here is "self" because no one will do it for us. Our employers or supervisors may provide resources to help, but we are responsible for our own development. The increasingly turbulent job environment means that people are likely to have multiple careers during their lives. Those who are continuous learning are more likely to make smooth career transitions than those who are not. This chapter examines the trend toward multiple careers and continuous learning.

In chapter 4, I argued that career motivation requires having clear career insight (e.g., clear career goals) and a meaningful career identity. These characteristics will encourage people to be evaluate their environments and learn what they need to know to be successful in their present careers, prepare for a new career, or both. However, as the cases described throughout this book indicate, people are often unprepared to face a career barrier. The barrier may arise suddenly and come as a shock, or it might arise slowly, miring the individual in a state of uncertainty and anxiety. People often have a loose conceptualization of their career direction. Some think they know what they want, but they articulate it in only very general terms. Others are unsure about what they want.

In order to find out how people conceptualized their career goals, I asked a group of talented employees enrolled in an executive masters degree program in technology management to indicate whether they had career goals. A computer systems consultant in his late twenties who is married and has one young child wrote:

> Starting my own business is at the top of the list, but there are many intermediate steps that I am actively pursuing. These include a little schooling in management, increasing my knowledge about the computer consulting field, and planning my company's first steps.

Another computer expert wrote:

My career goals are not very clear in my mind. I have eliminated some options, though. I do know that my current path is not what I truly want. I am a systems/software engineer with no way to grow at my current company. I think I want to be an executive where I can have a opportunity to make more money. That means being at a company where I can have the chance to grow. Or it means starting my own company.

A more certain individual was much more positive and goal oriented. He wrote:

Yes, I have very definite career goals. I plan to build my company up and become wealthy through the operations of my business activities. I would be a most unhappy person if I were to go bankrupt or found myself working for another person or company.

Here is what a young woman in the banking industry said:

My career goals became very clear for me last year when my employer announced its intentions to sell the business to another bank. By consolidating functions and eliminating duplication, the new owner would be able to recover the purchase price. My department would be consolidated with operations in another state. I saw this as an opportunity! My position will be abolished in 6 months. Knowing that I will be graduating shortly before that time, I intend to use my new degree as leverage in finding a new job at a higher salary. Now I get a great severance package AND I find my new job. Fortunately, I have a supervisor who realizes that I want to be on a "fast track," and she is willing to coach me. I learned a lot from her, and now I'm ready to move on. The timing is excellent!

Another participant wrote:

My career goals are somewhat tentative. I have been with a large organization now for over 30 years. My credentials include a couple of advanced degrees in engineering and many years as a group leader. My primary interests include challenging technical work, a certain amount of responsibility and authority, and freedom of action. My present position satisfies all of the above. However, I feel that sometimes I have more responsibility than authority. I have always been interested in new challenges, and at the present time, I am considering the possibility of doing consulting work on my own, initially part-time. Eventually, when I retire from my present job, I would like to continue with consulting. This is why I am pursuing a graduate degree in technical management.

Although these people have a general idea of their career goals, some more specific than others, they are all taking steps to advance their education. They do not know precisely what they want or what the future will demand; however, they are preparing in a general through advanced education. One person is doing so 30 years into his career. Many of them want control over their career destinies, so they want to be in business for themselves. Some of these individuals will have more than one career—perhaps in very different businesses. This is especially likely because they are in different technological fields. The basic management skills they are fine-tuning in their degree program will probably serve them well in a variety of areas of technology and economic conditions, and as variety of other personal and organizational factors change. In the following sections I consider how people evolve into multiple careers and how they engage in continuous learning.

Changing Careers

Douglas T. Hall, another well-known career researcher and writer, suggested that people are likely to go through a series of careers during their lives (Hall, 1996a, 1996b). The 30-year career working in the same company in the same type of job has gone the way of the buggy whip. Hall called this the "Protean" career after the Greek god Proteus who changed shapes to fit the situation. Each career is a cycle of exploration, trial, establishment, and mastery. People may move into entirely new areas (as when a police man or woman retires to become a school teacher or when a middle manager in the electronics industry opens a country inn). Some people may move into part-time work, as a man or woman might do when his or her children are young. A person may move from a technical to a managerial position.

The goal of a Protean career is psychological success. The career is managed by the person, not the organization. As such, companies do not provide structured career paths but rather opportunities for enriching education and challenging experience that enable self-development. The career therefore becomes a lifelong series of identity changes and continuous learning. People are successful because they know how to learn, and this is the key to their continuous employability.

The new work environment will require new skills. A group of human resource executives and executive recruiters agreed that future managerial careers will require the following:

- A knowledge-based technical specialty.
- Cross-functional and international experience.

- Competence in collaborative leadership.
- Self-management skills.
- Personal traits of flexibility, integrity, and trustworthiness. (Allred, Snow, & Miles, 1996)

Developing these skills will require continuous learning. I introduced this concept in chapter 6 and return to it now.

Continuous Learning

Continuous learning is the process of acquiring knowledge, skills, and abilities throughout one's career (London & Mone, in press). Recognizing this, an employer may provide support and indeed develop a culture that expects and reinforces continuous learning (Tracey, et al., 1995). However, we cannot count on working in such an environment, and people need to be on the outlook for trends in their organization and industry (or in new areas if a career change is in the offing). These trends provide direction for what they should be learning to do better today, to prepare for tomorrow, or both.

Career insight is one of three ingredients of career motivation along with resilience and identity. Insight may explain an individual's desire to participate in continuous learning. Insight requires recognizing the extent to which one has a learning gap between current and needed abilities, knowledge, or skills. People who are high in career insight are realistic about themselves and their career, and they are able to put these perceptions to use in establishing goals. Insight is enhanced when the situation encourages goal setting and provides guidance on how to achieve goals. Insight develops as people process information about possible job opportunities and career directions and feedback about their performance in comparison to clear standards or expectations.

Given the changes in career patterns I described earlier, employees must assume responsibility for their own learning and development. If they are fortunate, their employer will provide the resources to help, such as training programs and tuition reimbursement. However, most employees are on their own these days to track changing job expectations and career opportunities and their implications for continuous learning. Employees may even create their own learning activities. As a result, they must want to learn and have insight into the value of possible developmental activities.

Preparing for the Future

Continuous learning is a way to increase employees' value to the company in their current positions. If employees need to be laid off, then continuous learning increases their chances of finding employment elsewhere because they have up-to-date skills and knowledge.

An example of a joint union–management effort to support training in preparation for possible employee dislocations is the Alliance for Employee Growth and Development. Supported financially by AT&T and the Communications Workers of America, the Alliance funds training programs requested by employees at local sites. The employees determine the type of training they want based on information about skills needed by the company and in the outside job market. Examples of supported programs are tuition for computer training given at local community colleges and training centers set up on site at the plant for customized training programs. Chapter 7 provided a number of other examples of programs that enhance continuous learning.

Self-determined continuous learning is important for people in today's financially constrained, quality-oriented, rapidly changing companies. People need insight into their career goals and options and need to understand organizational goals, performance requirements, and what it takes to meet the organization's expectations today. They also require information about likely organizational directions, implications for future performance requirements, and what they need to do to meet these changing expectations. In some cases, the company will provide this information readily. These organizations realize that their employees need to keep up with organizational changes to ensure their continued contribution to the organization. In other cases, however, employees will have to seek out this information. As they interpret the information, they need to consider whether they might be better off preparing for other career directions.

Self-Management

People who are self-managing monitor and evaluate progress toward their goals on their own (Bandura, 1986). Self-managers are people who "know where they want to go in their lives, develop a plan for getting there, and execute the plan efficiently" (R. L. Williams, Verble, Price, & Layne, 1995; p. 495). Self-management involves establishing goals for oneself and then going out to accomplish them. This entails focusing on important tasks until they are completed, basing one's actions on clearly defined goals, and starting and finishing tasks on time (R. L. Williams & Long, 1991; R. L. Williams, Moore, Pettibone, & Thomas, 1992). The major steps in self-management are "selecting a goal, assessing progress toward that goal, developing a supportive environment for reaching the goal, using self-messages that

are supportive of reaching the goal, and implementing maintenance strategies" (R.L. Williams, Pettibone, & Thomas, 1991, p. 168).

When development is self-determined, people take responsibility for
their own learning. They determine what they need to know by evaluating
their environments. They consider what might happen in the future in their
industry, organization, or profession, and they judge the implications of these
trends for the skills and knowledge they will need to be successful. They
seek performance about their performance. They investigate opportunities
for development, and they set development goals. Then they evaluate their
progress. As they do so, they adjust their goals and learning behaviors as the
situation continues to change.

The Changing Nature of Work

I noted in the introduction that the career pattern of staying with one
employer for life and being involved in one job function or area of expertise
are going by the wayside. Today's career patterns are more disorderly,
unpredictable, and transitory. People move sideways, downward, and in and
out of different organizations (Inkson, 1995). Career advancement and
success does not just mean promotion anymore. There are fewer promo-
tional opportunities as organizations downsize and establish structures that
are more flexible and customer responsive. As a result, organizations are
creating new definitions for advancement. These may include bonuses,
tuition assistance, and job rotations to gain more experience. Individuals
need to understand these trends and what they mean for possible career
barriers and opportunities.

Ilgen and Pulakos (in press) described eight major changes in how work
is organized and accomplished. Mone and I considered implications of these
trends for new skill and knowledge requirements and the need for continuous learning (London & Mone, in press). Here are the trends, followed by
the skills they require:

1. *Work is increasingly done in process teams.* As a result, individuals should
   develop skills for listening, group problem solving, conflict resolution, negotiation, group leadership, cooperation, contribution, multiple roles of group
   members (source of timely information, knowledge, and skills), movement
   between teams, role as team leaders and members, spontaneity.
2. *Jobs are organized around projects, not function.* This suggest the need for a clear
   understanding of customer–supplier relationships within and between work
   groups, clear roles, identification with work process as well as function and
   profession, and the ability to work on more than one work process at a time.

3. *New technologies are emerging every day.* Employees should know how to manage and use diverse information, use technology to control and monitor work processes (technology as source of feedback), use technology to learn (gain information, observe others, and learn through simulations), work and communicate through a variety of technological media.

4. *Organizations have higher standards of performance.* People need to search for feedback for comparison to standards, understand performance dimensions (e.g., timeliness, quality, cost, efficiency), clarify individual performance, and understand how they contribute to meeting team goals and standards.

5. *Today's performance includes preparing for tomorrow.* People should seek information to identify skill gaps, recognize areas to improve current performance, keep up with advances in the profession, and anticipate how changes elsewhere in the firm and the industry may affect work demands and skill requirements.

6. *Employees (especially managers) face multiple constituencies with different expectations.* Employees have to balance diverse and increased demands, self-management and self-regulation skills, methods for resolving role conflict and ambiguity, and ways to integrate feedback information from multiple sources.

7. *Leaders need to be facilitators, coaches, and developers.* Leaders and managers must make the transition from work monitors and directors to coaches, developers, and facilitators. Employees should expect these behaviors from their leaders, and in choosing an employer, should evaluate whether the organization's leaders exhibit these roles.

8. *There are more opportunities for temporary and part-time work.* People who rely on part-time or temporary work need to adapt to changing environments, assess their own skills relative to changing work requirements, and assess the work environment to take advantage of changing career opportunities.

Career Enhancing Strategies. Given these trends, all employees need to be motivated to conduct ongoing self-assessment and, when necessary, reevaluate and alter their self-concept and change their behavior (London & Mone, in press). When organizational needs do not match employees' goals and skill sets, the employees may have to locate another job inside or outside the company, or will have to find another career track. Retraining and continuous learning will be important in any case. In general, key job skills for the future include an ongoing appetite for change, rapid decision making, the ability to manage and motivate oneself, and the willingness to take responsibility for one's own financial future (Luciano, 1995). Career-enhancing strategies include staying positive about workplace change, seeking accountability, getting ahead by moving sideways into other jobs that may have more advancement possibilities, finding a mentor, and protecting one's financial security. Other career-enhancing strategies include seeking advice and information about training and job assignments, developing work and career plans, learning new or developing existing skills, working extra hours, and networking (Feij, Whitely, Peiro, & Taris, 1995).

These career-enhancing strategies come alive in the experiences of recently displaced managers. Consider the advice of two managers who had lost their jobs and, after considerable emotional and financial pain, were struggling to open their own businesses. Here is what they had to say to young people entering the job market. A former production supervisor turned restaurant owner recommended, "Do the best you possibly can and learn as much as you can on the job so you can be more promotable. The more you know about the company, more promotable you make yourself" (D. Jones, 1996, p. 3B).

Finally, a former plant project engineer who opened a Jaguar restoration shop advised:

> First thing I'd say is save your money. A year's salary in the bank is necessary to survive in today's environment. Understand that every payday you and the company are even. Don't think anyone owes anyone anything. You can take your corporate security. To go out of business, I'd have to make 25% of my customers unhappy. To get fired, you only have to make your boss unhappy. (p. 3B)

IMPLICATIONS FOR ORGANIZATIONS

Human resource practitioners can design programs to help individuals cope with career barriers and help managers support subordinates facing career barriers. Training programs and self-assessment methods can help individuals:

- Analyze emotions and cope with them.
- Evaluate the situation realistically (make accurate attributions and forecast likely consequences).
- Identify viable coping strategies that deal with their emotions and affect the situation directly.
- Understand the environment and learn new skills that are increasingly important in organizations, such as networking and teamwork.
- Assess what was learned about him or herself and the career environment (their employer, job opportunities).
- Devise tracking mechanisms.

Overall, techniques that do the aforementioned, such as those described in chapter 7, help people establish and revise strategies to deal with career barriers more effectively. Human resource professionals design integrated human resource systems for goal setting, appraisal, feedback, and continuous learning all aimed at accomplishing the organization's goals. These processes inform employees about organizational objectives and their implications for skill requirements. This should include data about career opportunities in other parts of the organization as well as skills likely to be needed in the future.

Employees need the chance to enhance their skills for today and tomorrow. This is especially important for employees whose skills and knowledge base are becoming outdated rapidly. Organizations that support continuous learning will develop employees who are ready to contribute to the organization in different ways. These employees will be ready to create new ventures for continued and further company growth and profitability. When changing skill requirements or the need to cut costs lead to layoffs, those affected will be confident in themselves and ready to find opportunities elsewhere. In return, the organization will develop a reputation as a great place to work and learn, and will be able to attract the best talent. Human resource professionals can design systems to make this happen.

Human resource programs and policies can also address issues of employee treatment that create career barriers. Corporate policies and supervisor training should develop an organizational culture of fair and equitable treatment, supportive management, two-way communication, and equal opportunity. Human resource programs communicate top executives' expectations for how they want their business managed. Human resource professionals can inform top executives about what constitutes good management (i.e., fair and kind treatment of employees) and design programs that develop and reward good managers.

IMPLICATIONS FOR GOVERNMENT POLICY

Public policies in the form of federal and state legislation, executive actions, and judicial rulings affect how organizations treat their employees. This covers issues of harassment, fair and equitable treatment, and layoffs. The recognition of the pain caused by layoffs has led to public debate about the desirability of affecting organization's freedom to lay off people for purposes of restructuring. As it is, the government provides tax incentives and funds for training and retraining and mandates at least a 60-day notice of lay-offs. Retirement plans for sheltering before tax income give employees some additional financial security. Public attention to sexual harassment and whistleblowing cases has led to laws and court rulings on fair treatment.

These are positive signs. However, whatever progress has been made in the public arena has come after lobbying and media attention to the considerable pain and anguish from career barriers experienced by many individuals. In addition to support for people who have already suffered a career barrier, attention should be directed to avoiding career barriers through public policy. This can come from support for training employees who already have jobs and tax incentives and other mechanisms (e.g., business incubators) to encourage new business ventures within existing firms or for fledgling enterprises. Partnerships between business, government, and educational institutions can be quite successful.

UNANSWERED QUESTIONS

Research on career barriers will inform public policy, human resource programs, and individual actions. The concepts described throughout this book provide a rich set of ideas for further exploration. Here are some key questions for investigation:

- What are the ties between feelings and thoughts and cognitions and the effects of positive thinking and optimism on constructive action?
- How can destructive personal energy be rechanneled?
- Do people react differently to different career barriers—for instance, barriers caused by organizational and environmental circumstances compared to those caused by individual behaviors or actions (whether those of supervisors creating the barrier or the subordinate affected)?
- What are the relationships between individual characteristics, such as resilience and hardiness, to situational support?
- What career enhancement strategies work best to help people change their self-image and take positive actions to avoid career barriers?

CONCLUSION

The changing nature of work indicates that people must be attuned to their own developmental needs, and organizations must provide the enabling resources. Continuous learning is important for everyone, not just those who are in imminent danger of losing their jobs.

People and organizations may have to overcome barriers to continuous learning. People may resist learning and may need to be prodded to understand changing organizational requirements and evaluate their capabilities to meet them. Organizations may not want to invest resources in teaching skills that are not needed now. Managers may not view training as an important part of their subordinates' jobs. Solutions may lie in cooperative efforts between managers and subordinates at the departmental level. They can jointly analyze situational trends and their implications, establish plans for training and development, provide mutual support for people facing career barriers (those who are not performing well or who do not have the interest or capability to learn and adapt to the changing environment). Also, employees and companies need to be accountable for continuous learning. They must recognize and accept their responsibilities for continuous learn-ing and overcoming career barriers. They should evaluate themselves over time, track their progress, and be continuously on the lookout for perform-ance gaps. In addition, they can be creative in finding ways to apply continuous learning to cope with and avoid career barriers. This might entail finding new ways to learn, rechanneling people's capabilities to new ven-tures that create economic growth, and cooperating with other corpora-tions, government agencies, and universities to assist people facing career barriers.

Appendix A:
Additional Cases

The additional cases described here represent a number of different types of career barriers, some of which have not been covered elsewhere in the book. Two deal with limited career opportunities—for instance, discovering that ones chosen field does not have the opportunities for learning or advancement that one expected (Cases A.1 and A.9). Another case deals with dropping out from a career in science to follow a nontraditional lifestyle and then trying to restart a career later in life (A.13). Yet another case tells how blowing the whistle created a career barrier for the interviewee (A.4). Mental disability is the subject of another case (A.15). There are additional cases that describe the effects of poor supervision (A.7 and A.11), general organizational change (A.8), job loss from organizational downsizing (A.3, A.5, A.10, and A.14), and discrimination (A.2 and A.12).

ROUGH GOING IN EARLY CAREER (CASE A.1)

Young people sometimes have a tough time starting a career in their chosen field:

> *Kathy, age 25, has a bachelors degree in elementary education and special education. She hoped that the dual certification would help her find a position. Unfortunately, she was unable to find a teaching job after graduation. She served as a substitute teacher for 2 years, all the while trying to find a permanent appointment. She finally found a position in a private school in an area of specialty that is not exactly what she wanted. She continues to be frustrated by not being able to find a public school job in her area of specialization, which, she believes, is needed—especially in New York City. She remains idealistic in wanting to help children who need special assistance.*
>
> *Currently, Kathy is turning her energies to finishing a graduate degree. She recognizes the need to "network"—getting to know people in the city school system who might be able to help her find the type of position she wants.*

WHEN TENURE IS DENIED (CASE A.2)

The academic tenure process places unique demands on professionals at the start of their careers. After working hard for 6 years, the individual described here was at the mercy of a highly subjective and often political process:

> Ken is 40 years old. He and wife returned to graduate school 12 years earlier to obtain their PhDs and become professors. After receiving their degrees with distinction they both found positions at the same institution. She was granted tenure early, after only 5 years. A year later, he came up for tenure. He was approved unanimously by the faculty, and he sailed through the university's promotion and tenure committee and the dean's office. However, he was denied by the provost.
>
> Ken petitioned for a second review of the case, the provost agreed to have him reviewed a second time the following year. By then, the department had been organizationally moved under a different dean and promotion and tenure committee. Ken's department sought additional letters of recommendation from outside reviewers and worked hard to put together a supportive package. However, the new tenure advisory committee and dean imposed higher standards and denied tenure after another 9 months.
>
> By this time, Ken had lost all sense of self-objectivity. Ken and his wife had made a major commitment to the university, and they hoped that they would make this community their home. Ken believed the tenure process was unfair. In truth, his case was strong enough for tenure but had some minor weak points that justified denial. Ken could concentrate on nothing except how he would seek a legal remedy. He had great trouble even thinking about possible constructive career directions.

GETTING BACK INTO THE WORKFORCE (CASE A.3)

Resuming a career after having a family is often a difficult process:

> Laura is 47 years old, married (recently separated for 2 years and then reunited with her husband), and has two school-aged children. She has a varied career history, starting in early childhood education, leaving her job to stay home with her infants, trying interior design but finding that it did not pay well, and eventually taking a part-time job as a museum educator at a large research facility. This was 5 years ago. Since then, the job became full-time and then cut back again to 20 hours per week because of budget cuts.
>
> One career barrier that Laura confronted early on at the museum was a boss with a highly explosive and abusive personality. Laura's strategy, after much agonizing and consternation, was to confront the woman and establish their job boundaries. This seemed to work in getting the boss to avoid her. However, Laura feels that this altercation thwarted her chances for promotion. Now she is facing another career

barrier—the reduction in hours and the likelihood of further cutbacks. Because half of the museum staff has left, the remaining staff are struggling with the need to do more work than they are paid for to maintain high-quality programs. Laura feels that she has now overcome her fear and anxiety about the cutbacks.

WHISTLE BLOWING (CASE A.4)

Confronting an ethical problem and considering blowing the whistle is a "damned if you do, damned if you don't" situation. Doing so can create a career barrier. Not doing so means having to live with an unethical (and untenable) situation:

Linda, a 37-year-old social worker, was concerned about not following required procedure to protect case workers from infectious patients. The agency's policies clearly stated that caseworkers were not to interact with clients with tuberculosis unless the clients wore face masks and took other precautions to protect those around them. However, the director of the agency did not want to deny clients service because they refused to cooperate.

Linda voiced her concerns during the course of 8 months, but her concerns fell of deaf years. She was denied a promotion on the basis on not being a "team player" and told she would be denied further promotions until she changed her view. Linda's view is this: "With no way of promotion or growth within the department and my health constantly at risk, I am forced to find another job." She is depressed, has trouble concentrating, and dreads going to work. She cannot leave her job and lose the income, and finding another job is not easy.

BECOMING YOUR OWN BOSS (CASE A.5)

Hard work doesn't always pay off, but it is often the best thing people have going for them. When previously successful people lose their jobs, they find it appealing to become their own boss:

Maureen is a 49-year-old married woman with two children. After 17 years in the banking industry and moving into increasingly responsible positions, she lost her job when the bank merged and then sold her unit. As vice president she had been earning $75,000, supervised many employees, and was responsible for their training in the mortgage underwriting part of the business.

After the merger, Maureen was asked to train the employees and make the unit profitable. She trained the employees for 4 months and worked hard to ensure the success of the unit only to come to work one day to face a "lockout." The doors were locked and the employees were told to go to the main office. Once there, they were told that they were all terminated. Her unit had been sold to another firm. She felt "shocked and above all used." She had worked hard and received only positive feedback. There was not indication that the unit would be closed. She discovered later that the bank planned all along to sell the unit's portfolio and close it.

After 3 months without a job, Maureen found another position in a bank, only to leave that job a year later when the bank merged and she was offered a position in the new headquarters. This would mean a 2-hour commute each way. She decided never to put herself at the mercy of another institution again. She and a former coworker started a mortgage brokering business. She regretted that she never worked long enough in one firm to become vested in a retirement plan, although her husband will have a pension.

CONFRONTING HARASSMENT (CASE A.6)

Nancy is an African American attorney with an MBA degree. She is in her early 30s, is married, and has two children. Working on her first job in a prestigious law firm, she was harassed and treated her with disdain by her coworkers. For instance, she would ask for help or advice and, often times, was given incorrect information. She faced sarcastic and offensive comments about being an African American. She was excluded from certain activities and conversations. Nancy avoided saying anything about this to anyone at work becausee she wanted to keep the job. Working for a "good" law firm right out of law school would help her career in the long run. However, the situation was taking its toll on her family. She had little time for her children, and one son started to have problems in school, acting out and fighting with other kids. Her husband was supportive and understanding at first, but eventually he showed less concern. He had his own similar problems to deal with. After 7 months on the job, Nancy decided to quit. The senior partner of the firm was astounded to hear of the treatment she had received. He arranged for her to take a break from work for several months and then return. Meanwhile, he let his colleagues and staff know th at the harassment and discrimination would not be tolerated. The situation has been much more positive during the 2 years since returning from her leave of absence, although she still feels some tension while in the company of a few of her colleagues.

JOB CHANGE (CASE A.7)

Paula, a 55-year-old woman, has been married for 32 years and has four children. She has several degrees in nursing, including one she is currently earning. Three years ago, she left her job of 8 years as a part-time office RN. She felt she needed a change and was disappointed that her boss stopped contributing to the employees' retirement plan. She quickly found a well-paying job as an administrator at an adult home. However, after about 3 months on the job she began to experience conflicts with the owners. They were abusive to the staff, and their only concern was filling the facility with clients without regard to their welfare. Their concern for profits interfered with quality patient care and fair treatment of the staff. Paula left this position that had prestige and title and took several months off as a home care coordinator for a county nursing home. Fortunately, she is in a profession that is in demand.

CHANGING BUSINESS ENVIRONMENT (CASE A.8)

Changing economic and political conditions can affect the fate of a business, including the careers of its owners and employees. Changes in business may necessitate trying new business strategies and taking some risks. In this case, an entrepreneur needed to evaluate the business environment when a small manufacturing business made a successful, albeit rocky, transition from filling military contracts to serving the private sector. The case demonstrates the need to experiment and take some risks in order to find new business and career directions.

Patrick is the owner of a manufacturing firm that made parts for telecommunications and computer equipment largely for the defense industry. The firm was started by Patrick's father, who still worked for the company in the machine shop. Other family members worked for the firm as well. The company had grown considerably during the 1980s, tripling in size in about 4 years to about 150 employees. However, as government contracts dried up in the late 1980s, Patrick, in his 40s with a wife and family, faced the prospect of closing the company and finding another job or doing something to refocus the business. He reports being overwhelmed by the frustration and stress to the point of physical illness. He doubted his decisions and lost confidence in his ability to read the market. He had to lay off half of his employees initially, and later even more. His father was little support, and he kept most of his problems from his wife. When she asked what was happening, he usually jumped at her taking out his frustrations.

After about a year of this, Patrick had the chance to purchase another firm that made terminals for special uses in private businesses. He sold most of his current operation to buy the firm. Unfortunately, this turned out to be a highly competitive business. Prices dropped 60% as the market for the equipment was quickly saturated. Business picked up a bit after a year. However, most of his employees who were left did not deal well with the changes. Many were managers in their late 50s and 60s who were getting ready to retire, not start new projects. He felt constant pressure to motivate and encourage his top managers.

Currently, Patrick has 40 employees and 10 salespeople in five states. The employee pool is quite different from 2 years ago, with a greater focus on serving individual customers and an ability to deal with change better. Also, he makes sure that most employees are cross-trained to handle different jobs as needed. The firm is not profitable for the first time in 2 years.

LEGAL PROBLEMS (CASE A.9)

This case involves a woman who worked hard for many years only to be accused of a crime in an area of the business over which she had no control. Patricia was a 33-year-old woman, divorced with no children, with a BA degree. She worked for a food products importing firm for 8 years traveling worldwide. Nine months ago, she and her boss were fired when the company was raided by U.S. Customs, accused of defrauding the government by not paying the correct tariffs. The firm supposedly rerouted products through other countries with lower duty rates. Patricia was the buyer, and the trafficking department handled product delivery. The parent firm did not bother to interview her to hear her side of the story. She had trouble finding another job given the situation and was unemployed for 6 months. She faces indictment and could receive a prison term if found guilty.

Patricia was devastated when she was fired. She was angry and depressed for many weeks and even spoke of suicide. At this point, she is feeling better. Now she is working as a product coordinator for her former boss' wife's graphics firm. This job pays one-third her former salary and is boring. Realizing her unhappiness, her new employer offered to give her a different job with more responsibility and a higher salary as time goes on. She is ready to take control by sticking with her present job and make the best of a terrible situation.

WHEN THE ORGANIZATION RELOCATES
AND YOU DON'T (CASE A.10)

Sometimes it takes a while to realize the full ramifications of a situation. In this case, a top manager knew the firm was being relocated and that he would have a chance to move with the company but to a much lower paying position. This seemed to be a safety net until he realized it was not feasible. Panic set in until he was ready to discuss the situation with his family and begin the search for another job.

Paul was the controller for a small electronics assembly company in western New York State. His duties included supervising several clerks and a quality control specialist. His salary was approximately $50,000 per year with full health insurance, a small pension contribution, and several perks, such as a company car and free use of the company owner's condominium in Florida. He was 47 and married with two girls, ages 20 and 16. At the time, his wife was a medical receptionist and his older daughter was in her third year of college and planning to attend graduate school. His second daughter was a little more than a year away from college. He has an MBA in accounting and had worked for the company for 15 years. The owner of the firm suffered a heart attack and was disabled for about 5 months.

After the owner returned to work, the company's financial position deteriorated because of rapidly decreasing prices in the computer retail industry. Within a year, the owner sold the company to another electronics firm in California. A year after the sale, the new owners announced that the plant would be closed and consolidated in California. Paul was told he could move with the operations, but to the job of shipping and receiving supervisor with a $20,000 cut in pay, no pension contribution, and reduced health coverage. He declined the transfer.

As the controller for the company, Paul had advanced knowledge of the situation. He was one of the first to know that the facility would be closed and that the functions would be moved. It took about 9 months for him to find a new position. When he first learned of the plans to close the plant, he thought that the option of relocating was a possibility even with the lower salary. It was a safety net—but one that prevented him from taking action to find other employment.

As the plant was about to close and he recognized that relocating was not financially realistic, he felt a sense of panic. He recalls that this feeling lasted for about a week before he discussed the situation with his family and friends and began to explore other options. For about 2 months, the interviewee searched for another position. His severance package and unemployment insurance were enough to pay his bills for about a year and a half. He did some accounting work for a friend, and eventually found a job with a large firm at a slightly lower salary and a 1½ hour commute.

ABUSIVE SUPERVISOR (CASE A.11)

Bosses can be self-serving and malicious if it suits their purpose. Here, a promised promotion did not materialize when someone else got the job. Then the new boss set out to get the employee.

Roberta is a "30 something" divorced woman employed in a public relations firm. After her divorce and move back to her hometown, she had a sequence of diverse administrative-type jobs. Eventually, she found a job as an administrator of the fundraising office of a local college. She also volunteered in fundraising efforts for several local causes, such as the public radio station. She made quite a few contacts and was offered an excellent position in industry. However, the college's provost convinced her to stay. The college was in the midst of planning a major fund-raising event, and he did not want to lose her. He promised that she could be a candidate for the director of the development office, a job that was soon to be vacant. He convinced her that she would be a "perfect candidate" for the job. In the meantime, the provost gave her a modest raise to stay.

When the job was posted, the provost changed his story. He said that the successful candidate would have to have an undergraduate degree. Roberta was just several months away from completing her degree part-time, and she applied for the job noting that. However, she did not get the job. Instead, someone with connections but no college degree was hired. Roberta discovered this when a coworker came in with someone new and told the interviewee that she did not have to attend the next meeting because this other person, her new boss, would go.

This was disappointing, and things went from bad to worse. Several months later, the new boss brought Roberta up before the school's grievance committee complaining that she was bringing work home. The boss complained that Roberta was bringing work home when she was not feeling well or when she had a deadline to meet. The grievance committee supported Roberta and ruled that her boss had no basis for complaint. Another incident occurred when the boss gave Roberta time off for a personal appointment. When she returned, the boss was irate, screaming that she was late. At this point, Roberta gathered up her things and quit on the spot. The provost offered to arrange another position for her, but she refused. She married her boyfriend, completed her degree, and found a job in a public relations firm.

DISCRIMINATION (CASE A.12)

Some organizational cultures seem to promulgate negative treatment of employees. For instance, the U.S. Postal Service has a long history of rigid rules, standard procedures, and inflexibility. This is also the case in some military-like training environments, such as police academies. Here is someone who had both experiences in succession:

Shirley, 39 years old with no children has been living with her significant other for the past 7 years. She received an associates degree 17 years ago, and just last year completed her bachelors degree. She is currently pursuing a masters degree in management. Her career began with a series of positions in retail sales and she spent 5 years delivering baked goods to grocery stores. This was a physically demanding job so, at age 29, she took the Civil Service test and was offered a job as a letter carrier with the U.S. Postal Service. The Postal Service has recently been cited for its rigid job specifications and supervision, and this interviewee experienced what it is like to work under these conditions. One of her coworkers who was training her pointed to the time clock and told her, "When you start at the Post Office you leave your brain at the door and pick it up 30 years later." Shirley found rampant favoritism, and there was no way to advance. Supervisors stood behind her while she sorted the mail and timed her every move. Many times they yelled, "faster, faster." They followed her on routes, and threatened write-ups and suspensions.

One day while delivering mail in her truck, Shirley was hit head-on by another vehicle. She sustained a shoulder injury. She was harassed from the moment of the accident. The postmaster did not want her taking any time off from work. He even insisted on trying to be at every doctor's appointment she went to. She was back at work within a week and a half and assigned to phone duty. When she was well enough to go back to delivering mail, they moved her work station right outside the supervisor's office so that he could constantly watch her. Her union was no help. Meanwhile, Shirley had taken other civil service exams and she gained entrance to the county police academy. She left the Postal Service after 4 years, and at age 33 started to train to become a police officer. At the academy, Shirley felt she was again the target of harassment. It was worse than boot camp. She was constantly picked on; for instance, a police officer who was training her constantly yelled that her shoes were not shined properly. She would spend 3 hours a night shining her shoes. One day in physical training, the officer took her aside and made her go through cruel physical stunts. Suddenly she felt severe pain in her injured shoulder from her delivery truck accident. The officer would not let her stop. He continued to make her do flips landing on the injured shoulder for another half an hour. She reported the injury and left for a doctor's office. She had endured 3 weeks of training. The doctor told her she needed to rest the shoulder for 10 days. This was unacceptable to the police academy, and she felt she was coerced to resign. Had she not resigned, she realized later that she could have collected disability and then gone into another class. She felt helpless, was angry with herself for letting herself be intimidated, and felt "emotionally overwhelmed." Shirley is now back in retail sales working as a convenience store manager.

GETTING BACK ON TRACK AFTER TRYING THE UNCONVENTIONAL (A.13)

Having a free lifestyle is great for a while, but it makes it all the more difficult to achieve stability later in life. This is the case of a 42-year-old man who left a scientific career 15 years earlier to pursue a life that was more in line with his values and beliefs. Living a Bohemian lifestyle was fine until he and his wife, now responsible for their young adopted son, realized it was time to settle down. However, he is having trouble finding employment commensurate with his education and skills in a highly competitive job market:

Stan had a troubled childhood. His father abandoned his mother and brother when Stan was 7. A bright and physically able teenager, he dropped out of high school varsity football and also decided not to attend West Point. He received his BS in physics and masters in materials science from Stanford and went to work for a large electronics company in the Silicon Valley. He stayed there for 3 years and then transferred to a computer firm as a research technician. He stayed there for 5 years. He quit this job when he was 27 years old and had been married for about 6 months. Stan decided to leave science because he was becoming increasingly disillusioned with where he saw science leading humanity, and he needed to integrate his personal beliefs with his work. He had become involved in the disarmament movement, and he was active politically with speaking engagements, writing articles, and protesting weapons research. Stan and his wife traveled across country to Woodstock, NY where he found a job as a carpenter's apprentice. This proved to be a great creative outlet and allowed him to live a free lifestyle. They purchased a run-down waterfront cottage on Long Island, which gave him an opportunity to hone his new carpentry skills. For the next 10 years, he and his wife would work during half the year and travel during the other half. He learned to cross-country ski in upstate New York,

*backpack on the island of Jamaica, and play the guitar in Berkeley, CA. After he
and his wife adopted their son during a trip to Central America, they moved to a
farm commune in Colorado for 2 years where he helped renovate a cathedral. Living
with 150 people took its toll on their marriage, and when their son turned 5, Stan
and his wife returned to their home on Long Island to establish a more stable lifestyle.
Also, Stan was beginning to feel a need to return to science.*

*During the next 3 years, Stan had trouble finding work. He eventually began waiting
tables to make money. He felt lost, and could not find the strength to regain direction.
He later began doing computer and office management work for local contractors.
He was disappointed when he was dismissed from a job he thought would be
permanent after a project was completed. He is currently looking for employment.
Although his wife earns enough to support the family, he feels a need to do more
with his life and make a larger contribution to the family's financial welfare. His
wife has been urging him not to settle for the first job that comes along. She thinks
he should explore different alternatives—perhaps his own software design business—rather than break his back working for others who will use him up and spit
him out.*

ANOTHER CASE OF DOWNSIZING (CASE A.14)

After 20 years of working for the same company in the same job, the prospect
of finding other employment is daunting:

*Sheila is a 39-year-old married mother of three boys, aged 3 through 12. She had
worked as an airline reservation clerk for almost 20 years in Manhattan. When the
airline closed the office, she was offered a relocation to another state, but her
husband's job made this impossible. She did need the income and was not looking
forward to starting over again with another company or starting a new and different
career.*

*Therefore, Sheila applied for a flight attendant position. This meant being away for
a 5-week training program, after which she had to call in every day to see what her
assignment would be. This could last several years until she had enough seniority
to be assigned a permanent schedule. With much organizing and help from her
husband, a new babysitter, and family members who lived close by, Sheila has been
able to manage.*

*Sheila confessed that she doesn't deal with change very well. Leaving her family for
the training and starting a new career at her age was very stressful. She lost 10
pounds in 5 weeks, and felt physically ill during most of the training, but she passed
with flying colors. As a flight attendant, she never knows where she will be flying or
how long she is going to stay. She must wear a beeper so she can be accessible to the
airline at all times. Despite her success, she sees this as a band-aid fix. She does not
see how she can keep up this lifestyle for long.*

OVERCOMING A DISABILITY (CASE A.15)

Mentally handicapped individuals have careers. However, the criteria for success are different. Also, staying employed and learning new skills takes tremendous support. Barriers arise when these individuals cannot get jobs, face inflexible work schedules and regimens, and confront intolerant co-workers. Mentally challenged people appraise their situations, have emotional reactions, and initiate action—even if it is simply telling a caseworker that they are unhappy:

Norman is a mentally challenged (mildly retarded) employee. His speech is a little difficult to understand but with close listening is intelligible. He is considered to be a "high-functioning" individual. He does not make decisions for himself, and in many cases does not have the capacity to do so in a meaningful way. Much of this information was verified and supplemented by his job coach. He is 41 years old, lives in a group home, and is supervised by a job coach and case manager. Norman does stock and maintenance work 3 days a week for a total of 15 hours. His duties include binding books, cleaning, delivery and pick-up of materials on campus, and keeping his work area neat. He had been on this job for only 4 months at the time of the interview. In the past, he worked as a grounds laborer at a local beach during the summer and had another maintenance position with the special school he attended as a child.

The major career barrier Norman has faced is employers who are unwilling to hire people with mental disabilities. When he is hired, he finds little support and little flexibility—for instance, in scheduling work hours. Also, he faced other employees who felt that he was taking a job which could have been filled by a "normal" person. Norman is aware that he is "different" than others, but he does not get down on himself because of it. His job coach and case manager do what they can to make Norman's employment situations match Norman's capabilities and his interests. Norman tells his case manager when he wants to change jobs or when things are not working out.

His current situation is excellent. Norman has the freedom to complete the tasks in the sequence he wishes, with the understanding that they must be done. He has moved from 80% of work time under supervision by the job coach provided by his agency to 20% with most supervision and training of new tasks now performed by the employer. He has a development plan that calls for him to learn how to read a map and how to check and verify inventory. Also, he is improving his interpersonal skills through increased contact with others in the organization.

Appendix B:
Catalog of Cases

This is a summary of the cases that appear at the beginning and end of chapters 1–6 and in Appendix A. The cases are organized by type of career barrier in line with the categories of career barriers outlined in chapter 1. Note that these categories do not cover all the types of career barriers mentioned in chapter 1, only those represented in the cases collected for this study. Also, a case could fall under more than one category—for instance, when increased job demands and an abusive supervisor occur together. Each case has a code in parentheses at the end of the description. This refers to the chapter and case number where the full case description appears. So, for example, case 1.2 is the second case in chapter 1; A.1 is the first case in the Appendix A.

TYPES OF BARRIERS REPRESENTED
IN THE CASES

General organizational/environmental barriers
    Limited career opportunities
    Technological change
Specific (local) organizational, environmental, and situational barriers
    Job demands
    Poor supervision
    Organizational change
Organizational actions that affect specific individuals
    Organizational downsizing—job loss
    Whistleblowing
General individual barriers
    Physical or mental disability
    Low motivation
    Desire for a different lifestyle
Job-specific individual barriers
    Poor job performance

Non-job-related individual barriers
Discrimination or unfair treatment

CATALOG

Limited Career Opportunities

A young person in early career made a major career transition. An engineer, he saw few opportunities in the defense industry where he was employed. He quit, enrolled in law school full-time, and specialized in intellectual property law, which allows him to build on his engineering background. (2.8)

An experienced medical technologist was dismayed by poor support for career advancement. After surveying his profession and finding a similar situation at other hospitals, he left his job after 12 years to sell medical equipment. (3.2)

A divorced man who was stuck in a boring job looked for career alternatives that would use his creativity. He took several years to explore career alternatives and get some training. Then, with the financial and emotional support of his wife, he accepted a series of jobs that led to starting his own business. (6.2)

A young, highly trained and motivated person could not find the teaching job she wanted. (A.1)

People can be the unwitting victims of others' crimes. When this happens on the job, they lose their reputations and livelihoods. In this case, a woman in her 30s lost her job and faced indictment over a situation in a part of the business she did not control. (A.9)

This case shows the ups and downs of working in an industry that is highly influenced by regional economic conditions. A union plumber had a career of on-again-off-again work. At age 51, he could not see any alternative but to stay in his field and face long periods of unemployment. (4.3)

Technological Change

A young single mother made a career change from being a proofreader in a publishing company to being a paralegal. New technology gave her an excuse to get out of a dead-end position and learn a new profession. However, she did not make the transition until forced to. (2.5)

Job Demands

This case is an example of a young occupational therapist who faced increased job demands to do more with less. In her spare time, she investigated opening a private practice. She felt the excitement of exploring new career directions and the frustration and exhaustion of a higher work load. Although she was excited about the prospects of a the private practice, she recognized that it may not be realistic. (2.6)

A highly educated woman in her early 30s found her job as a university administrator highly stressful. Unable to cope with the situation, she took a leave of absence and eventually resigned. (3.1)

Poor Supervision

A young woman faced poor supervision and a demanding work environment. She retreated to more education as a safe haven. Although she explored new career possibilities, she did not learn how to deal with job stress. (6.1)

A hard-working young woman reported to supervisors who took advantage of her competence and career motivation. (7.4)

This is an example of someone who was disappointed by poor supervision and management style by the owners of the business. A nurse-administrator of an adult home found the owners to be abusive toward the staff and the clients. (A.7)

When people in power behave in a self-serving way, they may be kind or cruel depending on their purpose. In this case, a "30 something" divorced woman worked for someone who made promises that did not materialize, acted unfairly, and imposed unreasonable demands. (A.11)

Organizational Change

A 47-year-old administrative clerk in a medical office faced the situation in which a pleasant and profitable work environment established during a 12-year period was disrupted by partners who betrayed the senior doctor when he fell ill. She remained loyal to the senior doctor and helped him reestablish his practice. (1.4)

A middle-aged woman who had been in the same job for 14 years took a downgrade and accepted civil service status to avoid being laid off when her university employer cut its staff. She recognized what was happening and took action to protect her job security. (2.9)

Rather than lose his job after a company merger and downsizing, this 48-year-old divorced man accepted a transfer to another region of the country. Although he knew the downsizing was coming, he saw no other alternative but to stay with the firm and see what happened. The result was positive. (4.1)

Changing environmental conditions affected the viability of a business and the owner's decision to stick with the business for his own career and that of many of his employees. This case demonstrates the importance of persistence. It also shows that reorganization can create opportunities. (A.8)

Organizational Downsizing—Job Loss

A 58-year-old married man worked for a defense contractor as an electrical engineer before being laid off in an organizational downsizing. This is a classic case of a the displaced engineer. After some retraining, he became a software consultant. (1.1)

A man in late career was forced to retire by a new boss. The case shows that a positive attitude can contribute to finding other satisfying employment. (1.2)

A midcareer executive faced sudden unemployment. He should have seen it coming, but did not. After 21 weeks of dedicated job search, he found another position, but at a lower salary and a longer commute. (1.5)

A young family man put up with a stressful job for 6 years until his was laid off when the firm went bankrupt. During the 6 years, he could see that the firm's owner was bleeding the firm's profits and investing less and less in the business. Any opportunities for career development in the firm dried up. However, he waited until he lost his job before seeking retraining and finding another position. (2.3)

A young person stayed with a sinking ship and delayed facing a job search until she was unemployed. (2.4)

Knowing what to expect when searching for a job can keep a person motivated. This individual faced a job loss and cancer at the same time and overcame both. (5.2)

A middle-aged woman with young children returned to the work world and learned to stand up to a supervisor with whom she did not get along. Several years later, she faced a cutback in her hours due to a cost-cutting measure in the organization. This case shows a caring person who thought deeply about interpersonal relationships in her personal and work life. It shows how tenacity and commitment to family can support someone through tough times. (A.3)

A married woman in mid life lost her job after 17 years of increasingly responsible jobs in the banking industry. The case shows that hard work is important, but not always enough. She discovered that becoming her own boss was the best solution, and fortunately she had a spouse who could tide the family over financially as her new business got off the ground. (A.5)

This is a typical case of an older, experienced, and educated man who lost his job and had the intelligence and support to find another. After an initial feeling of panic, he shared his feelings with his family and came to grips with the situation. He found a new job with a lower salary and a long commute but with a good company. (A.10)

The prospect of losing one's job leads people to desperation. Instead of being laid off when the firm closed the branch office, this mother of three young children took an assignment that required constant travel. (A.14)

Whistleblowing

This is the case of a social worker who was forced to deal with clients who had infectious diseases and were unwilling to take the required precautions to protect those around them. The department director refused to deny service to these clients, putting the social workers' health at risk. Her continued complaints have fallen on deaf ears. Her choice was to stay and risk her health and future career advancement or quit. (A.4)

Physical or Mental Disability

Another success story, this case shows a woman who continued to work in a stressful job despite a severe debilitating illness. (5.3)

Mentally challenged individuals hold jobs and evaluate the barriers they confront. This case shows how a mildly retarded man was able to learn on the job and take on more difficult tasks, with the support of a caseworker and a flexible organization. He complained when the work was too difficult, and let his caseworker know when he felt ready to change jobs. (A.15)

Low Motivation

A man in midlife moved from job to job. He eventually realized that he could not wait and hope for the best, but, rather had to make things happen through more aggressive actions. (3.3)

An unskilled worker in a rural area who lost his job languished after he had trouble finding permanent employment. Only 25 years old, he was already divorced, remarried, and responsible for two young stepchildren. (4.2)

Desire for a Nontraditional Lifestyle

A 42-year-old man had difficulty getting back on track after following a nontraditional path. Becoming disillusioned with his career in science at age 27, he quit his position as a research technician. He and his wife pursued a carefree lifestyle for 15 years until they wanted more financial stability and a return to their nuclear family. Ultimately, he faced a competitive job market and is now having trouble finding permanent employment. (A.13)

Poor Job Performance

A man under 30 came to grips with the fact that his job performance was under par despite having received favorable feedback from others. He also had to face his wife's demands that he make more money. (2.10)

A young family woman became disillusioned with the stress of her chosen profession. A new job that promised to be exciting turned sour when she could not get along with her boss. Unemployed at the time of the interview, she was working with a career counselor to find a career direction that would offer a more supportive and less demanding work environment. (6.3)

Discrimination or Unfair Treatment

A 30-year-old junior attorney was given low-level assignments that precluded advancement or learning. Promises of advancement and better assignments never materialized. This appeared to be a classic case of gender discrimination. (1.3)

A person can be the unwitting victim of others' actions with little recourse but to withdraw from the situation. Here a barrister who was unjustly accused of illegal activity decided to change his life and career. (2.1)

Others' jealousies can fester and make the person powerless in the face of unfair treatment. A woman recently promoted to supervisor had trouble managing and received little support from the department. (2.2)

A project manager in the construction business lost a good job when the firm went belly up due to the owner's bad debts. Unfortunately, his next job ended similarly, in that the firm took advantage of his skills and then dumped him when he was no longer needed. His principal concern was how losing his job would be seen by others. (2.7)

Aggressiveness can pay off when fighting the political machine in big-city government. A woman in late career avoids being forced out by using all of her political muscle. (5.1)

An assistant professor was denied tenure and had trouble giving up the appeals process and moving on with his life. (A.2)

Discrimination can affect an individual's life and career. An African American woman who is an attorney (and also has an MBA) faced discrimination, harassment, and periods of stress in her first law position. (A.6)

Some work environments are notorious for their rigid and often abusive treatment of employees. This case describes a young woman who faced debilitating and harsh treatment first working for the U.S. Postal Service and then as a recruit in a police academy. (A.12)

Appendix C:
Case Description and Rating Forms

CASE DESCRIPTION FORM

(completed by the interviewer for each person interviewed)

1. Age: _____ under 30   2. Gender: _____ male
        _____ 30–39   _____ female
        _____ 40–49
        _____ 50–59   3. Occupation: _____
        _____ 60 or older   _____

4. Highest education: _____ some high school or high school degree
                      _____ some college or college degree
                      _____ some graduate work or graduate degree

5. Current marital status: ___married ___never married
                           ___divorced ___widowed

6. No. of children: _____

7. What was the nature of the situation? (check the response that best applies)
   _____job loss _____handicap _____relocation _____career change
   _____new position in the same company_____demotion _____job stress
   _____other_____

8. How long ago did the situation begin? _____years _____months

9. Has it been resolved (e.g., the person found another job, learned to live with the handicap, etc.)? (circle one) *yes   no*

10. When the situation occurred, it (check one) _____happened suddenly with little or no warning _____arose slowly until the individual realized that something had to be done.

11. When the situation first occurred, what was the interviewee's dominant emotion? (check the one that best applies)
_____fear _____anger _____denial _____sadness
_____frustration _____resignation
_____other (please indicate)_____

12. Did the interviewee have a realistic and apparently accurate view of the situation? (circle one) *yes no*

13. Did the interviewee have a clear explanation for why the situation occurred? (circle one) *yes no* If yes, did the interviewee attribute the primary cause to (check one) _____him/herself
_____factors beyond his/her control

14. The interviewee believed that he/she (circle one) *could could not* do something him or herself to overcome the barrier or bring the situation under control.

15. The interviewee had identified (circle one) *no a few many* actions he or she could take to overcome the barrier or resolve the situation.

16. How would you describe the interviewee's coping strategy (or strategies)? (check the one response that best applies)
_____proactive _____reactive

17. Would you say the coping strategies are (check the one response that best applies) _____constructive _____ dysfunctional
_____destructive

18. Did the interviewee's appraisal of the situation and coping strategies (check one)
_____change over time as the interviewee developed a more realistic or accurate appraisal of the situation
_____ remained about the same until the situation was resolved

CAREER ASSESSMENT POSTINTERVIEW
RATING FORM

Respondent (circle one):   Interviewer   Interviewee

Indicate whether each of the following is high, medium, or low by placing circle around your response (*Note: Scale labels in parentheses were not printed on the questionnaire.*)

(*Resilience*)
1. H M L Resilience—ability to overcome career barriers
2. H M L Self-efficacy—ability to make positive things happen
3. H M L Need for achievement—desire to excel

(*Insight*)
4. H M L Self-knowledge
5. H M L Knowledge about the job
6. H M L Knowledge about the employing organization
7. H M L Knowledge about the profession
8. H M L Current career opportunities for the future

(*Identity*)
9. H M L Commitment to the job
10. H M L Commitment to the employing organization
11. H M L Commitment to the profession
12. H M L Participates in continued training

(*Support for Resilience*)
13. H M L Rewards for doing a good job
14. H M L Ability to control what is done on the job
15. H M L Authority to make decisions

(*Support for Insight*)
16. H M L Availability of information about the organization
17. H M L Availability of performance feedback
18. H M L Encouragement from the supervisor or others for career planning

(*Support for Identity*)
19. H M L Likely future value of remaining with the employer
20. H M L Likely future value of staying in the same job
21. H M L Likely future value of staying in the profession

22. H M L Likely future value of changing jobs (staying in the same profession but moving to a new job with another employer)

(Stress)
23. H M L Current feelings of stress
24. H M L Current career satisfaction (coded inversely)

Appendix D:
Relationships Between Appraisal, Coping, and Career Motivation

After each interview, the interviewee and interviewer separately completed a rating form that asked about the individual's career motivation (items comprising career resilience, insight, and identity scales), situational support for career motivation, and current feelings of satisfaction and stress. In addition, the interviewer completed a form describing the interviewee's experience (biographical characteristics), emotions, appraisal, and coping mechanisms. These forms are presented in Appendix C. This resulted in seven sets of variables listed in Table D.1. After describing the sample, I provide a summary of the major findings and their implications. Then I present a technical description of the results preceded by a brief explanation of the meaning of the statistics for interested readers.

BIOGRAPHICAL CHARACTERISTICS

The study is based on an opportunity sample of people known by the interviewers to have experienced a career barrier. The goal was to obtain a diverse sample representing different types of career barriers. In total, 90 interviews were conducted. Fifteen percent of the sample was under 30 years of age, and 33% were in their 30s. Forty-nine percent were in their 40s or 50s. Just over half (51%) were women. Fifty-five percent were professionals, such as attorneys, engineers, professors, teachers, or nurses. Managers (CEOs, controllers, and middle managers) were included in this category. Most were well-educated (86% had some college, had completed college, or had done some graduate work), and married (68%). Forty-one percent had no children, 12% had one child, and 47% had two or more children. For further analyses, marital status was coded 1 = not married, 2 = married. Also note that the occupational variable formed a continuum from highest to lowest skilled (attorney or top executive coded 1, engineer or manager coded 2, administrator coded 3, skilled occupational worker coded 4, clerical worker coded 5, unskilled worker coded 6), and so was included as a continuous variable in further analyses.

TABLE D.1

List of Variables by Category

---

1. *Bio*
    Age
    Gender
    Occupation
    Education
    Marital status
    Number of children

2. *Career barrier characteristics*
    Job loss (2 = job loss, 1 = other career barrier)
    Resolved at time of interview (1 = yes, 2 = no)
    Speed by which the barrier arose (1 = suddenly, 2 = slowly)
    Clarity of explanation (1 = clear, 2 = unclear)

3. *Emotions*   .
    Fear
    Anger
    Frustration

4. *Stress*

5. *Cognitive appraisal*
    Realistic view of the situation (1 = yes, 2 = no)
    Cause (1 = blames self, 2 = blames factors beyond ones control)
    Ability to resolve the situation (1 = could do something oneself, 2 = could not do something oneself)

6. *Coping*
    Identified actions to overcome the barrier (1 = no, 2 = a few, 3 = many)
    Coping (1 = proactive, 2 = reactive)
    Effects of strategies (1 = constructive, 2 = dysfunctional, 3 = destructive)
    Change strategy over time (1 = changed, 2 = remained about the same)

7. *Career motivation and support for career motivation*
    Resilience
    Insight
    Identity
    Support for resilience
    Support for insight
    Support for identity

OVERVIEW OF MAJOR FINDINGS
AND THEIR IMPLICATIONS

The intercorrelations among the variables provide considerable insight into the nature of career barriers and individuals' reactions to them. Job loss, compared to the other career barriers in the sample, tended to be sudden, generated anger and blaming others, distorted reality, left people at a loss about what to do, and had a damaging effect on career motivation. Thus, job loss should be treated as a more severe situation than other career barriers, requiring special attention and support to help people find other jobs and resume their careers. Barriers that arose slowly seemed easier to take. People saw how they influenced the situation and what they could do about the situation. Those who understood the reason for the barrier felt they had more control over it. Hence plenty of warning and clear explanations are likely to help people determine how to cope with a career barrier.

Individual characteristics may influence reactions to career barriers. People who were more educated seemed to have more realistic views or more proactive and constructive coping strategies. Women were better able to cope and adjust their coping strategies to fit the changing situation compared to men.

Much attention has been given to managerial downsizing. However, career barriers in this sample were more stressful for occupational employees, such as clerks and construction workers. This suggests that organizations and government agencies should provide emotional support as well as training and redeployment for blue-collar workers.

People who saw themselves as a cause of the barrier were better able to cope. Being proactive was frustrating but less stressful than being reactive. In general, people should be encouraged to develop accurate attributions for a career barrier with special attention to how they might have influenced the barrier's occurrence. They might not be the principal cause of the barrier (for instance, a plant buyout and relocation), but they should understand the role they played in how the barrier affected them (for example, they did not maintain their skills, which in turn made it difficult to find another job). People need to understand how they affected the barrier because this will lead them to determine actions they can take to turn around the situation.

Maintaining career motivation (especially the elements of resilience and identity) was important to feeling less stress, being more realistic, and being proactive. People needed information about available opportunities in order to identify coping actions. Resilience, insight, and identity and support for these elements of career motivation were important to coping constructively. This suggests that programs to help people overcome career barriers should pay attention to performance rewards, organizational information and performance feedback, and convincing arguments that the future is bright.

TECHNICAL PRESENTATION
OF THE RESULTS

In the following sections, I examine each set of variables in turn. As I do this, I present the correlations between the variables within and between the sets. I placed these results in this appendix because they are somewhat technical. However, a bit of explanation will help the interested novice understand the results. The relationships are based on correlations (denoted by r). A positive correlation indicates that people who are high on one variable tend to be high on the other (or vice versa). A negative correlation indicates that people who are low on one variable tend to be high on the other. Correlations range from -1 to +1. A correlation of 0, or close to 0, indicates that the variables are not related. Some of the variables are combinations of various items that were rated by the interviewees. I report the extent to which the components are consistent (called an index of reliability, denoted by the term "alpha"). All correlations mentioned below are significant (at the p .05 level or better) unless otherwise noted. This means that there was only a 5% probability or less that a correlation of that size would have occurred by chance alone. Sample characteristics are presented in Table D.2. The means, standard deviations, and intercorrelations for all the variables are presented in Table D.3.

CAREER BARRIER CHARACTERISTICS

Chapter 1 described a range of career barriers. Although diverse career barriers were represented in the current sample, 39% involved job loss usually due to organizational downsizing, 23% involved a career change, and 15% involved job stress such as poor supervision or increased work demands. Other career barriers included relocation (for instance, moving with the company or a spouse; 2%), physical or mental handicap (5%), transfer to a new position in the same company (9%), or demotion (7%). For 26% of the sample, the situation occurred within 1 year of the interview; for 57% it had occurred between 1 and 5 years earlier; and for 17% it had occurred more than 5 years earlier. Most of the participants (74%) indicated that the situation had been resolved by the time of the interview (for instance, the person found another job). Most (63%) indicated that the career barrier arose slowing, whereas the rest said it happened suddenly with little or not warning. Most had a clear explanation for why the situation occurred (83%, as judged by the interviewer).

Because 39% of the sample had experienced job loss, the career barrier measure was recoded for further analysis into two groups (job loss = 2; other career barrier = 1). This allowed comparing the experience of job loss to other types of career barriers.

Other career barrier characteristics included whether the career was resolved or not at the time of the interview (coded 1 = yes, 2 = no), how quickly the career barrier arose (coded 1 = happened suddenly with little

TABLE D.2

Sample Characteristics

1. Age: 15% under 30
    33% 30–39
    32% 40–49
    17% 50–59
    3% 60 or older

2. Gender: 49% male
    51% female

3. Occupation: 55% professional (e.g., lawyer, engineer, professor, teacher, nurse, manager)
    45% nonprofessional (clerical, administrative, trade)

4. Highest education:
    14% some high school or high school degree
    38% some college or college degree
    48% some graduate work or graduate degree

5. Current marital status:
    68% married
    18% never married
    12% divorced
    2% widowed

6. Number of children: 41% no children
    12% one child
    27% two children
    14% three children
    6% four or more children

7. Nature of the career barrier:
    39% job loss
    5% handicap
    2% relocation
    23% career change
    9% new position in the same company
    7% demotion
    15% job stress (poor supervision, increased work demands)

8. How long ago the situation began:
    14% 6 months or less
    12% between 6 months and a year
    57% more than 1 and less than 5 years
    17% more than 5 years

9. Was the situation resolved at the time of the interview (e.g., the person found another job, learned to live with the handicap, etc.)?
    74% yes
    26% no

10. How the situation occurred:
    37% happened suddenly with little or no warning
    63% arose slowly until the individual realized that something had to be done

or no warning, 2 = arose slowly until the individual realized that something had to be done), and whether the interviewee had a clear explanation for why the situation occurred (coded 1 = yes, 2 = no).

TABLE D.3
Means, Standard Deviations, and Intercorrelations

	Means	Sds	1	2	3	4	5	6	7	8	9	10	11	12	13	14	15	16	17	18	19	20	21	22	23	24	25	26
Biographical characteristics																												
1. Age	2.61	1.04	---																										
2. Sex	1.51	.51	-.26	---																									
3. Occupation	3.16	1.69	.01	-.08	---																								
4. Education	2.32	.71	-.13	.11	-.27	---																							
5. Marital status	1.68	.47	.33	-.22	.13	-.06	---																						
6. # children	1.35	1.39	.61	-.25	.01	.10	.52	---																					
Career barrier characteristics																												
7. Job loss	1.39	.49	.16	-.26	.20	-.46	.10	.23	---																			
8. Resolved	1.26	.44	-.25	-.06	.16	.02	-.09	-.21	.02	---																		
9. Warning	1.63	.49	.05	.17	-.06	.20	-.00	.03	-.23	-.02	---																	
10. Explanation	1.17	.38	-.01	-.01	-.09	.09	-.08	-.25	.03	.21	-.11	---																
Emotions																												
11. Fear	1.16	.37	.07	.06	.04	-.11	-.11	.05	.03	-.05	-.18	.06	---															
12. Anger	1.20	.41	.10	-.01	.06	.14	.04	.04	.28	-.12	-.31	.08	-.22	---														
13. Frustration	1.28	.45	-.15	-.01	.03	.01	.09	-.14	-.28	.15	.27	.15	-.27	-.32	---													
14. Stress	2.07	.57	-.11	-.10	.30	-.18	.05	-.09	.14	.39	-.17	.07	-.08	.06	.03	---												
Appraisal																												
15. Realistic	1.22	.42	-.02	-.15	-.13	.18	.11	.01	.34	.25	-.17	.30	-.01	.07	-.08	.35	---											
16. Cause	1.79	.41	.12	-.01	.09	-.02	.11	.22	.27	-.05	-.26	-.02	.03	.26	-.09	.02	-.11	---										
17. Self-initiative	1.47	.50	.13	-.14	.08	-.01	.21	.17	.32	.11	-.12	-.13	-.11	.14	-.07	.10	.17	.37	---									

TABLE D.3 continued

	Means	Sds	1	2	3	4	5	6	7	8	9	10	11	12	13	14	15	16	17	18	19	20	21	22	23	24	25	26
Coping																												
18. Number of actions	1.89	.61	.13	.13	-.01	.22	-.04	-.04	-.19	-.10	.22	-.06	.18	-.10	.02	.06	-.09	-.38	-.46	---									
19. Proactive	1.47	.50	.00	-.08	.24	-.36	.02	.06	.33	.10	-.03	.05	.15	-.03	-.23	.27	.39	.02	.29	-.27	---								
20. Effects	1.32	.62	-.06	-.24	.22	-.38	.04	.07	.24	.15	.09	.11	-.07	.01	.02	.24	.50	.04	.15	-.26	.52	---							
21. Flexibility	1.40	.49	.06	-.22	-.05	-.26	-.09	-.07	.23	-.01	-.09	-.12	-.02	-.05	-.17	.03	-.02	.27	.09	-.04	.20	.04	---						
Career motivation																												
22. Resilience	2.52	.40	-.01	.18	-.17	.48	.00	-.10	-.43	-.17	.18	-.16	-.07	-.12	-.02	-.35	-.50	-.21	-.14	.05	.36	-.46	-.13	---					
23. Insight	2.51	.36	.32	-.02	-.22	.30	.18	.21	-.11	-.02	.18	-.17	-.03	-.09	-.11	-.06	-.09	-.04	.06	.09	-.10	-.25	.14	.34	---				
24. Identity	2.33	.39	-.09	-.01	-.10	.48	-.07	-.06	-.30	-.13	.25	-.18	.11	-.23	-.11	-.36	-.25	-.36	-.10	.27	-.23	-.37	-.07	.57	.21	---			
Support for . . .																												
25. Resilience	1.94	.52	.03	-.12	-.16	.33	.02	-.01	-.20	-.10	.14	-.35	.01	-.33	.05	-.26	-.26	-.15	.02	.15	-.16	-.28	.18	.45	.32	.61	---		
26. Insight	1.90	.49	-.17	.01	-.09	.33	-.08	-.05	-.26	.05	.03	-.22	-.03	-.24	-.11	-.13	-.03	-.23	-.19	.27	-.16	-.22	.12	.21	.20	.51	.65	---	
27. Identity	2.02	.47	.10	.06	-.21	.30	.11	.12	-.21	-.37	.26	-.18	.02	-.16	-.11	-.45	-.32	-.10	-.11	.13	-.25	-.26	.04	.43	.16	.53	.38	.30	

Note: n = 90; Codes: Occupation 1 = clerical and occupational, 2 = professional and managerial; Marital status 1 = not married, 2 = married; Job loss 1 = other career barrier, 2 = job loss; Career barrier resolved at time of interview 1 = resolved, 2 = not resolved; Warning 1 = happened suddenly, 2 = arose slowly; Explanation was clear 1 = yes, 2 = no; Realistic and accurate view of the situation 1 = yes, 2 = no; Cause 1 = self, 2 = factors beyond interviewee's control; Self-initiative 1 = could do something him- or herself to overcome the barrier, 2 = could not; Number of actions identified 1 = none, 2 = few, 3 = many; Proactive 1 = proactive, 2 = reactive; Effects 1 = constructive, 2 = dysfunctional, 3 = destructive; Flexibility 1 = change appraisal and coping strategy over time, 2 = appraisal and coping strategy remained about the same until the situation was resolved. Correlations: .22 and higher p < .05, .28 and higher p < .01, .35 and higher p < .001.

175

In general, a career barrier that arises slowly but is recognized suddenly may be just as shocking as one that is announced suddenly. Indeed, one man who knew that his office was relocating well in advance did not panic until it suddenly hit him that relocating was not feasible for his family. Nevertheless, the distinction between slowly emerging and suddenly announced career barriers applies to most of the cases. Job losses tended to happen more suddenly than other career barriers ($r = -.23$).

Also, having a clear explanation for why the situation arose may be a factor of the individual as much as the situation in that the reason may be clear but the individual may not see it. For convenience, I included clarity of explanation as a situational characteristic because it defined the nature of the situation for the interviewees. Situations that had not been resolved at the time of the interview tended to have unclear explanations for why they occurred ($r = .21$) because people were still in the midst of understanding them.

Career Barrier With Biographical Characteristics

The characteristics of career barriers tended not to be related to biographical characteristics of the sample with a few exceptions. People who had lost their jobs were less well educated ($r = -.46$). People who had lost their jobs or had a clear explanation for the barrier tended to have more children ($r = .23$ and $r = -.25$ respectively). These latter correlations are of a low magnitude and are descriptive of the sample, but not necessarily reflective of a general trend.

EMOTIONS

The interviewers asked about the interviewees' dominant emotion when the barrier first arose. The most frequently cited feeling was frustration (28%). Other common feelings were fear (16%), anger (21%), and resignation (12%). Eight percent felt sadness, and another 8% seemed to deny the problem. Seven percent reported some other response, such as panic or depression.

The most frequently mentioned emotions—fear, anger, and frustration—were studied further by creating three dummy variables (fear, coded yes or no; anger, coded yes or no; and frustration, coded yes or no).

Emotions With Biographical Characteristics

Fear, anger, and frustration were not significantly related to any of the biographical characteristics.

Emotions With Career Barrier Characteristics

People were more likely to be angry when they lost their jobs (compared to the other career barriers) or when the career barrier arose suddenly ($r = .28$ and $r = -.31$ respectively). People were more likely to be frustrated when faced with other career barriers or when the career barrier arose slowly ($r = -.28$ and $r = .27$ respectively). Fear did not vary by type of career barrier.

STRESS

The satisfaction item was coded inversely to form an index of dissatisfaction. This was correlated with the stress item ($r = .37$ based on a combination of interviewer and interviewee ratings). Interviewer and interviewee measures of stress were highly related $r = .71$). The interviewer and interviewee ratings were averaged to form a single stress index (*alpha* = .72).

Stress With Biographical Characteristics

Occupational employees (clerks, carpenters, etc.) experienced more stress than those in more responsible, professional positions ($r = .30$).

Stress With Type of Career Barrier

There was only one significant relationship between a career barrier characteristic and stress. People experiencing career barriers at the time of the interview were under more stress than those for whom the situation had been resolved ($r = .39$). Job loss was not more stressful than other career barriers ($r = .14$, n.s.).

Stress With Emotions

Stress was not significantly related to fear, anger, or frustration.

APPRAISAL

Chapter 1 described clarity as one of the dimensions of a career barrier. It refers to the individual's understanding of the barrier's causes and consequences. Chapter 2 reviewed how people integrate their cognitions and feelings to appraise the barrier. In this study, appraisal was assessed by three items on the case description form: Did the interviewee have a realistic and apparently accurate view of the situation (coded 1 = yes and 2 = no)? Did the interviewee attribute the primary cause to him-/ or herself (coded 1) or factors beyond his or her control (coded 2)? (This question applied only to those who had a clear explanation for why the situation occurred.) The interviewee believed that he or she could (coded 1) or could not (coded 2) do something him or herself to overcome the barrier or bring the situation under control.

Most of the people experiencing career barriers seemed to have a realistic and apparently accurate view of the situation (68%). Only one-fifth of the sample blamed themselves for the barrier; 80% blamed factors beyond their control. Not surprisingly, the more people blamed others for their situation, the more they felt that they could not do something themselves to overcome the barrier ($r = .37$).

Appraisal With Biographical Characteristics

The appraisal variables were not significantly related to any of the biographical characteristics.

Appraisal and Career Barrier Characteristics

Other reactions were different for people who lost their jobs compared to those who experienced other career barriers. People who lost their jobs were less likely to have a realistic view of the situation, more likely to blame external factors (not themselves), and more likely to believe there was nothing they could do themselves to overcome the barrier or resolve the situation ($r = .34$, $r = .27$, and $r = .32$ respectively).

Not surprisingly, people who had not resolved the situation at the time of the interview were less realistic about the situation ($r = .25$). When the barrier arose slowly, individuals were more likely to see themselves as a primary cause ($r = -.26$). Those who had an unclear explanation for the barrier also had an unrealistic view of their situation as judged by the interviewer ($r = .30$).

Appraisal With Emotions

The relationships between the appraisal and emotion variables were not significant.

Appraisal With Stress

People who had an unrealistic view of the situation had higher stress ($r = .35$)

COPING

Four variables from the case description form measured coping: The interviewee had identified no (coded 1), a few (2), or many (3) actions he or she could take to overcome the barrier or resolve the situation. The interviewee's coping strategy was proactive (coded 1) or reactive (coded 2). Effects of the coping strategy were constructive (coded 1), dysfunctional (2), or destructive (3). Finally, the interviewee's appraisal and coping strategies changed over time as the interviewee developed a more realistic or accurate appraisal of the situation (coded 1) or remained about the same until the situation was resolved (coded 2).

Although more interviewees had a realistic view of the career barrier and an accurate understanding of the reasons why it occurred (see earlier), they were not as certain about what to do. Less than half (46%) believed they could do something themselves to overcome the barrier or bring the situation under control. Forty-one percent believed they could not do something themselves, and 13% were unsure. One fourth of the interviewees had identified no actions they could take to overcome the barrier or resolve the situation. As stated earlier, 74% of the situations had been resolved by the time of the interview. Therefore, those who were in the midst of coping with the clear barrier did not have a clue about what to do. Of those who had identified some actions they could take, 61% felt that there were a few things they could do, and only 14% felt that there were many things they could do, including eliciting the help of others. About one-half the sample took a proactive stance (52%), whereas the other half were reactive—that is, waited for things to happen to resolve the situation (48%, as judged by the interviewer). Most coping strategies (76%) seemed to be constructive. Sixteen percent were categorized by the interviewer as dysfunctional, and 8% as destructive. Sixty percent indicated that their appraisal of the situation and coping strategies changed over time as they developed a more realistic or accurate appraisal of the situation. The rest indicated that their appraisal and coping strategies did not change over time.

The more actions identified, the more proactive and constructive the coping ($r = -.26$ and $r = -.27$ respectively). Proactive coping tended to be also viewed as constructive ($r = .52$).

Coping With Biographical Characteristics

Women were more likely to use constructive coping strategies and change their strategies as the situation evolved ($r = -.24$ and $r = -.22$). Clerical and occupational employees were more likely to use reactive strategies ($r = -.24$) that are destructive or dysfunctional ($r = .22$) compared to professional and managerial employees. More educated individuals were more likely to use proactive and constructive coping strategies ($r = -.36$ and $r = -.38$ respectively) and change their strategies over time ($r = -.26$).

Coping With Career Barrier Characteristics

People who had lost their jobs were more likely to be reactive ($r = .33$), engage in dysfunctional strategies ($r = .24$), and not adjust their coping strategy over time ($r = .23$). When the barrier arose slowly, people had identified more actions for overcoming the barrier ($r = .22$).

Coping With Emotions

Those who used a more proactive strategy were more frustrated ($r = -.23$) perhaps because they anticipated that more things would happen as a result of their initiatives.

Coping With Stress

Stress was higher for people who adopted more reactive and dysfunctional coping strategies ($r = .27$ and $r = .24$ respectively).

Coping With Appraisal

Having a realistic view of the situation was positively related to coping proactively and constructively ($r = .39$ and $r = .50$ respectively). People who blamed factors beyond their control identified fewer actions to resolve the situation ($r = -.38$). People who blamed factors beyond their control were more likely to maintain the same coping strategy over time ($r = .27$) handicapping themselves further. Not surprisingly, people who took more actions felt they could do something themselves to overcome the barrier ($r = -.46$), while people who were reactive felt they could do very little ($r = .29$).

CAREER MOTIVATION AND SUPPORT
FOR CAREER MOTIVATION

The postinterview measures of career motivation scales (the career resilience, insight, and identity scales), support for career motivation, current stress, and current satisfaction were completed by the interviewee and independently by the interviewer. The correlations between the interviewee and interviewer ratings ranged between .37 and .71, so the scales were calculated by averaging items from the interviewer and interviewee ratings. The reliabilities (alphas) for the resulting career motivation, support for career motivation, and stress measures were all sufficiently high (greater than .72).

The measures of the components of career motivation were moderately intercorrelated. People who were high on resilience (i.e., the ability to overcome career barriers) were also high on identity (e.g., commitment to the employing organization; $r = .57$) and, to a lesser degree, insight (e.g., self-knowledge, knowledge of the job; $r = .34$). Insight and identity were not significantly related ($r = .21$). Support for resilience (e.g., receiving rewards for doing a good job) was positively related to support for insight (e.g., the availability of performance feedback; $r = .65$) and support for identity (e.g., likely future value of remaining with the employer; $r = .38$). Support for identity was also higher when there was support for identity ($r = .30$).

Each support variable tended to be important to all the career motivation measures, suggesting that overall, support in the work environment is important to career motivation. Support for resilience was positively related to resilience ($r = .45$), insight ($r = .32$), and identity ($r = .61$). Support for insight was not significantly related to resilience ($r = .21$) or identity ($r = .20$), but was positively related to identity ($r = .51$) indicating that having information about oneself and the organization contributes to feelings of commitment. When support for identity was high, so were resilience and identity ($r = .43$ and $r = .53$, respectively).

Because these measures were collected at one point in time, the results do not provide an indication of causality. Different relationships may emerge between the support and motivation variables over time. A longitudinal study (i.e., following the same people over time) would be necessary to determine the effects of each support variable on each element of career motivation. This would determine, for instance, whether support for resilience increases resilience and not insight and identity.

Career Motivation and Support With Biographical Characteristics

People who were older were higher on insight ($r = .32$). Finding that older people are wiser about themselves and the environment is not surprising. The only other significant relationships between biographical characteristics and career motivation and support for career motivation involved education, which was positively related to all the career motivation and support variables. People who were more educated were higher on resilience, insight, and identity ($r = .48$, $r = .30$, and $r = .48$ respectively). Also, people who were more educated received higher support for resilience, insight, and identity ($r = .33$, $r = .33$, $r = .30$ respectively). (Career motivation and support for career motivation may be the reason why educated people were able to cope with career barriers constructively; $r = -.38$, between education and coping constructively—a lower rating means more constructive coping).

Career Motivation and Support With Career Barrier Characteristics

Job loss seemed to have a more severe effect on career motivation and perceived support for career motivation than the other career barriers. Specifically, those who lost their jobs, compared to another career barrier, were lower in resilience and identity ($r = -.43$ and $r = -.30$ respectively). Job loss was not related to stress ($r = .14$, n.s.). Thus, to speculate, job loss may affect resilience and identity, which in turn may affect stress. Neither job loss nor insight were related to stress, indicating that awareness of oneself and the environment does not seem to vary by career barrier or have a differential effect on stress. The support variables were not highly related to type of career barrier except, interestingly, for support for insight ($r = -.26$). Job loss may lead to having less information (or, stated another way, more ambiguity), but having less information does not matter for resilience, identity, or stress.

Again to speculate, these correlations suggest that information alone will not help make people feel better about themselves or able to overcome the career barrier, especially when it comes to job loss. Job loss, more than the other career barriers, is likely to depress resilience and identity regardless of the support for these elements of career motivation. Although job loss is likely to mean little environmental support for resilience and identity (but not significantly so, perhaps because people find support from sources outside the job), the high relationships between support and career motivation variables reported earlier in this chapter suggest that extra support may be needed to bolster resilience and identity for people who lose their jobs.

There was less support for identity for when the situation had not been resolved at the time of the interview ($r = -.37$). Thus, not surprisingly, people who were actually in the midst of dealing with a career barrier when they were interviewed had less hope for the future. Other than that, career motivation and support were not related to whether or not the career barrier had been resolved at the time of the interview.

How fast the career barrier arose was not related to feelings of resilience and insight or support for these elements of career motivation. However, when the career barrier happened slowly, identity and support for identity were higher than when the career barrier happened suddenly with little or no warning ($r = .25$ and $r = .26$ respectively). Thus, barriers that happen suddenly seem to have a stronger (more framebreaking) effect on the individual's sense of commitment to job, career, and profession.

Having a clear explanation for the career barrier was related only to support for resilience. People who had a clear explanation for the barrier had higher support for resilience ($r = -.35$). Thus, people who felt they understood the reason for the career barrier also felt they had more control over the situation. Being sure people affected by a career barrier know why it happened to them is likely to be important to their feeling that they can overcome the barrier.

Career Motivation and Support With Emotions

Regarding emotional reactions, feelings of fear and frustration were not significantly related to the motivation or support variables. However, anger was higher when identity was lower ($r = -.23$) and support for resilience insight were lower ($r = -.33$ and $r = -.24$ respectively). This suggests that people felt more angry when their identity was lower and when there was less environmental support, especially for insight and resilience.

Career Motivation and Support With Stress

The career motivation and support variables were low when stress was high. Specifically, stress was negatively related to resilience and identity ($r = -35$

and $r = -.36$ respectively) but not to insight ($r = -.06$, n.s.). Also, stress was negatively related to support for resilience and support for identity ($r = -.26$ and $r = -.45$ respectively) but not to support for insight ($r = -.13$, n.s.). Thus, insight and support for insight did not seem to be important to feelings of stress, whereas resilience and identity (and support for these elements of career motivation) were. Insight may have affected motivation indirectly through resilience, identity, or both. These results suggest that people who have strong commitment to the job, career, or profession and believe in themselves are likely to feel less stress when they encounter a career barrier than those who have weak commitment and weak self-confidence. Giving people information to help them understand themselves and the situation is not likely to lessen feelings of stress.

A regression analysis predicting stress based on the career motivation and support variables provides some further insight to this process. The overall R was .51 ($R^2 = .22$, p < .01). However, only support for identity contributed significant unique variance to stress. (The b weights were not significant for the other variables.) This indicates that giving a person a reason to be optimistic about the future is particularly important to reduce stress in facing a career barrier.

Career Motivation and Support With Appraisal

Having a realistic and apparently accurate view of the situation was important to career motivation and support variables, particularly those involving resilience and identity. People seemed to be more realistic when they were high on resilience ($r = -.50$) and there was support for resilience ($r = -.26$). Also, people seemed to be more realistic when they were high on identity ($r = -.25$) and there was support for identity ($r = -.32$). This may have been because a large portion of the sample had experienced job loss, which had negative relationships with resilience and insight, and people who had lost their jobs were less realistic ($r = .34$).

People who were low in career identity were likely to blame the career barrier on factors beyond their control ($r = -.36$). Maintaining one's sense of identity is likely to result in a greater understanding of how one contributed to the barrier. As reported earlier, barriers that happen slowly are likely to be attributed to internal causes. Also, recall that barriers that happen quickly are related to lower feelings of identity. As a consequence, the suddenness of career barrier may prompt people to blame others as their sense of identity is weakened. This is all the more reason for avoiding sudden announcements of bad news.

Career Motivation and Support With Coping

People who maintained their sense of identity felt they had more options open to them ($r = .27$). Also, support for career insight (i.e., having information about one's performance and the organization as well as support for career planning) was positively related to feeling that there were more options available ($r = .27$).

People who were higher in resilience and identity were more proactive in their coping strategies ($r = -.36$ and $r = -.23$ respectively). Therefore, resilience and identity were important to maintain. This is reinforced by the finding that constructive coping was significantly related to all the career motivation and support variables. People were more constructive who were higher in resilience, insight, and identity ($r = -.46, r = -.25, r = -.37$ respectively). Also, people were more constructive when there was higher support for resilience, insight, and identity ($r = -.28, r = -.22, r = -.26$ respectively). Thus, having strong support from the work environment and strong career motivation were important to responding to a career barrier constructively. Also, as suggested from the findings regarding education reported earlier, people with higher education were more likely to have the motivation and support to respond constructively. Unfortunately, the people in this sample who had lost their jobs were less well educated ($r = -.46$), so coping was most difficult for them.

Changing coping strategies over time in response to the career barrier was not significantly related to career motivation or support for career motivation.

SUMMARY

Here is a review of the key findings. Job loss was different in a number of respects from the other career barriers. In particular:

- Job loss tended to happen more suddenly than other career barriers. Job loss and suddenly occurring barriers generated anger, whereas other types of barriers and slowly emerging barriers generated frustration. People who lost their jobs were less likely to have a realistic view of the situation, were more likely to blame external factors (not themselves), and were more likely to believe there was nothing they could do themselves to overcome the barrier. People who lost their jobs were more likely to adopt a reactive, dysfunctional strategy and were unlikely to adjust their strategy over time.
- Job loss seemed to have a more severe effect on career motivation and perceived support for career motivation than the other career barriers.

Specifically, those who lost their jobs, compared to another career barriers, were lower in resilience and identity.

Other characteristics of career barriers may influence appraisal and coping. Specifically:

- When the barrier arose slowly, individuals were more likely to see themselves as the primary cause. Also, when the barrier arose slowly people had identified more actions for overcoming the barrier.
- People who felt they understood the reason for the career barrier also felt they had more control over the situation. This highlights the importance of having a clear explanation for a career barrier.

Biographical characteristics affected appraisal and coping:

- More educated individuals were more likely to use proactive and constructive coping strategies.
- Women were more likely to use constructive coping strategies and change their strategies as the situation evolved.
- Career barriers were more stressful for clerical and occupational employees than professionals or managers. Clerical and occupational employees were more likely to use reactive strategies that were destructive or dysfunctional compared to professional and managerial employees.

How people appraised the career barrier was related to their coping strategies:

- The more people blamed themselves for their situation, the more they felt that they could do something themselves to overcome the barrier. People who blamed factors beyond their control identified fewer actions to resolve the situation and were more likely to maintain the same coping strategy over time possibly making the situation worse.
- Stress was higher for people who adopted more reactive and dysfunctional coping strategies ($r = .27$ and $r = .24$ respectively).
- Having a realistic view of the situation was positively related to coping proactively and constructively.

Finally, career motivation and support for career motivation were related to appraisal and coping:

- People who were high in resilience and identity (and have support for resilience and identity) were likely to be less stressed by the career barrier, have a more realistic view of the situation, and be more proactive than those low in resilience and identity. People who were low in career identity were likely to blame the career barrier on factors beyond their control. People who maintained their sense of identity felt they had more options open to them.

- Support for career insight was positively related to feeling that there were more options available.
- People who were high in resilience, insight, and identity and support for these elements of career motivation were likely to cope constructively.

TOWARD A MODEL OF REACTIONS TO CAREER BARRIERS

As an initial test of a model of reactions to career barriers, I aggregated several of the variables to reduce the data set to nine indexes:

1. *Experience:* This was a combination of age, education, and professional/managerial jobs. Occupation was recoded into two levels: 2 = professional and managerial jobs and 1 = nonprofessional (clerical and occupational) jobs. Age, education, and the new occupational variable were standardized and averaged to form the experience index.

2. *Strength of barrier:* The barrier characteristics (the recoded job loss variable, barrier not resolved at time of interview, barrier arose suddenly, and unclear explanation) were averaged. Job loss (i.e., job loss versus other career barriers) was included because job loss seemed to be a stronger, more traumatic career barrier from relationships reported earlier. Strength of career barrier, therefore, incorporates elements of costs (range of effects as well as financial costs) and certainty or irreversability—characteristics of career barriers described in chapter 1.

3. *Motivation:* The measures of resilience, insight, and identity were averaged.

4. *Support for career motivation:* The three support variables were averaged.

5/ 6. *Emotions:* Anger and frustration were included here because the earlier analyses showed that these were more important to the appraisal variables than fear. Because only one emotion could be recorded as dominant, if an interviewee was viewed as angry then the interviewee would not be viewed as frustrated, and vice versa. (That is, these are dummy variables.) As a result, they cannot be averaged and need to be examine separately.

7. *Stress:* This was the same index reported earlier.

8. *Appraisal:* This was the average of have a realistic viewpoint, self-attribution as the cause of the barrier, and believing that self-initiative is possible (there is something the interviewee can do him- or herself to deal with the barrier). Blaming oneself does not necessarily mean that the appraisal is realistic. However, coupling realism with self-attribution and believing that self-initiative can pay off should be associated with constructive coping strategies. Note that because of the way the variables were coded, the lower this appraisal index, the more positive the appraisal (realistic, recognition of self-involvement, and opportunities for self-initiative).

9. *Coping*: Number of actions identified was recoded as a two-level variable combining "a few" and "many" and inverting it so that having some actions in mind was coded 1 and having no actions was coded 2 (to be consistent with the other variables in this index). Effects was also made a 2-level variable (1 = constructive, 2 = not constructive combining dysfunctional and destructive). These were averaged with being proactive and changing strategies as the situation evolved. Thus the lower this coping index, the more positive the coping.

The means, standard deviations, and intercorrelations for these nine indexes are presented in Table D. 4. The more experienced individuals were less likely to suffer strong barriers (in terms of job loss or suddenly appearing barrier), were higher in motivation and support for motivation, and were lower in stress ($r = -.32, r = .48, r = .39$, and $r = -.27$ respectively). More experienced individuals also coped more positively ($r = -.36$). The stronger the barrier, the less the support for motivation and the more the anger and stress ($r = -.38, r = .27$, and $r = .33$ respectively). Also, the stronger the barrier the more negative the appraisal and coping ($r = .46$ and $r = .28$ respectively). Career motivation and support for motivation were highly related ($r = .62$). People who were higher on motivation were lower in stress and more positive in appraisal and coping ($r = -.34, r = -.33$, and $r = -.37$ respectively). People who were higher in support for career motivation were less likely to be angry ($r = -.36$) and feel stress ($r = -.30$). Also, support for motivation was related to having a positive appraisal ($r = -.29$). People

TABLE D.4
Means. Standard Deviations, and Intercorrelations for the
Reduced Set of Variables

	Means	Sds	1	2	3	4	5	6	7	8
1. Experience	.00	.60	----							
2. Barrier strength	1.29	.26	-.33	----						
3. Career motivation	2.45	.30	.48	-.42	----					
4. Support for career motivation	1.95	.39	.29	-.38	.62	----				
5. Anger	1.20	.41	-.10	.27	-.20	-.34	----			
6. Frustration	1.28	.45	-.02	-.17	-.10	-.05	-.32	----		
7. Stress	2.07	.57	-.27	.34	-.34	-.30	.06	.03	----	
8. Appraisal	1.49	.29	-.11	.46	-.33	-.29	.30	-.17	.20	----
9. Coping	1.34	.31	-.36	.28	-.37	-.16	.01	-.17	.17	.51

Note: $r = .22$ or higher $p < .05$, $r = .28$ or higher $p < .01$, $r = .35$ or higher $p < .001$.

whose dominant emotion was anger were more negative in their appraisal ($r = .30$). Frustration and stress were not significantly related to appraisal or coping. Appraisal and coping were positively related ($r = .51$).

Some Caveats. Because these measures were all collected at the same point in time, the relationships do not prove causality. A significant relationship between any two variables may be due to a causal link one way or the other or to the influence of one or more other variables. Because several groups of variables stem from the same method, response biases could influence the correlations. (Recall that the career motivation, support for career motivation, and stress indexes were derived from the interviewer and interviewee questionnaire, and the other measures were derived from the interviewers' completing the case description form.) Research is needed to test this model on larger samples with data collected over time.

Modeling the Relationships. Given these caveats and the modest size of the data set, sophisticated causal path analyses would not be appropriate. Nevertheless, the correlational results and some simple regression analyses can be used to develop several proposed models for future research on variables that predict coping. Figure D.1 depicts three models predicting coping, appraisal, and stress separately based on the correlations. Stress seemed to be an independent reaction, at least one that was not related to coping or appraisal. Feeling stress may not enhance or diminish an accurate and realistic appraisal and constructive coping, although it may affect other aspects of one's life not investigated here, such as health and family relationships. For each criterion (coping, appraisal, and stress), I ran a regression analysis to determine the joint effects of the set of predictors in each model and identify which variables make a unique contribution to each criterion. The models and results of the regression analysis are described in the following:

The model predicting coping proposes that the dominant factor in constructive coping is a realistic and accurate appraisal. Career motivation and experience increase the likelihood of constructive coping. Stronger career barriers are more likely to engender dysfunctional coping. The regression analysis predicting coping was significant ($R^2 = .34$, $p < .01$), however, only appraisal resulted in significant unique variance (accounting for 28% of the variance in coping). Research is needed to explore the effects of career motivation, experience, and the nature of the career barrier in determining coping strategy. Research compares the supportive effects of career motivation on coping for people facing different career barriers.

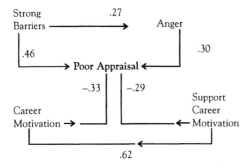

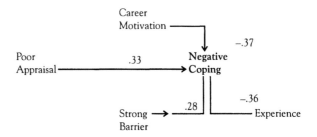

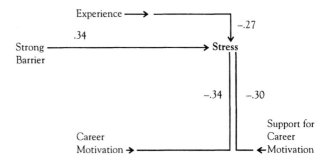

Fig. D.1. Models predicting appraisal, coping, and stress with bivirate correlations.

The model predicting appraisal suggests that appraisal is likely to be more accurate and realistic when career motivation and support career motivation are high. Strong career barriers generate anger and less accurate appraisal, and anger may further reduce appraisal accuracy. The regression analysis predicting appraisal was significant ($R^2 = .32$, $p < .01$ with only the strength of the barrier contributing significant unique variance to appraisal.

The model predicting stress argues that stronger barriers generate more stress. However, more experienced people and those with higher career motivation and support for career motivation feel less stress. The significant regression equation ($R^2 = .27, p < .01$) revealed two variables that contributed significant unique variance to stress: the strength of the barrier and support for career motivation. This suggests that the stressful effects of tough career barriers may be lessened by a work environment which supports career motivation (e.g., provides information about career opportunities, reason to have some optimism about the future, and authority to make decisions).

A bare-bones model based on the variables that contribute significant unique variance (that is, variance apart from the other variables) is shown in Fig. D.2. This does not mean that the other variables are not important to stress, appraisal, and coping, and future research is needed to determine how they contribute. However, the model suggests at least that the strength of the career barrier affects appraisal, which in turn influences coping. Strong career barriers produce stress that can be lowered by support for career motivation.

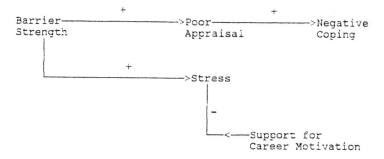

Fig. D.2. Bare-bones model based on variables that make a unique contribution to stress, appraisal, and coping.

References

Abramson, L. Y., Seligman, M. E., & Teasdale, J. D. (1978). Learned helplessness in humans: Critique and reformulation. *Journal of Abnormal Psychology, 87*, 49–74.

Allred, B. B., Snow, C. C., & Miles, R. E. (1996). Characteristics of managerial careers in the 21st century. *Academy of Management Executive, 10*(4), 17–27.

Archer, J., & Rhodes, V. (1993). The grief process and job loss: A cross-sectional study. *British Journal of Psychology, 84*, 395–410.

Armstrong-Stassen, M. (1994). Coping with transition: A study of layoff survivors. *Journal of Organizational Behavior, 15*, 597–621.

Ashford, S. J. (1989). Self-assessments in organizations: A literature review and integrative model. *Research in Organizational Behavior, 11*, 133–174.

Ashford, S. J., & Cummings, L. L. (1983). Feedback as an individual resource: Personal strategies of creating information. *Organizational Behavior and Human Performance, 32*, 370–398.

Azrin, N., Besalel, V., Wisotek, I., McMurrow, M., & Bechtel, R. (1982). Behavioral supervision versus informational counseling of job seeking in the Job Club. *Rehabilitation Counseling Bulletin, 25*, 212–218.

Baillie, P. H., & Danish, S. J. (1992). Understanding the career transition of athletes. *Sport Psychologist, 6*(1), 77–98.

Bandura, A. (1986). *Social foundations of thought and action: A social cognitive theory.* Englewood Cliffs, NJ: Prentice-Hall.

Baumeister, R. F., & Scher, S. J. (1988). An ecological perspective on integrating personality and social psychology. *Journal of Personality and Social Psychology, 53*, 1222–1228.

Beach, L. R., & Mitchell, T. R. (1990). Image theory: A behavioral theory of decision making in organizations. In B. Staw & L. L. Cummings (Ed.), *Research in organizational behavior* (vol. 12, pp. 1–41), Greenwich, CT: JAI.

Beiser, M., Johnson, P., & Turner, R. J. (1993). Unemployment, underemployment and depressive affect among Southeast Asian refugees. *Psychological Medicine, 23*, 731–743.

Bennett, G. J., Jr. (1995, June 12), Employment assistance. *C&EN: Newsletter of the American Chemical Society. 29*, 50–51.

Berger, S. M. (1977). Social comparison, modeling, and perseverance. In J. M. Suls & R. L. Miller (Eds.), *Social comparison processes: Theoretical and empirical perspectives* (pp. 209–234). Washington, DC: Hemisphere.

Bernard, M. E., & DiGiuseppe, R. (1994). Rational-emotive consultation: The missing link to successful consultation. In M. E. Bernard & R. DiGiuseppe (Eds.), *Rational-emotive consultation in applied settings* (pp. 1–31). Hillsdale, NJ: Lawrence Erlbaum Associates.

Bird, B. J. (1989). *Entrepreneurial behavior.* Glenview, IL: Scott, Foresman.

Black, D. R., & Loughead, R. A. (1990). Job change in perspective. *Journal of Career Development, 17*, 3–9.

Blau, G. J. (1985). The measurement and prediction of career commitment. *Journal of Occupational Psychology, 58*, 277–288.

Blau, G. J. (1988). Further exploring the meaning and measurement of career commitment. *Journal of Vocational Behavior, 32*, 284–297.

Blau, G. J. (1989). Testing the generalizability of a career commitment measure and its impact on employee turnover. *Journal of Vocational Behavior, 35,* 88–103.

Blau, G. J., Paul, A. A., & St. John, N. (1993). On developing a general index of work commitment. *Journal of Vocational Behavior, 42,* 298–314.

Blix, A. G., Cruise, R. J., Mitchell, B. M., & Blix, G. G. (1994). Occupational stress among university teachers. *Educational Research, 36*(2), 157–169.

Brewer, M. B., & Weber, J. G. (1994). Self-evaluation effects of interpersonal versus intergroup social comparison. *Journal of Personality and Social Psychology, 66,* 268–275.

Brockner, J., Konovsky, M., Cooper-Schneider, R., & Folger, R. (1994). Interactive effects of procedural justice and outcome negativity on victims and survivors of job loss. *Academy of Management Journal, 37,* 397–409.

Brown, D. (1995). A values-based approach to facilitating career transitions. *Career Development Quarterly, 44,* 4–11.

Browne, M. W. (1995, July 4). Supply exceeds demand for Ph.D.'s in many science fields. *The New York Times,* p. 16.

Burke, M. J., Brief, A. P., George, J. M., Roberson, L., & Webster, J. (1989). Measuring affect at work: Confirmatory analyses of competing mood structure with conceptual linkage to cortical regulatory systems. *Journal of Personality and Social Psychology, 57,* 1091–1102.

Campion, M. A., Cheraskin, L., & Stevens, M. J. (1994). Career–related antecedents and outcomes of job rotation. *Academy of Management Journal, 37*(6), 1518–1542.

Caplan, R., Vinokur, A., Price, R., & van Ryan, M. (1989). Job seeking, re-employment, and mental health: A randomized field experiment in coping with job loss. *Journal of Applied Psychology, 74,* 759–769.

Carver, C. S., & Scheier, M. F. (1981). *Attention and self-regulation: A control-theory approach to human behavior.* New York: Springer.

Carver, C. S., & Scheier, M. F. (1982). Control theory: A useful conceptual framework for personality-social, clinical, and health psychology. *Psychological Bulletin, 92,* 111–135.

Carver, C. S., & Scheier, M. F. (1990). Origins and functions of positive and negative affect: A control-process view. *Psychological Review, 97,* 19–35

Catalano, R., Dooley, D., Wilson, G., & Hough, R. (1993). Job loss and alcohol abuse: A test using data from the Epidemiologic Catchment Area. *Journal of Health & Social Behavior, 34,* 215–225.

Cohler, B. J. (1991). The life story and the study of resilience and response to adversity. *Journal of Narrative & Life History, 1*(2–3), 169–200.

Compton, W. C., Seeman, J., & Norris, R. C. (1991). Predicting hardiness: A search for the parameters of deep cognitive structures. *Medical Psychotherapy: An International Journal, 4,* 121–129.

Conlon, D. W., & Ross, W. H. (1993). The effects of partisan third parties on negotiator behavior and outcome perceptions. *Journal of Applied Psychology, 78,* 280–290.

Crites, J. O. (1978). *Career maturity inventory: Theory and research handbook.* (2nd ed.). New York: McGraw-Hill.

Davis, J., & Rodela, E. S. (1990). Mid-career transition. *Prevention in Human Services, 8*(1), 205–218.

Dawis, R. V., & Lofquist, L. H. (1984). *A psychological theory of work adjustment.* Minneapolis: University of Minnesota Press.

Dion, K. L., Dion, K. K., & Pak, A. W. (1992). Personality-based hardiness as a buffer for discrimination-related stress in members of Toronto's Chinese community. *Canadian Journal of Behavioural Science, 24,* 417–536.

Dubin, S. S. (1990). Maintaining competence through updating. In S. L. Willis & S. S. Dubin (Eds.), *Maintaining professional competence* (pp. 9–43). San Francisco: Jossey-Bass.

D'Zurilla, T. J. (1986). *Problem-solving therapy: A social competence approach to clinical intervention.* New York: Springer.

Eby, L. T., & Buch, K. (1994). The effect of job search method, sex, activity level, and emotional acceptance on new job characteristics: Implications for counseling unemployed professionals. *Journal of Employment Counseling, 31*(2), 69–72.

Eby, L. T., & Buch, K. (1995). Job loss as career growth: Responses to involuntary career transitions. *Career Development Quarterly, 44,* 26–42.

Egeland, B., Carlson, E., & Stroufe, L. A. (1993). Resilience as process. *Development & Psychopathology, 5,* 517–528.

Ekman, P. (1992). An argument for basic emotions. *Cognition and Emotion, 6,* 169–200.

Ellis, A., & Harper, R. A. (1975). *A new guide for rational living.* North Hollywood, CA: Wilshire.

Epstein, S. (1980). The self-concept: A review and proposal of an integrated theory of personality. In E. Staub (Ed.), *Personality: Basic issues and current research* (pp. 82–132). Englewood Cliffs, NJ: Prentice Hall.

Evan, D. R., Pellizzari, J. R., Culbert, B. J., & Metzen, M. (1993). Personality, marital, and occupational factors associated with quality of life. *Journal of Clinical Psychology, 49,* 477–495.

Fedor, D. B., Rensvold, R. B., Adams, S. M. (1992). An investigation of factors expected to affect feedback seeking: A longitudinal field study. *Personnel Psychology, 45,* 779–805.

Feij, J. A., Whitely, W. T., Peiro, J. M., & Taris, T. W. (1995). The development of career-enhancing strategies and content innovation: A longitudinal study of new workers. *Journal of Vocational Behavior, 46,* 231–256.

Feldman, D. C., & Bolino, M. C. (1996). Careers within careers: Reconceptualizing the nature of career anchors and their consequences. *Human Resource Management Review, 6*(2), 89–112.

Festinger, L. (1954). A theory of social comparison processes. *Human Relations, 7,* 117–140.

Fine, S. B. (1991). Resilience and human adaptability: Who rises above adversity? *American Journal of Occupational Therapy, 45,* 493–503.

Fiske, D. W., & Taylor, S. E. (1991). *Social cognition* (2nd ed.). New York: McGraw-Hill.

Florian, V., Mikulincer, M., & Taubman, O. (1995). Does hardiness contribute to mental health during a stressful real-life situation? The roles of appraisal and coping. *Journal of Personality and Social Psychology, 68,* 687–695.

Folkman, S., & Lazarus, R. S. (1988). *The manual for the ways of coping questionnaire* (research ed.). Palo Alto, CA: Consulting Psychologists Press.

Forgas, J. P. (1994). The role of emotion in social judgments: An introductory review and an affect infusion model (AIM). *European Journal of Social Psychology, 24,* 1–24.

Forgas, J. P., Bower, G. H., & Moylan, S. J. (1990). Praise or blame? Affective influences on attributions for achievement. *Journal of Personality and Social Psychology, 59,* 809–819.

Frijda, N. H. (1988). The laws of emotion. *American Psychologist, 43,* 349–358.

Fry, B. J. (1991). Working with uncooperative spouses. *Journal of Career Development, 17,* 265–270.

George, J. M., & Brief, A. P. (1995). *Motivational agendas in the workplace: The effects of feelings on focus of attention and work motivation.* Tulane Working Papers Series, A. B. Feeman School of Business, Tulane University, New Orleans.

Gibbons, F. X., & Gerrard, M. (1991). Downward comparison and coping with threat. In J. Suls & T. A. Wills (Eds.), *Social comparison: Contemporary theory and research* (pp. 317–345). Hillsdale, NJ: Lawrence Erlbaum Associates.

Goethals, G., & Darley, J. (1977). Social comparison theory: An attributional approach. In J. M. Suls & R. L. Miller (Eds.), *Social comparison processes: Theoretical and empirical perspectives* (pp. 259–278). Washington, DC: Hemisphere.

Gosse, V. F., Sullivan, A. M., Ross, A. S., & Simmonds, A. J. (1992). Evaluation of the goal oriented adult learning (GOAL) program. *Psychosocial Rehabilitation Journal, 15*(4), 97–100.

Gregory, R. J. (1995). Rubbish man—alleviating the personal impact of economic misfortune: An opportunity to expand the role of rehabilitation counseling. *Journal of Applied Rehabilitation Counseling, 26*(2), 54–59.

Gussow, M. (1996, March 23). In a writer's physical loss, the miracle of creativity. *The New York Times*, p. 13.

Hall, D. T. (1976). *Careers in organizations*. Santa Monica, CA: Goodyear.

Hall, D. T. (1987). Career development in organizations: Where do we go from here? In D. T. Hall (Ed.), *Career development in organizations* (pp. 332–352). San Francisco: Jossey-Bass.

Hall, D. T. (1996a). Protean careers of the 21st century. *Academy of Management Executive, 10*(4), 8–16.

Hall, D. T. (1996b). *The career is dead—long live the career: A relational approach*. San Francisco: Jossey-Bass.

Heatherton, T. F., Polivy, J., Herman, C. P., & Baumeister, R. F. (1993). Self-awareness, task failure, and disinhibition: How attentional focus affects eating. *Journal of Personality, 61*, 49–59.

Heilbronn, F. S. (1992). The use of Hatha Yoga as a strategy for coping with stress in management development. *Management Education & Development, 23*(2), 131–139.

Heppner, M. J., Multon, K. D., & Johnston, J. P. (1994). Assessing psychological resources during career change: Development of the career transitions inventory. *Journal of Vocational Behavior, 44*(1), 55–74.

Herriot, P., Gibson, G., Pemberton, C., & Pinder, R. (1993). *Journal of Occupational & Organizational Psychology, 66*, 115–123.

Hill, T., Lewicki, P., Czyzewska, M., & Boss, A. (1989). Self-perpetuating development of encoding biases in person perception. *Journal of Personality and Social Psychology, 57*, 373–387.

Holland, J. L. (1985). *Making vocational choices*. Englewood Cliffs, NJ: Prentice-Hall.

Holmes, B. H., & Werbel, J. D. (1992). Finding work following job loss: The role of coping resources. *Journal of Employment Counseling, 29*(1), 22–29.

Howard, A., & Bray. D. W. (1981). Today's young managers: They can do it, but will they? *The Wharton Magazine, 5*(4), 23–28.

Howard, A., & Bray, D. W. (1988). *Managerial lives in transition: Advancing age and changing times*. New York: Guilford.

Hutchings, J., & Gower, K. (1993). Unemployment and mental health. *Journal of Mental Health, 2*, 355–358.

Ilgen, E. R., & Pulakos, E. D. (Eds.). (in press). *The changing nature of work performance: Implications for staffing, personnel actions, and development*. San Francisco: Jossey-Bass.

Imbimbo, P. V. (1994). Integrating personal and career counseling: A challenge for counselors. *Journal of Employment Counseling, 31*(2), 50–59.

Inkson, K. (1995). Effects of changing economic conditions on managerial job changes and careers. *British Journal of Management, 6*(3), 183–194.

Jerusalem, M. (1990). Temporal patterns of stress appraisals for high- and low-anxious individuals. *Anxiety Research, 3*, 113–129.

Johnson-Laird, P. N., & Oatley, K. (1989). The language of emotions: An analysis of a semantic field. *Cognition and Emotion, 3*, 81–123.

Jones, D. (1996, February 19). Life after a plant closing. *USA Today*, p. 3B.

Jones, J. (1991–1992). Specifying the temporal relationships between job loss and consequences: Implications for service delivery. *Journal of Applied Social Sciences, 16*(1), 37–62.

Jones, P. S. (1991). Adaptability: A personal resource for health. *Scholarly Inquiry for Nursing Practice*, 5 (2), 95–108.

Kanfer, R. (1990). Motivation theory and industrial/organizational psychology. In M. D. Dunnette & L. M. Hough (Eds.), *Handbook of industrial and organizational psychology*, 2nd ed., vol. 1 (pp. 75–170. Palo Alto, CA: Consulting Psychologists Press.

Kaplan, B. (1991). Animadversions on adversity, ruminations on resilience: A quasi-commentary on Bertram J. Cohler's article, "The life story and the study of resilience and response to adversity." *Journal of Narrative & Life History*, 1 (2–3), 201–211.

Karl, K. A., & Kopf, J. M. (1993, August). *Will individuals who need to improve their performance the most, volunteer to receive videotaped feedback?* Paper presented at the Annual Meeting of the Academy of Management, Atlanta.

Katzell, R. A., & Thompson, D. E. (1990). Work motivation: Theory and pratice. *American Psychologist*, 45, 144–153.

Kaufman, H. G. (1982). *Professionals in search of work*. New York: Wiley.

Kelly, H. H. (1972). *Causal schemata and the attribution process*. Morristown, NJ: General Learning Press.

Kernan, M. C., & Lord, R. G. (1991). An application of control theory to understanding the relationship between performance and satisfaction. *Human Performance*, 4, 173–185.

Klarreich, S. (1993). RET: A powerful tool to turn a traumatic job termination into an enlightening career transition. *Journal of Rational-Emotive & Cognitive Behavior Therapy*, 11(2), 77–89.

Kobasa, S. C. (1979). Stressful life events, personality, and health: An inquiry into hardiness. *Journal of Personlity and Social Psychology*, 37, 1–11.

Kobasa, S. C., Maddi, S. R., & Kahn, S. (1982). Hardiness and health: A prospective study. *Journal of Personality and Social Psychology*, 42, 168–177.

Kolb, D. A. (1984). *Experiential learning: Experience as the source of learning and development*. Englewood Cliffs, NJ: Prentice-Hall.

Kramer, M. W. (1993a). Communication and uncertainty reduction during job transfers: Leaving and joining processes. *Communication Monographs*, 60(2), 178–198.

Kramer, M. W. (1993b). Communication after job transfers: Social exchange processes in learning new roles. *Human Communication Research*, 20(2), 147–174.

Krausz, M., & Reshef, M. (1992). Managerial job change: Reasons for leaving, choice determinants, and search processes. *Journal of Business & Psychology*, 6, 349–359.

Langer, E. J. (1975). The illusion of control. *Journal of Personality and Social Psychology*, 32, 311–328.

Larson, J. R., Jr. (1988). The dynamic interplay between employees' feedback-seeking strategies and supervisors' delivery of performance feedback. *Academy of Management Review*, 14, 408–422.

Last, L., Peterson, R. W. E., Rapaport, W., & Webb, C. (1995). Creating opportunities for displaced workers: A center for commercial competitiveness. In M. London (Ed.), *Employees, careers, and economic growth* (pp. 210–233). San Francisco: Jossey-Bass.

Latack, J. C., Kinicki, A. J., & Prussia, G. E. (1995). An integrative process model of coping with job loss. *Academy of Management Review*, 20, 311–342.

Lawler, K. A., & Schmied, L. A. (1992). A prospective study of women's health: The effects of stress, hardiness, loss of control, Type A behavior, and physiological reactivity. *Women & Health*, 19, 27–41.

Lazarus, R. S. (1991). *Emotion and adaptation*. New York: Oxford University Press.

Leana, C. R., & Feldman, D. C. (1992). *Coping with job loss: How individuals, organizations, and communities respond to layoffs*. Lexington, MA: Lexington.

Levine, S. R., Wyer, R. S., & Schwarz, N. (1994). Are you what you feel? The affective and cognitive determinants of self-judgments. *European Journal of Social Psychology, 24*, 63–78.

Levy, P. E., Albright, M. D., Cawley, B. D., & Williams, J. R. (1995). Situational and individual determinants of feedback seeking: A closer look at the process. *Organizational Behavior and Human Decision Processes, 62*, 23–37.

Logue, A. W. (1995). *Self-control: Waiting until tomorrow for what you want today.* Englewood Cliffs, NJ: Prentice-Hall.

London, M. (1983). Toward a theory of career motivation. *Academy of Management Review, 8*(4), 620–630.

London, M. (1985). *Developing managers: A guide to motivating and preparing peopple for successful managerial careers.* San Francisco: Jossey-Bass

London, M. (1988). Organizational support for employees' career motivation: A guide to human resource strategies in changing business conditions. *Human Resources Planning, 11*, 23–32.

London, M. (1990). Enhancing career motivation in late career. *Journal of Organizational Change Management, 3*, 58–71.

London, M. (1993a). Relationships between career motivation, empowerment and support for career development. *Journal of Occupational and Organizational Psychology, 66*, 55–69.

London, M. (1993b). Career motivation of full- and part-time workers in mid and late career. *The International Journal of Career Management, 5*(1), 21–29.

London, M. (1995a). *Self and interpersonal insight: How people learn about themselves and others in organizations.* New York: Oxford University Press.

London, M. (1995b). Giving feedback: Source centered antecedents and consequences of constructive and destructive feedback. *Human Resource Management Review, 5*, 159–188.

London, M. (1995c). *Employees, careers, and job creation: Developing growth-oriented human resource strategies and programs.* San Francisco: Jossey-Bass.

London, M. (1996). Redeployment and continuous learning in the 21st Century: Hard lessons and positive examples from the downsizing era. *Academy of Management Executive, 10*(4), 67–69.

London, M., & Mone, E. M. (1987). *Career management and survival in the workplace.* San Francisco: Jossey-Bass.

London, M., & Mone, E. M. (in press). Continuous learning. In E. R. Ilgen & E. D. Pulakos (Eds.). *The changing nature of work performance: Implications for staffing, personnel actions, and development.* San Francisco: Jossey-Bass.

London, M., & Noe, R. A. (1997). Career motivation theory: An update and directions for research and practice. *Journal of Career Assessment, 5*(1), 61–80.

Luciano, L. (1995). Five smart ways to get ahead today. *Money, 24* (3), 118–123.

Lyons, J. A. (1991). Strategies for assessing the potential for positive adjustment following trauma. *Journal of Traumatic Stress, 4*, 93–111.

Maddi, S. R., & Hess, M. L. (1992). Personality hardiness and success in basketball. *International Journal of Sport Psychology, 23*, 360–368.

Maddi, S. R., & Khoshaba, D. M. (1994). Hardiness and mental health. *Journal of Personality Assessment, 63*, 265–274.

Magnusson, K. C., & Redekopp, D. E. (1992). Adaptability for transitions: Components and implications for intervention. *Canadian Journal of Counseling, 26*, 134–143.

Mallinckrodt, B., & Bennett, J. (1992). Social support and the impact of job loss in dislocated blue-collar workers. *Journal of Counseling Psychology, 39*, 482–489.

Mandler, G. (1990). A constructivist theory of emotion. In N. S. Stein, B. L. Leventhal, & T. Trabasso (Eds.), *Psychological and biological approaches to emotion* (pp. 21–43). Hillsdale, NJ: Lawrence Erlbaum Associates.

Marin, P. A., & Splete, H. (1991). A comparison of the effect of two computer-based counseling interventions on the career decidedness of adults. *Career Development Quarterly, 39,* 360–371.

Masten, A. S., Best, K. M., & Garmezy, N. (1990). Resilience and development: Contributions from the study of children who overcome adversity. *Development & Psychopathology, 2,* 425–444.

McAuliffe, G. J. (1993). Constructive development and career transition: Implications for counseling. *Journal of Counseling & Development, 72*(1), 23–28.

McCall, M. W. (1994). Identifying leadership potential in future internationl executives: Developing a concept. Special issue: Issues in the assessment of managerial and executive leadership. *Consulting Psychology Journal: Practice & Research, 46,* 49–63.

McCall, M. W., Jr., Lombardo, M. M., & Morrison, A. M. (1988). *The lessons of experience: How successful executives develop on the job.* Lexington, MA: Lexington.

Melamed, T. (1996). Validation of a stage model of career success. *Applied psychology: An international review, 45*(1), 35–65.

Merja, H. (1995). The role of work-related causal attributions in occupational crisis. *Journal of Psychology, 129*(2), 167–180.

Miller, M. V., & Hoppe, S. K. (1994). Attributions for job termination and psychological distress. *Human Relations, 47,* 307–327.

Mirsky, J., & Barasch, M. (1993). Adjustment problems among Soviet immigrants at risk: II. Emotional distress among elderly Soviet immigrants during the Gulf War. *Israel Journal of Psychiatry & Related Sciences, 30*(4), 233–243.

Morrison, E. W., & Bies, R. J. (1991). Impression management the feedback-seeking process: A literature review and research agenda. *Academy of Management Review, 16*(3): 522–541.

Murphy, S. T., & Zajonc, R. B. (1993). Affect, cognition, and awareness: Affective priming with optimal and suboptimal stimulus exposures. *Journal of Personality and Social Psychology, 64,* 723–739.

National Advisory Mental Health Council Behavioral Science Task Force. (1995). Basic behavioral science research for mental health: A national investment. *Psychological Science, 6,* 192–202.

Nelson, T. D. (1993). The hierarchical organization of behavior: A useful feedback model of self-regulation. *Current Directions in Psychological Science, 2,* 121–126.

Neubauer, P. J. (1992). The impact of stress, hardiness, home and work environment on job satisfaction, illness, and absenteeism in critical care nurses. *Medical Psychotherapy: An International Journal, 5,* 109–122.

Newman, B. K. (1995). Career change for those over 40: Critical issues and insights. *Career Development Quarterly, 44*(1), 64–66.

Noe, R. A., Noe, A. W., & Bachhuber, J. A. (1990) Correlates of career motivation. *Journal of Vocational Behavior, 37,* 340–356.

Noe, R. W., & Ford, J. K. (1992). Emerging issues and new directions for training research. In G. R. Ferris & K. M. Rowland (Eds.), *Research in personnel and human resource management* (Vol. 10, pp. 345–384). Greenwich, CT: JAI.

Nowack, K. M. (1991). Psychosocial predictors of health status. *Work & Stress, 5,* 117–131.

Organ, D. W. (1988). *Organizational citizenship behavior: The old soldier syndrome.* Lexington, MA: Lexington.

Osipow, S. H., & Fitzgerald, L. F. (1993). Unemployment and mental health: A neglected relationship. *Applied & Preventive Psychology, 2*(2), 59–63.

Pedersen, P., Goldberg, A. D., & Papalia, T. (1991). A model for planning career continuation and change through increased awareness, knowledge, and skill. *Journal of Employment Counseling, 28*(2), 74–79.

Pemberton, C., Herriot, P., & Bates, T. (1994). Career orientations of senior executives and their implications for career guidance. *British Journal of Guidance & Counseling, 22*(2), 233–245.

Perrez, M., & Reicherts, M. (1992). *Stress, coping, and health: A situation-behavior approach; Theory, methods, applications.* Seattle: Hogrefe & Huber.

Powers, W. T. (1973a). Behavior: The control of perception. Chicago: Aldine.

Powers, W. T. (1973b). Feedback: Beyond behaviorism. *Science, 179,* 351–356.

Price, R. H. (1992). Psychosocial impact of job loss on individuals and families. *Current Directions in Psychological Science, 1*(1), 9–11.

Price, R. H., & Vinokur, A. D. (1995). The Michigan JOBS Program: Supporting career transitions in a time of organizational downsizing. In M. London (ed.). *Employees, Careers, and Economic Growth* (pp. 191–209). San Francisco, CA: Jossey-Bass.

Prussia, G. E., Kinicki, A. J., & Bracker, J. S. (1993). Psychological and behavioral consequences of job loss: A covariance structure analysis using Weiner's (1985) attribution model. *Journal of Applied Psychology, 78,* 382–394.

Rife, J. C., & Belcher, J. R. (1994). Assisting unemployed older workers to become reemployed: An experimental evaluation. *Research on Social Work Practice, 4,* 3–13.

Rosow, J. M., & Zager, R. (1988). *Training: The competitive edge.* San Francisco: Jossey-Bass.

Rouiller, J. Z., & Goldstein, I. I. (1993). The relationship between organizational transfer climate and positive transfer of training. *Human Resource Development Quarterly, 4,* 377–390.

Ruch, M. C., Schoel, W. A., & Barnard, S. M. (1995). Psychological resiliency in the public sector: "Hardiness" and the pressure for change. *Journal of Vocational Behavior, 46,* 17–39.

Russo, J. E., & Schoemaker, P. J. H. (1992). Managing overconfidence. *Sloan Management Review, 33*(2), 7–17.

Rutter, R. (1993). Resilience: Some conceptual considerations. *Journal of Adolescent Health, 14*(8), 626–631.

Salancik, G. R., & Pfeffer, J. A. (1978). A social information processing approach to job attitudes and task design. *Administrative Science Quarterly, 23,* 224–253.

Salomone, P. R., & Mangicaro, L. L. (1991). Difficult cases in career counseling. *Career Development Quarterly, 39,* 325–336.

Sanger, D., & Lohr, S. (1996, March 9). The downsizing of America: A search for answers to avoid the layoffs. *The New York Times,* pp. A1, A12–13.

Saxton, M. J., Phillips, J. S., Blakeney, R. N. (1991). Antecedents and consequences of emotional exhaustion in the airline reservations service sector. *Human Relations, 44,* 583–595.

Schachter, S. (1964). The interaction of cognitive and physiological determinants of emotional state. In L. Berkowitz (Ed.), *Advances in experimental social psychology* (Vol. 1, pp. 49–82). New York: Academic Press.

Schein, E. H. (1978). *Career dynamics: Matching individual and organizational needs.* Reading, MA: Addison-Wesley.

Schein, E. H. (1990). *Career anchors: Discovering your real values.* San Diego, CA: Pfeiffer & Company.

Schleifer, L. M., & Shell, R. L. (1992). A review and reappraisal of electronic performance monitoring, performance standards and stress allowances. *Applied Ergonomics, 23,* 49–53.

Schmit, M. J., Amel, E. L., & Ryan, A. M. (1993). Self-reported assertive job-seeking behaviors of minimally educated job hunters. *Personnel Psychology, 46,* 105–124.

Schneider, B., Gunnarson, S. K., & Wheeler, J. K. (1992). The role of opportunity in the conceptualization and measurement of job satisfaction. In C. J. Cranny, P. C. Smith, &

E. F. Stone (Eds.), *Job satisfaction: How people feel about their jobs and how it affects their performance* (pp. 53–68). New York: Lexington.

Schwarz, N. (1990). Feelings as information. In E. T. Higgins & R. M. Sorrentino (Eds.), *Handbook of motivation and cognition: Foundations of social behavior, Vol. 2* (pp. 527–561). New York: Guilford.

Sinclair, R. C., Hoffman, C., Mark, M. M., Martin, L. L., & Pickering, E. L. (1994). Construct accessibility and the misattribution of arousal: Schachter and Singer revisited. *Psychological Science, 5,* 15–19.

Smither, J. W. (1995). Creating and managing an internal contingent work force of managerial and technical-professional employees. In M. London, (Ed.), *Employees, careers, and economic growth* (pp. 142–164). San Francisco: Jossey-Bass.

Solcova, I., & Sykora, J. (1995). Relation between psychological hardiness and physiological response. *Homeostasis in Health & Disease, 36,* 30–34.

Spekman, N. J., Goldberg, R. J., & Herman, K. L. (1993). An exploration of risk and resilience in the lives of individuals with learning disabilities. *Learning Disabilities Research and Practice, 8,* 11–18.

Spera, S. P., Buhrfeind, E. D., & Pennebaker, J. W. (1994). Expressive writing and coping with job loss. *Academy of Management Journal, 37,* 722–733.

Sperry, L. (1992). Recent developments in neuroscience, behavioral medicine, and psychoneuroimmunology: Implications for physical and psychological well-being. *Individual Psychology: Journal of Adlerian Theory, Research, & Practice, 48,* 480–487.

Staudinger, U. M., Marsiske, M., & Baltes, P. B. (1993). Resilience and levels of reserve capacity in later adulthood: Perspectives from life-span theory. *Development & Psychopathology, 5,* 541–566.

Stumpf, S. A. (1992). Career goal: Entrepreneur? *The International Journal of Career Management, 4*(2), 26.

Super, D. E. (1957). *The psychology of careers.* New York: Harper & Row.

Super, D. E. (1963). *Career development: Self-concept theory.* New York: CEEB.

Swanson, J. L., & Tokar, D. M. (1991). Development and initial validation of the career barriers inventory. *Journal of Vocational Behavior, 39,* 344–361.

Tracey, J. B., Tannenbaum, S. I., & Kavanagh, M. J. (1995). Applying trained skills on the job: The importance of the work environment. *Journal of Applied Psychology, 80,* 239–252.

Tsui, A. S., Ashford, S. J., St. Clair, L., & Xin, K. R. (1995). Dealing with discrepant expectations: Response strategies and managerial effectiveness. *Academy of Management Journal, 38,* 1515–1543.

Turban, D. B., Campion, J. E., & Eyring, A. R. (1992). Factors relating to relocation decisions of research and development employees. *Journal of Vocational Behavior, 41,* 183–199.

Uchitelle, L., & Kleinfield, N. R. (1996, March 3). The downsizing of America: On the battlefields of business, millions of casualties. *The New York Times,* pp. A1, A26–29.

Vancouver, J. B., & Morrison, E. W. (1995). Feedback inquiry: The effect of source attributes and individual differences. *Organizational Behavior and Human Decision Processes, 62,* 276–285.

Vinokur, A. D., van Ryn, M., Gramlich, E. M., & Price, R. H. (1991). Long-term follow-up and benefit–cost analysis of the jobs program: A preventive intervention for the unemployed. *Journal of Applied Psychology, 76,* 213–219.

Walton, S. J. (1990). Stress management training for overseas effectiveness. *International Journal of Intercultural Relations, 14*(4), 507–527.

Wanberg, C. R., & Marchese, M. C. (1994). Heterogeneity in the unemployment experience: A cluster analytic investigation. *Journal of Applied Social Psychology, 24,* 473–488.

Wanberg, C. R., Watt, J. D., & Rumsey, D. J. (1996). Individuals without jobs: An empirical study of job-seeking behavior and reemployment. *Journal of Applied Psychology, 81,* 76–87.

Watson, D., & Slack, A. K. (1993). General factors of affective temperament and their relation to job satisfaction over time. *Organizational Behavior and Human Decision Processes, 54*(2), 181–202.

Weiner, B., & Graham, S. (1989). Understanding the motivational role of affect: Life-span research from an attributional perspective. *Cognition and Emotion, 3,* 401–419.

Westman, M. (1990). The relationship between stress and performance: The moderating effect of hardiness. *Human Performance, 3,* 141–155.

Wiebe, D. J. (1991). Hardiness and stress moderation: A test of proposed mechanisms. *Journal of Personality and Social Psychology, 60,* 89–99.

Williams, K. J., Williams, G. M., & Ryer, J. A. (1990). The relation between performance feedback and job attitudes among school psychologists. *School Psychology Review, 19,* 550–563.

Williams, R. L., & Long, J. D. (1991). *Manage your life.* Boston: Houghton Mifflin.

Williams, R. L., Pettibone, T. J., & Thomas, S. P. (1991). Naturalistic application of self-change practices. *Journal of Research in Personality, 25,* 167–176.

Williams, R. L., Verble, J. S., Price, D. E., & Layne, B. H. (1995). Relationship of self-management to personality types and indices. *Journal of Personality Assessment, 64,* 494–506.

Williams, R. N. (1992). The human context of agency. *American Psychologist, 47,* 752–760.

Winefield, A. H., Tiggermann, M., & Winefield, H. R. (1992). Unemploynment distress, reasons for job loss and causal attributions for unemployment in young people. *Journal of Occupational & Organizational Psyhchology, 63,* 213–218.

Wolf, G., Casey, J., Pufahl, J., & London, M. (1995). Developing displaced engineers for job creation in high technology firms. In M. London (Ed.), *Employees, careers, and economic growth* (pp. 234–257). San Francisco: Jossey-Bass.

Wolf, G., London, M., Casey, J., & Pufahl, J. (1995). Career experience and motivation as predictors of training behaviors and outcomes for displaced engineers. *Journal of Vocational Behavior, 47,* 316–331.

Zajonc, R. B. (1980). Feeling and thinking: Preferences need no inferences. *American Psychologist, 35,* 151–175.

Zakowski, S., Hall, M. H., & Baum, A. (1992). Stress, stress management, and the immune system. *Applied & Preventive Psychology, 1* (1), 1–13.

Zalesny, M. D., & Ford, J. K. (1990). Extending the social information processing perspective: New links to attitudes, behaviors, and perceptions. *Organizational Behavior and Human Decision Processes, 47,* 205–246.

Author Index

A

Abramson, L. Y., 25, *193*
Adams, S. M., 64, *195*
Albright, M. D., 65, *198*
Allred, B. B., 136, *193*
Amel, E. L., 52, 73, *200*
Archer, J., 34, *193*
Armstrong-Stassen, M., 76, *193*
Ashford, S. J., 29, 50, 51, 64, *193, 201*
Azrin, N., 123, *193*

B

Bachhuber, J. A., 62, *199*
Baillie, P. H., 9, *193*
Baltes, P. B., 77, *201*
Bandura, A., 137, *193*
Barasch, M., 108, *199*
Barnard, S. M., 82, *200*
Bates, T., 106, *200*
Baum, A., 26, 111, *202*
Baumeister, R. F., 30, 49, *193, 196*
Beach, L. R., 28, *193*
Bechtel, R., 123, *193*
Beiser, M., 14, 34, *193*
Belcher, J. R., 123, *200*
Bennett, G. J., Jr., 122, *193*
Bennett, J., 91, *198*
Berger, S. M., 30, *193*
Bernard, M. E., 109, 110, *193*
Besalel, V., 123, *193*
Best, K. M., 76, *199*
Bies, R. J., 64, *199*
Bird, B. J., 117, *193*
Black, D. R., 12, *193*
Blakeney, R. N., 10, *200*
Blau, G. J., 62, *193, 194*
Blix, A. G., 11, *194*
Blix, G. G., 11, *194*
Bolino, M. C., 61, *195*
Boss, A., 30, *196*
Bower, G. H., 34, *195*

Bracker, J. S., 54, *200*
Bray, D. W., 60, 69, *196*
Brewer, M. B., 30, *194*
Brief, A. P., 27, 34, 46, *194, 195*
Brown, D., 104, *194*
Browne, M. W., 122, *194*
Buch, K., 11, 107, *195*
Buhrfeind, E. D., 109, *201*
Burke, M. J., 27, *194*

C

Campion, J. E., 91, *201*
Campion, M. A., 12, *194*
Caplan, R., 91, *194*
Carlson, E., 77, *195*
Carver, C. S., 29, *194*
Casey, J., 68, 114, *202*
Catalano, R., 75, *194*
Cawley, B. D., 65, *198*
Cheraskin, L., 12, *194*
Cohler, B. J., 16, *194*
Compton, W. C., 79, *194*
Conlon, D. W., 29, *194*
Crites, J. O., 62, *194*
Cruise, R. J., 11, *194*
Culbert, B. J., 80, *195*
Cummings, L. L., 64, *193*
Czyzewska, M., 30, *196*

D

Danish, S. J., 9, *193*
Darley, J., 30, *195*
Davis, J., 109, *194*
Dawis, R. V., 62, *194*
DiGiuseppe, R., 109, 110, *193*
Dion, K. K., 81, *194*
Dion, K. L., 81, *194*
Dooley, D., 75, *194*
Dubin, S. S., 94, *194*
D'Zurilla, T. J., 109, 110, *195*

Subject Index

A

Absenteeism, hardness relation, 81
Achievement
  needs and support, 92
  reinforcement and continuous learning culture, 94–95
Adaptability, job seeking, 73
Adjustment, career motivation model, 62
Adult learning theory, curriculum development at Center for Commercial Competitiveness, 116
Advancement
  new definitions, 138–139
  opportunities and support role in career motivation, 92, 101
Age
  discrimination
    career barrier, 4, 14–15
    cases, 163
    mature workers, 99
  emotional reaction to negative events, 32
  patterns of career motivation, 68
Agendas, setting/implementation and learning, 16
Alcohol abuse, unemployment, 75
Alliance for Employee Growth and Development, training employees, 137
Alternative recognition, interventions for appraisal/coping, 112
American Chemical Society, intervention and training, 122
Anger, *see* Emotions
Anticipation, career barriers, 15
Anxiety
  feedback seeking, 64
  job failure, 76
Apathy, job loss, 25
Applications, job seeking and coping strategies, 52
Appraisal
  career barrier interpretation, 35–38
  career motivation and support relationships, 184
  coping relationships, 180–181
  technical results of survey, 174, 178–179

Assessment
  continuous learning culture, 95–96
  goals and career barriers, 16–17
Athletes
  ceiling and career barriers, 9
  performance and hardness relationship, 81
AT&T, intervention and training, 116–117
Attributes, phase-specific of resilience, 78
Awareness, development, 16

B

Bankruptcy, interpreting career barriers, 33–34
Behavior
  emotional reactions to job loss, 26–27
  explanation for and thought processing, 28
  matching to goal and information processing about career barriers, 29
  self-defeating behaviors and coping strategies, 49, 56
Behavioral counseling, resilience patterns, 78
Behavioral/situational linkages, career motivation model, 62–64
Bias, judgment and information processing, 30
Biographical characteristics
  appraisal and coping relationships, 178, 180, 186
  career barrier relationships, 176
  career motivation and support relationships, 182
  emotions relationship, 177
  technical results of study, 169–170, 174
Blue-collar workers, coping strategies and career barriers, 132, 171
Boss, *see also* Executives; Manager
  role model and implications of career motivation, 69
  toughness and downsizing, 4
Brain power, channeling, 122
Business
  environment changing and new career directions, 149
  failure and career barriers, 9
  plans and entrepreneurship training, 119